DECADENT ORIENTALISMS

Decadent Orientalisms

The Decay of Colonial Modernity

David Fieni

FORDHAM UNIVERSITY PRESS
New York 2020

Copyright © 2020 Fordham University Press

All rights reserved. No part of this publication may be reproduced, stored in a retrieval system, or transmitted in any form or by any means—electronic, mechanical, photocopy, recording, or any other—except for brief quotations in printed reviews, without the prior permission of the publisher.

Fordham University Press has no responsibility for the persistence or accuracy of URLs for external or third-party Internet websites referred to in this publication and does not guarantee that any content on such websites is, or will remain, accurate or appropriate.

Fordham University Press also publishes its books in a variety of electronic formats. Some content that appears in print may not be available in electronic books.

Visit us online at www.fordhampress.com.

Library of Congress Cataloging-in-Publication Data available online at https://catalog.loc.gov.

Printed in the United States of America

21 20 19   5 4 3 2 1

First edition

for Nancy
for Ella
for Margot

CONTENTS

Introduction: Orientalist Decadence   1

Part I   (DIS)INTEGRATING SEMITISM: FRENCH AND ARABIC IN THE TWILIGHT OF THE OTTOMAN EMPIRE

1. French Decadence, Arab Awakenings: Figures of Decay in the *Nahda*   31
2. Al-Shidyaq's Decadent Carnival   52
3. From Dreyfus in the Colony to Céline's Anti-Semitic Style   68

Part II   WORKING THROUGH POSTCOLONIAL DECADENCE

4. Resurrecting Colonial Decadence in Independent Algeria   97
5. Algerian Women and the Invention of Literary Mourning   118
6. Virtual Secularization: Abdelwahab Meddeb's "Walking Cure" and the Immigrant Body in France   136

Conclusion: Toward a Contrapuntal Double Critique of Colonial Modernity   159

Acknowledgments   173
Notes   177
Select Bibliography   203
Index   215

Decadent Orientalisms

INTRODUCTION
Orientalist Decadence

> During that period [the seventh and eighth centuries], Greek science played a role among the Syrians, the Nabataeans, the Harranians, and the Sassanid Persians that was quite analogous to that which European science has been playing in the Orient for a half-century.
>
> —ERNEST RENAN, *Averroès et l'averroïsme*

> As a medicine for human society, [reason's] success when truly tried is so manifest that not even the blind and the deaf can deny or gainsay it. All that the objection just elaborated leads to is this: a physician treated a sick man with medicine and he recovered: then the doctor himself succumbed to the disease he had been treating. In dire straits from pain and with the medicine by him in the house he has yet no will to use it. Many of those who come to visit him or seek his ministrations or even gloat over his illness could take up the medicine and be cured, while he himself despairs of life and waits either for death or some miraculous healing.
>
> —MUHAMMAD 'ABDUH, *Risalat al-tawhid*

> What seems most important in the question of the modern Arab and Muslim renaissance is its relation to decadence.
>
> —ABDELKEBIR KHATIBI, "Pensée-autre"

The first two decades of the twenty-first century have occasioned a veritable renaissance of indictments of decadence directed at and coming from Arabs and Muslims. A multitude of voices around the world accuse "the West" of moral decadence, indicated by causes as diverse as its excessive consumption and wealth, its immorality and lack of religiosity, its views on women and gender roles, its disregard for the rule of law, or its inhumane detention and abuse of vulnerable populations. Meanwhile, the "War on Terror" still being waged by the United States and its allies has explicitly declared and implicitly endeavored to affirm the decadence of Arabs and

Muslims. A speech delivered by George W. Bush to a group of supporters on Veterans' Day of 2005 rather lucidly illustrates the fantasmatic logic of these mirrored discourses of decadence:

> This fight we have joined is also the current expression of an ancient struggle—between those who put their faith in dictators, and those who put their faith in the people.... Tyrants and would-be tyrants have always claimed that regimented societies are strong and pure—until those societies collapse in corruption and decay. Tyrants and would-be tyrants have always claimed that free men and women are weak and decadent—until the day that free men and women defeat them.[1]

Bush rehearses the well-worn rhetoric (common to medieval crusaders and contemporary political scientists) of "an ancient struggle" between incompatible civilizations: in this case, it is the *demos* that is pitted against the Oriental despot, represented here by former Iraqi president Saddam Hussein. Earlier in the same speech, Bush masks this banal and inflammatory language with two "politically correct" observations: that the Islamist enemy identified by the US government has distorted the concept of "jihad," and that there is a difference between "Islamo-fascism" and "the religion of Islam." He conflates the ideology of the Islamist enemy with "the ideology of communism," both of which would be united as the sworn adversaries of "free men and women" everywhere. Just beneath the half-hearted ideological screen, one sees that it is pure might—military or "terrorist"—that ultimately proves the decadence of the despotic other.

The wildly imaginative historical and ideological revisions articulated in this speech are even more striking for their similarity to Islamist discourses of decadence, which make many of these same claims while also abusing history in like fashion. Take the example of *Dabiq*, the glossy magazine published by the group that calls itself the Islamic State, which contains numerous articles denouncing "Western Decadence." An issue from summer 2016 diagnoses the causes of this decadence by pointing to the European scientists and thinkers whose ideas have undermined the religious morality of society. A caption beneath a photo of Sigmund Freud tells us that Freud was "one of the engineers of Western Decadence," and the accompanying text affirms that "the teachings of Darwin, Marx, Nietzsche, Durkheim, Weber, and Freud made their way into most Western societies through educational systems and media industries designed to produce generations void of any traces of the fitrah [innate nature].... They destroyed the basis of religiosity ... and what it entailed of morality and society." The speech by President Bush and the IS magazine article share a set of familiar rhetorical moves: They both divide the world into East and West, condense history to diagnose decadence, and then attribute blame. Both declarations sow the seeds of decadence and decay within their ideological opponent: Bush's (implicitly) "Oriental" "Islamo-fascism" and *Dabiq*'s "Western secular" tradition are both doomed to collapse; Bush and *Dabiq* both conceive of the enemy as an inherently defective entity, one designed to fail. This, then, is the prime directive of what I am calling *decadent Orientalism*: not simply that the "Orient" be constituted by its own decadence—its own supposed internal logic of decay, disintegration, and regression, but that the particular way of conceiving of planetary space and society as locked in a battle between a homogenized "Orient" and a homogenized "Occident" entails this kind of "decadent" thinking, where the other half of a world already cleaved in two itself suffers a continual process of internal fracturing. Orientalism is thus necessarily a style of power, as Edward Said has famously asserted, and this style is constituted by the will to fracture and division. The essence of the object of its knowledge—the Orient—is thus to unmake itself, according to its peculiar ontology of unbecoming.

Focusing on the nexus between the Arab world and France, *Decadent Orientalisms* performs a genealogy of the forms of contemporary Orientalist decadence seen in both the speech by Bush and Islamist rhetoric by tracing such self-reflecting discourses back to the nineteenth century, and then following them forward again into our contemporary moment of crisis. The mirroring effect seen in the juxtaposition of Bush and IS ideological claims also operates in the epigraphs from Ernest Renan and Muhammad 'Abduh, which illustrate two models for explaining how knowledge has been appropriated for ideological purposes over time and across the globe. Whereas Renan's academic assertion emphasizes the predominant influence of Greco-European historical agency, 'Abduh's allegory of contagion affirms the power of reason as an autonomous force over and against the ailing will of the stricken physician, who here represents something like the totality of the Islamic *ummah*'s will to heal. Both conceive of the transmission of reason as a function performed by culturally specific agents of influence and contagion. This book ultimately displaces both these narratives by locating them in another theoretical structure. The historical framework in which this structure may be articulated is the intersection of Orientalism and decadence in intellectual and literary history, precisely because Arabic intellectuals such as 'Abduh were only able to secure their modernity by first bearing witness to their own "Oriental decadence."

Three closely related phenomena serve as points of arrival that motivate the book's historical excavations of the bond between Orientalism and decadence: the Algerian Civil War of the 1990s, the 9/11 attacks and subsequent "War on Terror," and the accelerated renewal of Islamophobia in France and beyond. *Decadent Orientalisms* decodes the symptoms on the ideological skin covering the social body with a view to detecting the deep structure of Orientalism pulsing beneath and organizing the animosities of our contemporary moment. This book focuses on the modalities of power in language peculiar to the conflicted history of France and the Arab world, from the nineteenth-century *nahda*, or "Arab renaissance," in the Mashreq to the contemporary Maghreb and its diasporas. Chapters 1–3 probe selected moments in the history of what Said called the "Semitic object" (or, in the words of Gil Anidjar, the "Semitic hypothesis"): the invented object of European pseudo-knowledge that created a forced grouping together of Arabs, Jews, and other peoples whose languages shared morphological similarities. From the start, "Semites" were conceived as being "decadent," that is, as possessing an essence that would somehow be both unchanging and characterized by a kind of inherent degenerative force. The first three chapters delineate and critique the process of dis-integrating the elements of this fabricated "Semitic" object. Chapters 4–6 focus on writers and thinkers from the Maghreb who provide a critique of these discourses and offer productive ways of working through the dead end of Orientalist decadence.

Whereas Part I explores questions emerging from philology, the philosophy of history, and civilizational discourses rooted in the nineteenth century and focusing on interactions between France and the Mashreq, Part II sets up the book's effective focus, which is the ways that Orientalist decadence continues to haunt the relationship between France and the Maghreb in the postcolonial era. By drawing out a thread from Renan to Céline and the Dreyfus affair, this book not only provides a French genealogy of European anti-Semitism but also brings into relief the role of French colonialism in sculpting racial attitudes in both the metropole and among the different populations in the countries of the Maghreb. In this sense, *Decadent Orientalisms* completes Said's early elaborations on the Oriental figure of the Semite by identifying and analyzing specific moments and texts that would prove to be transformative in the history of Jews and Arabs in relation to the postcolonial nation-state and postcolonial cultural production.

Introduction: Orientalist Decadence

My analysis stakes out a position within the larger project of colonial comparativism, a core concern of which has been the interrogation of the formal relationship between nationalist liberal thought and intellectual projects within the colonial world. The juncture of Orientalism and decadence provides a specific inflection of the problem of nationalism in the colony, which, as Partha Chatterjee has argued, "produced a discourse in which, even as it challenged the colonial claim to political domination, it also accepted the very intellectual premises of 'modernity' on which colonial domination was based" (30). The challenge of reading the discursive formations and deformations resulting in the collision of Orientalism and colonial modernity lies precisely in the difficulty of imagining a relationship that is at once intimate and radically separate. This book analyzes this dynamic and contradictory "relationship" (which is also in many ways an utter lack of relationality) in a variety of specific configurations and contexts since the nineteenth century.

Decadent Orientalisms graphs out a triangulation of its three central concepts—decadence, Orientalism, and colonial modernity—to critique the pervasive and lasting assumptions that continue to regulate not only *discourse* relating to Arab societies but also configurations of language, thought, and the disciplines that also power the much broader set of transactions pertaining to cultures, politics, and economies in these societies. The term "colonial modernity" here operates, as it has for a range of postcolonial scholars, as a critical tool for unearthing such assumptions, especially those relating to the Eurocentricity of the concept of modernity itself. Reading the colonial archive through the lens of colonial modernity reframes the transactional temporalities and spaces of colony, postcolony, and metropole, rendering visible the perspectives of those suffering the forms of subjection specific to colonialism and imperialism. In Gerard Aching's account of the term, not only does the concept of colonial modernity decenter Europe and North America as points of origin for modernity, but it also foregrounds the experience of the colonized and decolonizing as a source of critique and action. "Colonial modernity," Aching writes,

> can thus be conceived as an experience of subjugation—analogous to but not a mere duplicate of 'universal' modern subjectivity—that presses communities and individuals to reflect on and define their place in the world. . . . It is not an inherently peripheral version of "metropolitan modernity" but an experience of subjugation, thwarted contestation, and similar engagements between rulers and their subjects that hold out perilous yet creative possibilities for autonomous action and for sovereignty. (44)

This book thus considers the normative, rational, and positivist iterations of Orientalism *as* decadence and Orientals as ontologically manifesting a state of decadence, but also the powerful critique that emerges from the subject Orientalized *as* decadent, stunted, and peripheral. The Orientalized writers I discuss write from this position of the damages inflicted by Orientalism and cultural imperialism. As such, they testify to what David Lloyd calls the "unevenly distributed relation to damage and survival" (107) that marks the experience of subjugation at the nexus of coloniality and modernity. It should be said that this book does not use the term "colonial modernity" as the kind of fetishistic "alternative modernity" that Fredric Jameson has critiqued as obscuring Jameson's own affirmation that modernity *is* global capitalism, but rather, in the words of Tani Barlow, as a "speculative frame for investigating the infinitely pervasive discursive powers that increasingly connect at key points to the globalizing impulses of capitalism" (6). My goal is not simply to construct a new critique of colonial modernity but to connect the dots between the ways that Orientalized writers and thinkers have themselves reflected on their place in the world, and also to link up the creative possibilities that have emerged along the seams of the contradictions of colonial modernity in its perpetual state of disintegration and decay.

By giving an account of the *decay* of colonial modernity, *Decadent Orientalisms* opens an avenue of critique into the ways that the internal contradictions of colonial discourse and those of global capitalism feed on each other symbiotically. For if "the Orient" must be simultaneously the site of surplus and scarcity, it is precisely because such an ambivalence allows for discourses pertaining to civilization, culture, and race to map onto the expansionist demands of global capital in terms of markets, labor, and resources. The Oriental philologist "discovers" a defect in the Arabic language, the colonial administrator affirms an incompatibility between the indigenous population and the requirements of the modern citizen, and the expropriation of land, labor, and goods follows suit, as if by a kind of natural logic. This overmapping of superstructure and base cuts much deeper than something like a simple *justification* of imperialist exploitation and domination. As Fanon tells us, "in the colonies, the economic substructure is also a superstructure," which is why "Marxist analysis must be slightly stretched every time one has to deal with the colonial problem" (40). One of the core arguments that runs throughout this book thus concerns the dual nature of Orientalism as an affective discourse that collapses description and prescription, where what claims to be objective knowledge—about the inherent decadence of the Arab world, say—

Introduction: Orientalist Decadence   7

in fact contributes to the perpetually worsening state of affairs in Arab societies.

Reading decadence comparatively, while showing how decadence is always comparative, allows for a reconsideration of the stylistics of colonial power and suggests the need to rethink the relationship between power and the production of culture and knowledge in other ways than through the exhausted paradigms of benevolent influence, cultural contamination, or ambivalent hybridity. To think about French Orientalism without reference to what was actually happening in the Orient reinforces the paradigm that anti-Orientalist discourses seek to expose; to study Arabic thought and culture as being born of, or influenced primarily by, Europe reinforces a monolithic and fetishized notion of culture that obfuscates the relationship between ideology and power. One of the chief relevant criticisms of Edward Said's *Orientalism* (1978) has been its lack of non-European perspectives, a problem that Said first began to address in *Culture and Imperialism* (1992). However, this latter text focused mostly on twentieth-century responses to imperialism, what Said has famously called the "voyage in." The responses to both Europe and modernity in the nineteenth century in the so-called East remain largely underexplored in a truly comparative context, particularly given the striking coincidence of the idea of decadence in both literatures in the second half of the nineteenth century. It seems especially important to understand how the actually existing world that Orientalism sought to comprehend fully within its imaginary figurations—the real people and societies located by Europe as Oriental—configured their own understanding of decadence both with and against the strategies of European discourse. This book thus considers the "voyage in" of these other "belated travelers," beginning with those coming from the lands of the Ottoman Empire, whose belatedness was thrust upon them in the form of French prognoses of the Orient's decadence.[2]

The pluralized form Orientalisms in the book's title indexes an important feature of my argument relating to the consistency and coherence of the diverse set of practices, institutions, and perceptual frames that constitute what Said simply termed Orientalism in the singular. On one hand, it is the *apparent* consistency of Orientalism that betrays its status as an uncritical, false narrative. But this consistency is, of course, merely apparent, as Orientalism is by no means an internally coherent intellectual program but rather more akin to a war machine, a hegemonic armature of statements, positions, policies, and styles that are only beholden to the volatile and arbitrary dictates of imperial modes of sovereignty embedded in the cartographic imagination and culture at all levels. To pluralize the mechanisms of Orientalism in this way is to provincialize the claims of imperialist power and thus demonstrate the ad hoc nature of the grand narratives of colonial knowledge production: the "Semitic hypothesis," the inevitable march of Capital, the inherent secularism of European Christianity, the decadence of the "Oriental" mind, and so on. *Decadent Orientalisms* locates and critiques selected moments in this false narrative, not only at their point of dissemination (primarily in France) but also at their point of assimilation and critique (beginning in the Ottoman East and moving toward the Maghreb). This study shows that "Orientalism" is no more a single homogenous thing than the lived historical realities of the societies of the so-called "Orient" have ever been. Thus Ernest Renan's philological "solution" to the "Semitic Question" is one modality of Orientalist style, and the Decret Crémiuex of 1870 is another; the two strategies only intersect at the most crude point of the Orientalist thesis, where the inherent decadence of the homogeneous Orient would prove the ascendency of the homogenous Occident.

Before going any further, it is necessary to clarify what is meant by "decadence" in the context of the current study. The problem with decadence is that the term scarcely evinces any more concrete specificity than its equivalent in ethical discourse ("evil") or its counterpart in the language of aesthetics ("the grotesque"); to this quandary of the word's semantic drift can be added the divergent historical transformations that "decadence" has suffered in English and French (*décadence*) (to say nothing of its legions of Arabic synonyms). The discourse of decadence, like that of Orientalism, is ultimately a *style* of evaluating society and performing cultural adjudications. As I use the term, decadence is never a question of measuring collective health or vitality in some supposedly accurate fashion; rather, it is the way that these measurements take place. To critique the discourse of decadence, then, is to examine the entire apparatus of social critique and evaluation, an object of study whose vastness approaches the sublime.

The specific ideological construct that organized nineteenth-century academic Orientalism was the "Semitic object," the name Said gives to the product of European philology that united Jews and Arabs—and other "Semites"—under the banner of biological and linguistic degeneration.[3] Tracing the genealogy of Orientalism as it mutates from its nineteenth-century configurations into its twentieth-century forms is a way of narrating the fragmentation of the Semitic object into an array of microdiscourses that become embedded within the postcolonial map. To examine Orientalism as a decadent discourse in this sense—as a discourse that is both disintegrating internally and activating disintegration externally—requires a theoretical framework that can account for the ambivalence inherent in the concept of decadence itself. If Orientalism is a style of evaluation, then the hallmark of this style is its dual function as both a descriptive and a performative discourse. In other words, the Orientalist claims made by those seeking to legitimate European colonialism (William Jones, Silvestre de Sacy, Renan), German National Socialism (Ludwig Alsdorf, Paul Thieme),[4] or American Empire (Bernard Lewis) not only mobilize their ethnolinguistic evaluations of Indians, Egyptians, Jews, or Muslims in support of power, but they also assert these descriptions as ontological truth. These "ontological truths" about who, exactly, is decadent, may then circulate as distillations of the "medicine" of human reason (whether Greco-European or Indo-Germanic) whose "success," 'Abduh asserts, would be obvious even to the blind and the deaf. The dissemination of the truth of the Semitic object *in the colony* is one crucial if underexplored way that Orientalism has been able to accomplish the fragmentation and degeneration it only claims to describe. It is thus a decadent discourse both in the sense that it measures degeneration and decline but also because its very function, like that of the modern cluster bomb, is to break apart and to disperse its dangerous objects indiscriminately over a wide area.

The ambivalence that marks the discourse of the *nahda* derives, in part, from Orientalism's doubled function. The consciousness of the *nahda* as a liberating historical break is indissociable from the acute awareness of the state of decadence articulated in nineteenth-century Arabic thought. It would be far from the truth, however, to say that Arab and Islamic intellectuals simply adopted European models of historical decadence or social decline. Rather, Orientalist prognoses of decadence tended both to validate and intensify indigenous discourses of social evaluation. This complex relationship goes beyond issues of cultural translation, such as the continued attempts to transcribe the concepts of European political thought into the lexicon of Islamic jurisprudence.[5] More important than ideology was the material evidence of European wealth and disciplinary techniques, both of which served—for Arabic intellectuals like 'Abduh—as irrefutable evidence of the success of Europe's "remedy" for decadence. The "influence" of Europe upon many Arabic intellectuals' perception of the decadent state of Arabic culture was not the gift of European rationality, but rather the gift of its own shadow, obscuring the myriad forms of Arabic reason in the infinitely brighter light of *the* Enlightenment, while also exposing the inadequacy of the "lands ruled by the spirit of Islam."[6] Nor can European Orientalism be said to simply play the part of a tutor of

Enlightenment in the *nahda*; more important, I would argue, it served as a tutor of decadence. Khaled Fahmy makes a similar claim in the specific context of Egyptian legal "reform" during the nineteenth century, arguing that the transformation of the legal system "was inspired not only by liberal European ideas but also by a less enlightened aspect of this same 'modern' Europe, an aspect that taught rulers of Egypt how to tighten their grip over their subjects and how to make their rule more efficient and productive" (226). The very concept of the historical awakening of the *nahda* thus emerges in the intellectual climate of Orientalist decadence, which is primarily a technique of "dominating, restructuring, and having authority" (Said 1978, 3), not just *over* the Orient, but *within* the Orient in the absence of any visibly *other* colonial master.

Each chapter in this book develops a distinct theoretical paradigm to account for the specific texts and contexts put into play in my highly selective case studies. The critical methodology employed throughout aims to locate the reciprocal disfigurations produced by the authors and texts under consideration. Take, for instance, Friedrich Nietzsche, whose specter haunts the margins of these paradigms: He is at once a product of the "age of decadence" and the thinker who theorizes Empire radically *otherwise*, in many ways making possible our own discursive moment. Yet I do not simply seek to measure the *nahda* against Nietzsche, but rather to suggest that the decaying discourse of colonial modernity both erupts within and prefigures his concern with decadence, nomadism, genealogy, and the symptom. *Decadent Orientalisms* deconstructs specific oppositions, such as European form vs. Arabic content, or French theory vs. Arabic literature, thereby articulating the ways that *writing* thinks, following Stathis Gourgouris,[7] or how literature operates as theory in action. Especially when reading non-European texts, it becomes necessary to locate theory where it exists, whether that be philology, poetry, or theology. The distinctive critical frames I utilize allow me to articulate the intimately separate relationship between French and Arabic decadence in various ways: as a stalled awakening within the utopian dream palaces of European progress (Introduction and Chapter 1); as the dissolution of the colonial symptom in carnivalesque language play (Chapter 2); as a symptomatic fetish imported into the colony (Chapter 3); as the reanimation of Orientalist antagonisms in the postcolonial nation-state (Chapter 4); in the nationalization of loss, and the imperative that women, specifically, mourn this loss (Chapter 5); and finally as the virtual secularization of transnational Islam mobilized within global circuits of power (Chapter 6). These configurations suggest something of the contrapuntal structure of critique—adapted from Said's own critical method—within which this study seeks to relocate discourses of influence, contamination, translation, and Enlightenment.[8]

Historical Awakening as Defamiliarization

This introductory essay articulates a theory of awakening in history that will help us connect French, Arabic, and Islamic reformist discourses as they engage the ideas about decadence that were so prevalent during the fin de siècle in France and beyond.[9] Each subsequent chapter explores a key moment, figure, or juncture where the fate of the Orient itself would seem to be predestined to decline, regress, collapse, and fail; consequently, Arabic and Muslim responses and resistances to such a narrative are foregrounded throughout. The book's *longue durée* approach, beginning in the nineteenth century and ending in the twenty-first, aims to trace an arc that might provide not only a more global understanding of the juncture of French Orientalism and decadence, but also an appreciation of how Arabic and Islamic intellectuals conceived their own modernity amidst the rising din of European imperialism and the disintegration of the Ottoman Empire, and how imbricated discourses of awakening and somnolence, progress and regression, have inflected subsequent thinkers and authors.

The figures used in nineteenth-century French Orientalism to depict the East as decadent, as scholars before and after Edward Said have repeatedly shown, illustrate the range and elasticity of European repertoires for describing, managing, and dominating Europe's Eastern neighbors. These well-rehearsed subjects might be said to achieve a kind of critical mass in the French literary imagination with the Romantic obsessions of Chateaubriand, Lamartine, Hugo, and Nerval, whose imagined Orient provided the almost blank page onto which they could trace the contours of their own fantasies and desires. Romantic Orientalism morphed into the scientific Orientalist techniques of Ernest Renan, who forced the Orient, conceived as a static, dead branch on the human family tree, into the stalled second position in his pseudo-Hegelian dialectic of progress. For Renan, the ever-changing *telos* of this narrative of progress ultimately finds its home among the races of Europe, but only after having traversed, and disposed of, the rest of humanity on its way. Renan will serve as the primary theorist of Orientalist decadence, and substantial space will be devoted to working through his writing, both later in this Introduction and in Chapter 1. The literary versions of Orientalist fantasies that came to prevail in the second half the nineteenth century in writers such as Flaubert and Loti constituted a self-conscious effort to revive the ancient energies supposedly embodied in the figure of the decadent Oriental by "acting out" or playing the role, a cultural transvestism that was often conceived as an alternative to the homogeneity and mediocrity generated by the inexorable march of the kind of progress envisioned by Renan.[10] As an important moment in the genealogy of Orientalism, the decadent strain in French letters featured a continued exploitation of the East as tabula rasa for the European imagination, but also witnessed the denaturalization of national, historical, and gender categories whose relative stability was necessary to maintaining faith in European progress. In texts that belong to what has become the canon of the French decadent literary corpus— beginning with Flaubert, Baudelaire, and Verlaine, and continuing through Huysmans, Villiers de l'Isle d'Adam, Octave Mirbeau, and Rachilde (among others), one witnesses the dissolution of an authentic European subject of history, a dissolution that is often mediated through the Orient, the Oriental, and the "arabesque."[11] While the "coincidence" of decadence in both French and Arabic letters of the period served as a point of departure for the current text, this is not a book about the decadent French authors of the 1880s, but rather something else entirely. A brief discussion of French literary decadence nonetheless provides important context for, as well as something of a contrast to, the core concerns of Part I: philology and Islamic reformist discourse in the context of the *nahda*. At the same time as the French *décadents* are responding to progress by aestheticizing disease and textualizing hysteria, Arabic intellectuals are responding to both the declining Ottoman Empire and the ascending European powers by reinventing the Arab-Islamic past and asserting an authentic Arab subject as awakening in history. Beginning with al-Tahtawi's description of his educational mission to Paris, published in the 1830s, and continuing throughout the nineteenth century, a growing body of work in Arabic, while coming from an incredibly diverse pool of writers writing in a variety of geographical locations, with the range of opinions, attitudes, and styles to be expected from such a vast sampling, all agreed on one point: that the Arab world (or the East, Islam, etc) was in a state of decadence—*inhitat*— compared with both the current European powers and the Islamic past. The ways of configuring this decadence and of identifying the underlying reasons for decline were as numerous as the individual texts themselves.[12]

One way to articulate the relationship between the aforementioned French and Arabic writers would be to say that while the French were acting out the role of the Oriental in order to cure themselves of progress, their Arab and Muslim counterparts were trying on the role of the Occidental in order to cure themselves of decadence. Flaubert's Egyptian costume and Loti's lavish Turkish salon and clothing were extracted from an Ottoman Empire whose own dress codes were becoming officially westernized by the *tanzimat* reforms beginning in 1829.[13] While France was under the spell of *contes orientaux*, Muhammad 'Abduh was writing his Enlightenment-inspired version of Islamic jurisprudence, Jurji Zaydan was penning novelistic imitations of Sir Walter Scott, and Farah Antun was publishing his thoughts on secularism, inspired by Ernest Renan. The relationship seems to be one of mutual inversion and imitation: the Arabic writers understand themselves as truly "decadent," and aim at Western-inspired progress, while the French decadents feel overwhelmed by progress, and aim at Oriental decadence. The comparativist is thus presented with what appears to be a set of interlocking figures whose very symmetry betrays their constructedness. Such an understanding of this relationship envisions two entities yearning toward each other, dreaming in the direction of each other, yet completely missing one another. The unevenness of the relationship between Europe and the Arab world reminds us, however, that while the French turn to an imaginary, opulent East takes place in the context of the visible excesses produced by colonial capitalism, the Arabic glance westward takes place amidst the very material lack revealed through the comparison with European wealth and power.

As a way out of the mirrored hall of theories of cross-cultural influence and pseudo-dialectical notions of colonial tutelage, this introduction will first look at what is called *al-nahda* in conjunction with the concept of historical awakening suggested by Walter Benjamin in the notes collected for the *Arcades Project*. Before elaborating this theoretical juxtaposition, however, it is necessary to briefly look at the more standard uses of the term *nahda* in Arabic literary history and criticism.

The Arabic word most commonly used to describe the period in question has its own rich genealogy. According to what has become something like the standard historical account, *al-nahda* is most often considered to have been initiated in 1798 with the entry of Napoleon in Egypt and to have come to a close with the 1914 War and the end of the Ottoman Empire in 1922. It has therefore often been understood as a period marked by increasing contact with and the growing influence of Europe. The *Lisan al-'arab* dictionary defines *nahda as* "power and force"; Edward William Lane's nineteenth-century dictionary locates this power in the human being: the verbal root *nun-ha'-dad* its infinitive means "he rose, or stood up," or "sped, or hastened, to or towards, the people, or company of men," either in an act of simple departure, or in order to meet the enemy; the nominal form in Lane is defined as "a single act of rising" (2860); Reinhart

Dozy's supplement to Lane adds the sense of preparedness, of being in a state or condition to perform a given action (729). *Nahda* thus evokes a forceful and capable individual rising in haste to meet another. Such a definition provides a rough outline of the resonance that the term *nahda* provided for those, like Jurji Zaydan, Butrus al-Bustani, and Farah Antun, who sought to describe and configure the historical context in which they wrote and for those who continue to employ the term.

Nada Tomiche's article in the *Encyclopedia of Islam* rightly points out the problem with translating the term as "renaissance," as has often been done in both English and French treatments of the period. The first problem with this term is its obvious Eurocentric associations. This is not to say that the *nahdawis* did not conceive of themselves as the beneficiaries of Napoleon and Europe, but only that their conception of their relationship with European culture was more complex than any influence-model would indicate. (The fact that later critics are by no means required to rehearse the terms of literary history as it was conceived in its contemporary context is another important consideration, and one to which I will return later.) "The most eminent of the pioneers to speak of *Nahda*," Tomiche writes, was Zaydan, who associates the movement with "the beneficial contribution of the West to the East, a contribution which he sees as beginning with Bonaparte's invasion" (900). Both assertions—that Napoleon in Egypt marked the beginning of the "Arab Awakening"[14] (as the *nahda* is sometimes called in English), and that Europe acted as a kind of cultural benefactor to the Arab world—have since taken on the status of fact in many treatments of this period in Arabic literary and cultural history.[15] The second problem with conceiving of the *nahda* as a kind of "rebirth," Tomiche insists, is that *nahda* is most suited to the specific situation of Arabic literary history, which constituted a radical break from the past. This distinguishes it from the situation of Islamic reformism of the period, which often articulated its project as a return to the lost purity of the earlier Muslim community. While there is certainly some truth to her assertion that "Islamic scholars are not confronted by the same situation as that which faces literary historians," to separate the Islamic strain of late nineteenth-century Arabic thought from what might be called a more properly literary strain does not help us to understand why these two responses to historical phenomena developed as they did.

While the specific use of the term *nahda*, as outlined here, is an explicit element of Arabic literary writers' self-description, there is a substantial body of work by non-Arab Islamic scholars that also refers to the *nahda* or "awakening" of Arab or Islamic society at large. In his November 1882

"Lecture on Teaching and Learning" delivered in Calcutta, the Persian father of modern Islamic reformism, Jamal al-Din al-Afghani, began his address to "the youth of India" by declaring his joy that after "having awakened after a long sleep, [they] are reclaiming their inheritance and gathering the fruit of their own tree" (102). Here Afghani configures modernity in a way that is germane with the main currents of Islamic reformist thought for which he was an important antecedent. Aziz al-Azmeh argues that the discourse of this period was both unhistorical and overly concerned with the ideas of authenticity that have structured Islamic reform movements since Afghani and have since spread into pan-Islamic and pan-Arab discourse. The "truth" of the "authentic historical subject," al-Azmeh writes, "is an ontological truth, one whose resistance to the vagaries of time is demonstrated by the revivalist belief in its capacity for resuscitation" (88). "Time," he continues, "is therefore cleft between origins and corruptions, between authenticity and the snares of enemies" (89). Al-Azmeh conceives of Afghani's authentic Islamic subject as an engine of decadent faith in a way that is not completely irrelevant to *nahda* as the rising of the individual to meet an enemy. After the long sleep of inauthentic existence brought on by a variety of foreign influences (which we will elaborate later), the Islamic youth of India, in Afghani's understanding, have become again what they once were and are claiming what was theirs to begin with, conceived as an organic birthright ("the fruit of their own tree"). Indeed, for Afghani, the rights of the awakening individual are indivisible from the rights of the awakening nation, which he conceives as a "vitalistic body" (85).

What I hope to tease out in the rest of this section is that Afghani's conception of an authentic Islamic subject—and along with it the beginnings of modern pan-Islamic ideology—is, in part, complicit with the Renan's racist, Eurocentric, and Orientalist notion of the modern secular subject. While Al-Azmeh points out that Afghani gets his anthropomorphic vision of the nation from Islamic medieval philosophy, he also argues that Afghani's romantic notion of authenticity "lies at the intersection of a number of concepts that are foreign to classical Islamic thought," although the sources of Afghani's understanding of the authentic are hard to trace (85). Al-Azmeh suggests that such ideas could have reached Afghani in rather unsystematic ways—orally and through occasional references in newspapers—but also affirms the possibility that specific social or political conditions may foster the "spontaneous growth" of romantic nationalist concepts (85). In either case, Afghani's concept of an authentic subject of history may very well be derived, at least in part, from Enlightenment ideas, but its ideological derivation is less important, it can be argued, than the fact that these ideas are deployed in response to specific threats made against actual bodies, here in reference to Indian Muslims under British colonial rule. Afghani makes a similar point in his response to Renan of 1883, when he writes: "I am here pleading to M. Renan not the case of Islam, but rather that of many hundreds of millions of men who would thus be condemned to live in barbarity and ignorance" (39). Afghani appeals here to Renan's supposedly universalistic humanism by making his cause that of "many hundreds of millions of men," and not the abstract entity of Islam. Thus while the time of the authentic subject is conceived in terms of its lack of historicity, as self-identical and undisturbed as is a period of deep sleep, the event that awakens the sleeping body of Islam—the discovery of the narrative of European progress in the context of European colonial aggression—is conceived of as an event that causes this body to assert its own continuity in time, and even to demand entry into this time.

Beyond the problems presented by the Islamic intellectual's attempt to assimilate or translate European ideas is the question of how someone in Afghani's position uses the tools available to him strategically in response to specific situations. Reading the precarious contingencies of Afghani's position suggests one reason why the term *nahda* has only rarely been used to describe the various versions of Islamic reformism of the nineteenth century. The supposed return to an authentic Islamic past envisioned by Muhammad 'Abduh and others, was, as many have pointed out, not a return to any form of Islam that had existed in the past, but a profoundly new interpretation of Islamic law and theology.[16] In other words, the modernity of Afghani's Islam is carefully hidden behind the mask of Islamic authenticity. On the other hand, the intellectual and literary movement that has been affiliated with the term *nahda*, as Tomiche herself has shown, was also concerned with narrating an authentic Arab subject, but had more to gain by explicitly making claims to a rupture with the past and its own modernity.[17] While both the Islamic reformists and the *nahdawis* responded to events with innovations, those with a stake in Islam were especially careful to disavow the novelty of their response as a way of maintaining religious legitimacy.

It is here that playing *nahda* against Walter Benjamin may help to elucidate this kind of awakening in history that is conceived as the continuity of an authentic subject of history. Benjamin articulates his own historical materialist project as a way of violently disrupting the narrative of a self-identical subject of history, whose advancement toward a goal is self-evident; the effect of historical materialism, Benjamin famously asserts in his "Theses," is "to blast open the continuum of history" (263). He opposes this violent dislodging of self-complacent historical narrative to the naturalization of what he calls, after Bergson, "homogeneous time," which closely resembles the "empty" time of the authentic Islamic subject as understood by reformers like Afghani and 'Abduh. If the discourse of authenticity is an engine of decadent faith, it is also an engine of faith in progress. Benjamin equates the narrative of progress with the kind of historical narrative whose itinerary can only be mapped onto a blank page, and he erects his own project in contradistinction to such an emptying out of historical time: "The concept of the historical progress of mankind cannot be sundered from the concept of its progression through a homogeneous, empty time. A critique of the concept of such a progression must be the basis of any criticism of the concept of progress itself" (1999, 261). Following Benjamin, the aim of what follows will be to critique the different versions of this homogeneous time of progress in texts by Renan and Afghani, and to read the *nahda*, in spite of the claims its leading proponents made on its behalf, as a disruption of the continuous dream narratives of both French Orientalism and Arabic decadence.

If, as Marx asserts in a letter quoted in *The Arcades Project*, "the reform of consciousness consists *solely* in . . . the awakening of the world from its dream about itself" (456), the moment of awakening is decisive, as Benjamin indeed affirms. Benjamin deploys awakening to understand the abruptness of historical consciousness as distinct from the gradual becoming supposedly assured by European science. The articulation of awakening as a concept, like the rest of the material collected in the *Arcades Project*, has only come to us in fragmentary and tentative form, so my use of the idea here will be part reconstruction, part speculation, and part *détournement*, since Benjamin conceives of this concept as specific to the needs and material reality of European history. As Susan Buck-Morss writes in her book about the *Arcades Project*, Benjamin's own methodological concerns implicitly suggest the kinds of use that the future should make of his ideas: "It follows that in the service of truth, Benjamin's own text must be 'ripped out of context,' sometimes, indeed with a 'seemingly brutal grasp'" (340). To bring Benjamin into a discussion of Islamic reformism is no decontextualized theoretical gesture, however, as French articulations and manifestations of progress in the writings of Guizot and Renan, as well as the material reality of Paris itself as visible proof of this progress, were also important for likes of al-Tahtawi, Afghani, and 'Abduh.[18] As will become evident, my use of Benjamin for an analysis of modernity in Renan and thinkers of the *nahda* allows me to defamiliarize both *nahda* and European frameworks for thinking through colonial modernity.[19] While Benjamin's writing on history as awakening emerged out of his desire to "redeem" mass culture for revolutionary purposes,[20] I intend to use his ideas here in order to rethink the collectivities that were being invented in the late nineteenth century in Arabic/Islamic discourse: Afghani's pan-Islamic world and 'Abd al-Rahman al-Kawakibi's pan-Arab world. In both discourses, the awakening of the slumbering masses—of Arabs or Muslims—is conceived as both a radical break with the past and as a reaffirmation of its continuity.

Benjamin's notion of awakening was an attempt to do for history what Proust had done for the individual subject: to defamiliarize, in a sense, the everyday objects of existence, and thereby to charge them with renewed significance, a significance that was aesthetic for Proust, but political for Benjamin. For the awakening sleeper "politics attains primacy over history," Benjamin asserts. "The facts become something that just now first happened to us; to establish them is the affair of memory. Indeed, awakening is the great exemplar of memory: the occasion on which it is given us to remember what is closest, tritest, most obvious" (389). The sudden, jolting shock of awakening becomes the representative structure of memory here. Benjamin aligns the state of sleep with the state of childhood, and thus parallels the act of awakening to an act of childlike discovery, even as what is being "discovered," *as if* for the first time, is indeed what is "closest, tritest, most obvious," and most naturalized for the awakening subject. Buck-Morss rightly points out the literary quality of such an understanding of history, claiming that Benjamin's "theory [of dream and awakening] merges elements of Surrealism and Proust, Marx and Freud, with those of historical generations and childhood cognition in a blend that is bound together more by literary than logical means" (253).[21]

Alongside awakening as defamiliarization and popular history exists Benjamin's theory of history as allegory, in the special sense of the term that he developed in his works on German baroque drama and on Baudelaire.[22] The allegorical structure of awakening becomes especially clear in the following fragment, which likens the process of the individual's physiological awakening to the possibility of the collective's recognition of its own material history:

> The nineteenth century a spacetime [Zeitraum] (a dreamtime) in
> which the individual consciousness more and more secures itself in
> reflecting, while the collective consciousness sinks into ever deeper
> sleep. But just as the sleeper—in this respect like the madman—sets

out on the macrocosmic journey through his own body, and the noises and feelings of his insides, such as blood pressure, intestinal churn, heartbeat and muscle sensation (which for the waking and salubrious individual converge in a steady stream of health) generate, in the extravagantly heightened inner awareness of the sleeper, illusion or dream imagery, which translates and accounts for them, so likewise for the dreaming collective, which, through the arcades, communes with its own insides. (389)

This passage reveals an allegorical understanding of historical consciousness much in the way that Fredric Jameson conceives of a "political unconscious" that finds its allegorical expression in specific cultural forms.[23] Benjamin's understanding of the relationship of the material base of society to its ideological superstructure is, in this sense, allegorical. Just as the material state of the body (the "intestinal churn" caused by an overfull stomach) becomes translated into the images of dreams, so, too, do culture and ideology translate the material state of society into forms that are not simply *determined*, as mimetic reflections, for example, would be. Instead, Benjamin ironically denatures culture by describing it in terms of natural processes that are somehow beyond the reach of the conscious subject, the way that dreams reach beyond the physical body of the dreamer. What interests Benjamin is "the role of bodily processes around which 'artistic' architectures gather, like dreams around the framework of physiological processes" (1999, 391).

Such a translation of the material base into superstructure is allegorical in as much as there is no apparent organic connection between the signifier and signified, there is no necessary connection between a full stomach and the dream that may come from it, and more specifically for Benjamin here, there is no necessary, obvious, natural connection between the masses strolling through the Parisian *passages* and the iron and glass spaces through which they pass. This very incongruity, like the incongruities generated by the deliberately random juxtapositions of the surrealists, becomes, for Benjamin, an index of awakening from the dreamworld of the nineteenth century. Indeed, it would be difficult to make the relatively banal space of the Paris arcades any stranger than to think of them as the skeletal and intestinal structure of the social body. There is thus both a juxtaposition of the strange and the seemingly familiar here, and also a photographic superimposition of the two modes of perception, which comes out of Benjamin's singularly surrealist understanding of the dialectic, which, as Buck-Morss has pointed out, is primarily *visual*. For Benjamin, she writes, "'the dialectic' allowed superimposition of fleeting images, present and past, that made both suddenly come alive in terms of revolutionary meaning" (220).

This apparently incongruous juxtaposition of Benjamin's notion of awakening with the concept and practice of *nahda* allows us to revise both France's role as tutor and Greater Syria and Egypt's roles as pupil in the "Arab Awakening" of the nineteenth century, without simply reversing the poles of such a configuration, as many on both sides of the issue have done. Such a concept also prompts us to understand the awakening in history of the *nahda* as a sudden juxtaposition of local and European objects that effects a certain defamiliarization of Islam and Arabic culture; we can likewise conceive of certain forms of what has been called French decadence as a similar practice that seeks out the shock of otherness in order to denature the French or European self. Rather than viewing Napoleon as the agent that awakens a sleeping Orient, or seeing the Orient as the symbolic other that reinvigorates a decadent Occident, we see that both French decadence and Arabic awakening are responses to the material changes brought about by the colonial and capitalist modernity of the late nineteenth century.

Renan's Anti-Semitic Philosophy of History

The discourse of progress calls into being the discourse of decadence, and both function on the level of the kind of secular faith that Ernest Renan preached so tirelessly and eloquently throughout his career. In Renan, the discourses of progress, decadence, and Orientalism in the nineteenth century find their most celebrated, and their most symptomatic, expression. Here I focus on Renan's anti-Semitic philosophy of history both to frame the larger discussions that run throughout this book and to serve as prelude to his importance for Arab and Muslim thinkers, which is presented in Chapter 1. E. M. de Vogue's eulogistic assertion from 1893, the year after Renan's death, provides a fittingly grand claim about the famed Orientalist's importance to his century: "Renan was to the world of ideas," wrote de Vogue, "what Victor Hugo was to the world of forms: the universal mirror, the most diffused interpreter of ways of thinking of his age."[24] Renan's status as an intellectual giant would quickly cede place to a more symbolic understanding of him as the "charming poet of *Souvenirs de jeunesse* and as the one who denied the divinity of Jesus in *La vie de Jésus*" (Gore 1970, 298). The Dreyfus affair, cleaving French society between the Catholic right and the secular left, made him into a leftist figure, which he certainly was not; while the left ignored his rather reactionary and elitist political ideas, the Catholics ignored his effusive embrace of Christianity, which he came to understand as the motor of modern progress. Renan's influence reached well beyond France, as he and his works served as an important point of contact for many Arabic and Islamic thinkers, including Afghani, with whom he participated in the celebrated debate that will be analyzed in Chapter 1. Renan was also important for Farah Antun, one of the earliest sustained voices in favor of secularizing the societies of the Near East, and the translator who rendered Renan's *La vie de Jésus* into Arabic between 1901 and 1902. Antun also wrote a book on Ibn Rushd that closely followed the argument in Renan's *Averroès et l'averroïsme*. This book spawned a debate with 'Abduh in the newspaper he edited, *al-Jami'a*, that mirrored the Renan-Afghani debate in the *Journal des débats*.[25] The use that Antun made of Renan thus mirrors the misrepresentation that came to constitute Renan's legend in France: While Antun and Renan appeared to many readers as progressive men of the left, 'Abduh, who supported Afghani's critique of Islam while in Paris, makes Antun and Renan into enemies of religion, even though their versions of the secular retain a distinctly religious tone.

Gary Shapiro accounts for Renan's enormous appeal during his lifetime by the fact that "he allowed his readers to believe themselves scientific and even a bit skeptical, while still allowing them to indulge in religious sentiments" in a wholly "voluptuous" manner (1982, 215). Renan's philosophy of history represents, above all else, a disavowedly mixed discourse that brought together scientific positivism and sentimental religiosity in the comforting and familiar prose style for which he is famous. While Renan, in line with the long lineage of Enlightenment thinkers, asserts that humankind has only recently awoken from its long sleep of ignorance, he ultimately homogenizes the time of history by forcing all events to signify the inevitability of European progress, evaluating all past history either as useful and necessary links in the chain that binds his European audience together, or as being useful to gauge decadence and stunted growth. In the latter case, the degeneracy of other races, especially the Semitic, both proves European health and provides negative examples of how not to behave, think, and live as a nation. Renan can thus be made to stand in for the well-fed, bourgeois dreamer of Benjamin's allegory of awakening who, instead of defamiliarizing the objects of everyday existence, provides his readers with a false sense of familiarity with what is distant from them: the ancient history of Semitic peoples. In a move similar to al-Afghani's belief in a renascent Islamic subject, Renan conceives of the awakening of nineteenth century European science as a realization of its merely dormant potential.

In English language criticism, Renan's specter has resurfaced as Said's Orientalist Dr. Frankenstein in *Orientalism* and as the voice of French nationalist thought in the era of colonial expansion.[26] In France, however, Renan's legend has proven more resistant to the critical attitude that he himself championed. Take for example Jean Balcou's *Ernest Renan: Une biographie*, a rather "empathetic"[27] reading of Renan's life and work that won the 2016 Prix de la Biographie from the Académie Française, or the five-hundred-page publication of the *Mémorial Renan* in 1993, celebrating the contributions of Renan to the human sciences, and featuring sixteen pages of photographic plates of Renanalia, including *objets d'orient* collected during his archaeological mission in Lebanon, as well as the *penseur de Tréguier*'s death mask. While most of the contributors to the volume do take issue with certain facts, ideas, nuances, or positions articulated in Renan's oeuvre, only Bruno Etienne provides anything like a direct critique of Renan's overall project, citing his often brutal racism against "Semitic" and other non-European peoples, his "total condemnation of Islam," along with his practical ignorance of Arabic and of Islamic cultures, despite the grand claims he made about *l'arabe* and *l'islamisme* as Chair of Oriental Languages at the Collège de France (1993, 427–31). The inclusion of Etienne's critique in the book only confirms the capacity of Orientalist discourse to incorporate and thus tame dissenting views.

Renan's many flawed edicts about the meaning of Arabness, Islam, and what Said calls "the Semitic object," built in many cases on faulty or highly speculative scholarship,[28] are not simply occasional inaccuracies in his work but rather form the very basis of his thought. Renan's philological study of Semitic languages allows him to induce his theory of historical time and ultimately to relegate the prophetic and decidedly unphilosophical Semitic races to the prehistory of the narrative of progress. As Johannes Fabian has pointed out, such a "denial of coevalness" of non-Western societies is constitutive of Western anthropological discourse, to which Renan's unique understanding of philology is a close cousin.[29] Renan anthropomorphizes historical progress by making the common analogy between the life of an individual and the life of humanity, where everything and everyone before—or otherwise outside of—the great awakening of European science becomes catalogued as belonging to the infancy of mankind: "After having marched long centuries in the night of childhood, without a consciousness of itself and by the sole strength of its resilience, the great moment has come when it has taken, like the individual, possession of itself, when it has recognized itself, when it has felt itself to be a living unity" (1995 [1890], 95). Although Renan's philosophy of history appears

Hegelian, this is true only in the sense that mankind's progress consists in recognizing the *Geist* that was always there to begin with. While Renan's historical ideas share a surface resemblance with a Marxist understanding of history as awakening from a dream, Renan remains an idealist to the core. Whereas Benjamin likens the awakening subject of history to a child whose very disorientation generates the significance of what he remembers, Renan infantilizes those ("savages" and "Semites") who prove his own narcissistic and paranoid fantasies of Aryan and Celtic hygiene and potency.[30]

Renan's scientific idealism reveals itself most notably in his racial theories of human intellectual development, which have their source in his own romantic, egocentric view of himself as representing the healthy, "normal," and ideal subject of human adulthood. He repeats the gesture, common in the French nineteenth century, of locating the moment of humanity's self-recognition in the French Revolution, as the first act of a mature and autonomous entity:

> It has been scarcely a half century since humanity has understood itself and reflected. . . . It is the moment corresponding to that when the child, guided heretofore by spontaneous instincts, caprice, and the will of others, asserts himself as a free and moral person, responsible for his acts. (1995 [1890], 96)[31]

Like other thinkers before him, Renan sought to cancel out with one sweeping gesture all human history that preceded the French Revolution. The irrational period preceding the coming of humanity's self-consciousness, he argues, will one day only be seen as a "curious preface" to the chapters of human history that remain to be written.

This canceling out of non-Aryan history, which, in *The Future of Science*, Renan buries amidst that book's thirty pages of footnotes, deserves to be brought into the main body of his text and emphasized as a structural necessity that supports his faith in progress. The footnote bolsters a passage from the text that aims to legitimate slavery when it has served the work of "humanity." In the footnote, Renan explicates his hierarchy of racial values, which are elsewhere articulated in a much more restrained, scientific, and seemingly objective manner:

> We are indignant about the manner in which man is treated in the Orient and in the barbaric states, and the little value attributed there to human life. This is not so revolting, when one considers that the barbarian possesses little, and *en effet*, infinitely less worth than

civilized man. The death of a Frenchman is an event in the moral world; that of a Cossack is scarcely a physiological fact: a machine was functioning that no longer functions. And as for the death of a savage, it is scarcely a fact more considerable in the grand scheme of things than when the spring of a watch breaks, and even this last fact can have more serious consequences, if only because the watch in question fixes the thought and excites the activity of civilized men. What is deplorable, is that a portion of humanity is degraded to such a point that it counts scarcely more than the animal; for all men are called to a moral value. (1995 [1890], 520)

Renan transfers his reader's projected moral indignation at the despotic violence of "decadent" societies onto a kind of righteous anger over the subhumanity of such societies, which is to be understood as an accomplished scientific fact. He further masks the structural necessity of this kind of Orientalist racism for his faith in science with a somewhat disingenuously belated self-critique.

Renan affirms the total sovereignty of science and of *"la grande civilisation purement humaine,"* which, even when it appears to be in a state of decline, "will vanquish once again her vanquishers, forever in the same way, until the day when there will be no one left to vanquish and she will reign with full rights as sole mistress" (1995 [1890], 136). The absolute affirmation of a "purely human civilization," combined with the absolute disposability of savages and Semites functions quite harmoniously in Renan, despite his rather transparently particularized brand of universalism. Even when he evokes a supranational conception of human civilization, the human is always defined, in however obscured a fashion, against the nonhuman barbarians at the gate. Renan denies those who toil toward human perfection and civilization the right to claim their own work; such a refusal reveals what makes Renan's thinking merely pseudo-Hegelian, a kind of unconscious parody of Hegel.[32] Renan retains from Hegel's parable of the master and the slave the necessity of the slave's work, and the furtherance of spirit through such work, but he refuses the slave the self-consciousness, and the liberation, his work is supposed to earn him. "The freeing of blacks was neither won nor earned by the blacks, but by the progress of their masters' civilization," he asserts later in the text (396). Renan's version of the dialectic does not accurately predict the future—decolonization on a global scale—but it does validate Frantz Fanon's assessment of the breakdown of the dialectic in the context of colonialism, which consisted precisely in denying the slave the fruits of his or her own labor.[33]

Renan then implies that the labor done in the work of civilization will be divided unequally among European nations, from France to Russia, entirely erasing the work done by non-European others. While the sovereignty of the future as the absolute motivator of progress allows him to blur the differences between European nations, the genius of this civilization to come may indeed bear the mark of nationality and race, provided this nation is spiritually "superior." The hermeneutical circle of Renan's understanding of national and racial categories permits him to affirm nationality when it suits him and to transcend it when necessary. The strategic essentialism of this gesture functions not on the principle of solidarity with the oppressed, but with the affirmation of the "superior" nation. This becomes a vicious circle when read in conjunction with Renan's own quite reactionary politics, which have been understood as favoring whichever party was able to secure power at any given moment.[34] His philosophy of history disavows decadence by asserting a false universal, whose inclusiveness is adumbrated by the fluid national and racial identifications found everywhere in his work. Despite Renan's Hegelian intimations, he ultimately asserts the infallible health of the Indo-European scientist, simply affirming the superiority of the master, and denying the savage, barbarian, or Semitic worker the value of his or her own labor, thus precluding any claim he or she might have had in the future, in the work of progress, or in humanity itself.

The requirements of Renan's transdisciplinary, comparative approach to history force him to seek out scientific value in any and all objects that he encounters, while his reactionary idealism provides a ready-made narrative of relative value arranged in a rigid hierarchy. His ambivalence with regard to his chosen discipline, which is most often articulated in relation to the Hebrew language and Jewish history, is also prominent in his statements on Islam and Arabs. His 1852 thesis, published in 1862, *Averroès et l'averroïsme*, combines praise and condemnation throughout the sections on "*la philosophie arabe*," which, he tells us, "offers one of the very few examples of a very advanced culture suppressed almost instantly without having left any trace, and very nearly forgotten by the people who created it" (1949 [1852], 13). This still-born school of thought serves him well, however, as his thesis allows him, to paraphrase Said, to artificially revive the fetus of Arabic philosophy in the figure of the great Cordovan thinker, Ibn Rushd (Averroes), if only to inter it a second time in the demise of the Paduan scholastic philosophers. While Renan praises Ibn Rushd for his struggle against religious orthodoxy, he ultimately finds value only in his failure to correctly interpret Aristotle, whose works formed the basis for

Ibn Rushd's vast body of commentaries. "There will emerge from this study," Renan writes, "almost no result that contemporary philosophy might advantageously assimilate, unless it be the historical result itself" (17), which for Renan was failure and oblivion. Only Greece, Renan adds, and most certainly not the Semitic race, is authorized to give lessons in philosophy: "On the contrary, if instead of asking for doctrines from the past, we only ask for facts, periods of decadence and syncretism, periods of transmission and slow alteration, would hold more interest than periods of perfection" (17–18). Renan diagnoses the decadence of the Semitic race from a position that combines the supposed objectivity of positivist science with the subjectivity of the fascinated spectator, which as Said has pointed out, was Renan's "ideal role" (1979, 147).

Not only does Renan's artificially revived Ibn Rushd allow him to support his thesis about the degenerate Semitic race and the scourge of Islamic despotism, but he also exploits what he considers to be the triumph of Islamic orthodoxy over "Arab philosophy" in order to assert his own secular viewpoints against the Catholic Church in France.[35] Renan's double purpose forces him to pit the universal spirit of rationalism against the multiplicity of world religions, while also continuously extracting and secularizing the essence of Christian belief in order to fuel his scientific universalism. In attempting to explain how the early burst of philosophical activity was so quickly and effectively extinguished in Islam, he compares the persecution of rational philosophers in Arab lands to what happened in Catholic Spain (presumably during the Inquisition), and to what could have happened in the rest of Europe "if the religious revival at the end of the XVIIth century had quashed all rational development" (1949 [1852], 43).

While Renan's philologically legitimated philosophy of history purports to outline a theory of progress, it is shot through with his theory of regression and decline. We witness the same discursive doubling in the *nahda*. Although it has often been viewed as a mimetic discourse that merely reiterates or translates European theories of secular, humanistic progress into an Arab or Islamic context, it also translates and assimilates the disavowed "dark side of progress," namely, the racial, national, and thoroughly "secular" theories of decadence and degeneration current during the European fin de siècle. One is tempted to recast Benjamin's famous dictum regarding civilization and barbarism, and assert that there is no document of Enlightenment that is not at the same time a document of decadence.[36] Renan's pseudo-constructivist discourse will set the limits of future discourse regarding secularism, religion, and the postcolonial nation-state,

Introduction: Orientalist Decadence

while also anticipating the way that state actors will justify or dismiss violence in the age of postcolonial civil wars and the War on Terror.

His work reveals the equation of Orientalist decadence, *decadence* = *time* + *loss*, where *loss* is comparatively derived and *time* is fraught with repetitions, corruptions, homogeneities, and teleologies. The time of Orientalist decadence collapses trajectories of progress and regress. Renan brings to light the way that European discourses of degeneration, while often constructing typologies of normality and abnormality, of health and sickness, often succumbed to the very semantic slippage inherent in the ideas of decline, decay, degeneration, and decadence that informed them. As I demonstrate in Chapter 1, Afghani and 'Abduh are only two of the best-known examples of intellectuals who translated Renan's peculiar brand of French decadence into the context of Arabic (or Islamic) revival, and who also allow us to theorize the discourse of decadence as a powerful engine of anti-imperialist critique.

PART I

(Dis)integrating Semitism: French and Arabic in the Twilight of the Ottoman Empire

CHAPTER 1

French Decadence, Arab Awakenings
Figures of Decay in the *Naḥda*

Edward Said's unrelenting and unapologetic effort to rethink and transform the interrelated critical fields of philology, humanism, and the secular continues to give pause and, in some cases, causes great consternation to critics of his work. The question often posed is this: Why would such a staunch opponent of cultural imperialism persist in using the very methodologies that his work goes to such great lengths to dismantle? I would argue that it is on this same field of operations that the viability of Saidian "secular criticism," or even the continued value of anti-Orientalist critique for the twenty-first century, must be defended. The point of departure for this chapter is this crucial constellation of terms, specifically as they came to be articulated by the nineteenth-century French philologist Ernest Renan. For Said, Renan represented the apotheosis of the capture of secular, philological humanism for the metaphysics of colonial command. This chapter returns not just to Renan but also to his reception by thinkers confessing Arab and Islamic affiliations in the Ottoman fin de siècle, focusing primarily on the period from 1883 to 1902. The aim of this return to Renan and the trope of decadence is thus to demonstrate the necessity, from Said's perspective and for our own, of radicalizing, not abandoning, all three critical tasks: humanism, philology, and the secular.[1]

Why, then, decadence? My argument is that Orientalism uses decadence as the figure through which its positivist scientific claims become redistributed as performative speech acts, meaning its "truths" about Oriental decadence are distributed among the objects of its study ("Orientals") within the terrain over which it seeks textual (and ultimately, political) authority ("the Orient"). Yet at the same time, the situation I am trying to give an account of here is also one of asymmetrical defamiliarization, since the European epistemological structures that get embedded outside of Europe also get overcoded and altered, not just through the interference generated through translation but also more effectively—and belatedly, I should add—via the long processes of decolonization and anti-imperialist and anti-Orientalist critique. Of course, this mutual defamiliarization is asymmetrical, because the flow of ideas and armatures of representation from Europe eastward was often almost immediate and sometimes widespread, whereas the resurgent flow back toward Europe took more time, moving along the most improbable currents of transmission and dissemination (as I will describe in relation to Renan and Farah Antun), constituting a version of Nietzschean "nomad thought" avant la lettre. The thinkers and writers of the Arab *nahda* (awakening, or renaissance) I will be discussing—Jamal al-Din al-Afghani, Abd al-Rahman al-Kawakibi, and Antun—devised their texts at ground level, shifting their tactics on a dynamic field of operations in response to the rapidly adapting strategies of imperial geopolitics and ideology. The mutual defamiliarization effected by the thought of decadence was asymmetrical also in terms of what we would now call institutional support, an important part of which was access to the archive; the differences between Renan and his Arab and Muslim interlocutors illustrate this clearly. (In fact, it is through Renan's scholarship that Antun was first introduced to the works of the great twelfth-century Cordovan philosopher, jurisconsult, and polymath Ibn Rushd, or Averroes, a fact discussed later in this chapter.) In order to understand how "Islam became an object in the struggle of interpretive space" during the nineteenth century (al-Azmeh 1993, 106), this chapter begins with how Renan and Afghani use the archive as they conceive of race and religion as functions of the relationship between progress and decline. Whereas Renan's version of the secular conceals the intensely religious spirit of European nationalism, Afghani's instrumentalization of Islam exposes the political will emerging within the object of Europe's supposedly mute other. Renan imagines Europe's coming-to-consciousness within the twin enclosures of

Hegelian idealism and academic Orientalism. Afghani, al-Kawakibi, and Antun, on the other hand, redeploy elements of these discourses in order to "awaken" from the spell of decadence cast upon them, while also falling into the sleep of the homogenous time carried within the very idea of authenticity.

"There Is No Decadence"

Ernest Renan's *L'avenir de la science* (The Future of Science), written at the beginning of his career in 1848 but not published until 1890, two years before his death, represents the self-fulfilling prophecy of the science of the New Philology as it was practiced in Paris in the second half of the nineteenth century. In his 1890 preface, Renan validates ex post facto the predications he had made about the science of philology forty-two years earlier: "*En somme*," he writes, "*j'avais raison*."[2] The only error to which he admits, the core truth that he discovered and disseminated through his teaching and writing over the course of his career, was that, in 1848, he did not possess "a sufficiently clear idea of the inequality of the races" (1995 [1890], 71–72), which, by 1890, had been "verified" by both science and colonization: "The rights of each human family to a more or less honorable mention in the history of progress are more or less determined" (73).

The text has much to say about philology, progress, secularism, and race, but, crucially, Renan disavows the validity of the concept of decadence. He writes, "There is no decadence from the point of view of humanity. Decadence is a word that must be definitively banished from the philosophy of history" (1995 [1890], 136). Just as the concept of decadence must be cut from the lexicon of progress, so, too, must the category of nationality. The one exception to these apparently sovereign rules is that there is, in fact, decadence at the level of race and nation. He continues, "We only call upon the principle of nationality when the oppressed nation is superior in spirit to the oppressor. Absolute partisans of nationality can only be narrow-minded. Human perfection is the goal. From this point of view, civilization always triumphs" (136). The relative, hierarchical values of the different "human families" are not mere accidents of Renan's personal prejudices, however, but rather serve to illustrate the function that racial and national categories serve within his philosophy of history. For there to be no decadence from the point of view of "human" history, Renan simply has to excommunicate the nonhuman elements from his secular temple of history. The idea of decadence, he argues, "only has meaning from the restricted view of politics and nationalities" (137). "When specific races atrophy," he continues, "humanity has reserve power to supplement these weaknesses" (137). Such a confession is typical of his writing, which would expose as the errors of others the very limits of his own thought: the purportedly universal category of "humanity" is, for Renan, absolutely dependent on race, nationality, and the possibility of their degeneration and decline.

Despite traces of social-constructivist gestures that his philological training seems to have left on his thought, Renan ultimately upholds a religious hierarchy that he supports primarily through his racial typology. This becomes especially clear in his celebrated study of Ibn Rushd, which offers positivistic support for his thesis about the incompatibility between the Arab mind, Islam, and a rational secular viewpoint. Renan's cancellation of the Semitic and affirmation of the Indo-European, as critics have pointed out, reads like a parody of Hegel.[3] "Enclosed," Renan writes, "like all Semitic peoples, in the narrow circle of lyricism and prophecy, the inhabitants of the Arabian Peninsula have never had the least idea about what might be called science or rationalism."[4] While Renan superficially intimates the event of medieval Arabic philosophy as a moment in the dialectic of human progress, his text ultimately denies it even the dimmed glory of such a role: "Arab Aristotelianism, personified by Averroes, was one of the great obstacles encountered by those then working so actively to found modern culture among the ruins of the middle ages" (1949 [1852], 289). The ancient science of the Greeks "returned" to the West (164) despite, not because of, the great age of Arabic philosophy (292). The difference between Oriental fatalism and Euro-Christian resistance to fate becomes the very "knot of the problem" for Renan, who explains that "the entire struggle is now taking place between the old and the new ideas of theism and morality" (1995 [1890], 102). The passage continues,

> We are here at the sacred line where doctrines part ways; one point of divergence between two lines coming out from a center places the infinite between them. It should at least be remembered that theories of progress are irreconcilable with the old theodicy, that they have no meaning apart from attributing divine action to the human spirit, in a word, by admitting as the primordial force in the world the reformative power of spirit. (1995 [1890], 102)

The least surprising aspect of this passage is the way that Renan allocates religion and science as radiating from the same source. Renan's oeuvre testifies to the fact that, as Said pointed out, the "secularizing tendency" that he represents did not seek to remove "the old religious patterns of human history and destiny" but rather to reconstitute, redeploy, and redistribute them in new frameworks.⁵ Nor does Renan's admission to his sister that *L'avenir de la science* would be his "profession of scientific faith" quite come as a revelation, as the text itself is explicit enough concerning the thoroughly Catholic nature of Renan's secularism. Renan further reveals the uncanny resemblance between his version of secularism and Christianity in his attempt to preempt the indignation of the religious reader who would accuse him of heresy: "'Oh, no!' I would say to him: 'I am your brother'" (1995 [1890], 111). It is this kind of partial sincerity that evokes for Nietzsche Renan's "broad smirk of the cleric," which Nietzsche considers to be one of Renan's "lies of seduction"; "like all priests," Nietzsche adds, "he becomes dangerous only when he falls in love" (1998, 43).

The legerdemain of Renan's "philological" method ultimately allows him to equate race with religion by employing the generalized migrancy of identifications, affiliations, and meanings common to so many forms of Orientalism, continuing through to the present day. Renan accomplishes this equation in order to explain Oriental decadence and Occidental progress: "The religions of the Orient say to man: 'Suffer Evil.' European religion may be summed up in this word: 'Fight Evil.' This race is indeed the daughter of Japheth: she is bold against God" (*Cette race est bien fille de Japet: elle est hardie contre Dieu*) (1995 [1890], 102). What he had explained elsewhere in terms of the universality of reason caught in a battle against religion, he here explains in terms of a monolithic Orient, whose multiplicity of similar religions reinforces the "lyrical and prophetic" essence of the Oriental mind that created them. Against this unphilosophical Orient, Renan posits a single European race-religion. By referring to the latter as the "daughter of Japheth," Renan reproduces, however ironically, the biblical genealogy of all human races, one of the sons of Noah being Japheth, whose offspring, according to exegetes, had spread westward to people Europe. Renan's historical projection thus reproduces the distortions of T-O maps from medieval Europe that distributed the world's people according to an edenic origin and the subsequent racial-tribal diasporas of biblical myth.⁶

What is truly remarkable about Renan's geometry of secular difference is the *sacredness* of the separation between the theory of Providence and that of progress, a sacredness that consists in progress's very irreconcilability with and difference from Providence. Such a sanctification of difference manufactures an infinite chasm between the time of European progress, which is also the time of Renan's writing, and the time of the other, a chasm that Johannes Fabian has famously dubbed "allochronism."⁷

Renan's visualization of this temporal divergence attempts to establish the hygiene of secularism in a way that reinscribes the gestures of divine medieval cartography as an act of chronotopic faith. While he asserts the categorical purity of his secular scientific viewpoint as distinct from religious perspectives, he simultaneously argues for the proximity of Christianity to rational science and maps "the religions of the Orient" as its antipodes. Such an avowal of purity obviously masks the mixed nature of Renan's own comparativist discourse, which grafts together lexical and theoretical elements from a variety of genres and disciplines ranging from philology and philosophy to theology and sentimental narrative, all in its attempt to provide a universal and secular philosophy of history. At the site where language, race, and religion—the positive symptoms of decadence—are knotted together, Renan conceives what can only be called *a political theology of the color line*, making it so internal to the logic of colonial modernity that it would lastingly remain scarcely perceptible beneath debates about race or language or secularism, considered in isolation from one another. Renan's deep Orientalism thus fuses race to religion under the rubric of anti-Semitic decadence. Such is the genesis of the Orientalist secular.

Renan vs. Afghani

Despite the disingenuous disavowal of decadence by Renan, his brand of Orientalist decadence was the very banner under which Arab and Muslim intellectuals first gained access to colonial modernity. The price of entry was a confession of decadence. That is to say that, from the outset, the Orientalist perspective tended to conceive of intellectual exchanges with such interlocutors as abstractly ideological battle royals—between West and East, secularism and religion, or science and Islam. Such was the case in the celebrated debate between Renan and the Persian Islamic reformist Afghani, which took place in 1883. This classic Orientalist ideological smoke screen—West vs. East—obscures the very different conditions that obtained with regard to the production of each man's discourse. A brief comparison of Renan's and Afghani's positions in their respective intellectual spheres in 1883, when their famous exchange on "Islam and Science" took place, can help clear some of this ideological smoke. On the one hand, there is Renan, whose understanding of history shows that he fashions himself to become a symptom of his own age, race, and nation: he construes the supposed vitality of his own Celtic heritage, mixed with his modern, rational, and French perspective, into signs of humanity's health and vitality. He is a man proud in his identifications (Celtic, French, male), confident enough in his place (Paris, the Sorbonne), and secure enough in his position (Grand-officier de la Légion d'honneur since 1880, member of l'Académie Française since 1878) to openly assert his anticlerical ideas during his blunt attacks on Arabs and Islam.

On the other hand, there is Afghani. While Renan trumpets his Celtic heritage, Jamal al-Din bears the pseudonym he adopted in 1869, "al-Afghani"—"the Afghan"—possibly as a way to conceal his Persian Shi'ite origins and to dissimulate the influence on him of certain heterodox philosophical trends associated with Shi'ism.[8] Renan is aware of Afghani's semi-covert Persian heritage, by which he justifies his guarded admiration for Afghani, who, after all, would not then be a degenerate Semite but a healthy Indo-European. Afghani, on the other hand, asserts the past greatness of the Arab people and counters Renan's European concept of race (as something determined primarily by science) with a broader concept of race that considers the role of language and culture in the construction of the category "Arab."[9] As Renan becomes more and more certain of the rigidity of racial categories over the course of his career, Afghani exemplifies their malleability, even as he engages Renan in the intellectual arena that the latter has determined, in his language, and in his city. Renan's institutional security and settled contentment contrast sharply with Afghani's cosmopolitan, nomadic life of exile. Most likely born and raised in northwest Iran (Keddie 1968, 11), Afghani spent substantial time in Afghanistan, Egypt, India, Russia, Istanbul, London, and Paris, involved in sometimes secret activities that forced local authorities to keep track of him and deport him when they deemed it necessary. While Renan's wide-ranging literary interests reveal the scope of this "armchair scholar's" (the phrase is Nietzsche's) textual preoccupation of the globe, Afghani's career brings to light the networks of contact made possible by the dissolution of the Ottoman Empire as it confronted its neighbors to the west and to the east, while also revealing the fluidity of individual political positions called forth by the volatility of colonial European and late Ottoman geopolitics.

Whereas the elite French philologist discovers lost authors, fashioning a proprietary relationship to "his Arabs," using "his" Arabic to explain the decadence of the Arabs or declaring the impossibility of "Arab science" to an actual Arab or Muslim, the practitioners of the *nahda*, or *nahdawis*, deploy a variety of critical tools in their bricolage of tactics, which I consider in this book variously under the titles of *nahda*, awakening, carnival, traversal of fantasy. The Sorbonne debate remains especially significant for the diagram it gives us of the ways that French Orientalism set the terms and conditions, both in the world and in the text, of the great transactional exchange of ideas that constituted the *nahda*.

Renan's understanding of secularism redistributes religious patterns of history in order to disguise the profound antagonism between the secular and the religious that his legend has come to signify in France. He refuses the universal truth of the gospels while affirming the particular pedigree of rationalism entrusted by the Christian legacy to the Aryan race. Renan reminds us that the development of the idea of secularism in Europe is indissociable from the ideologies of Orientalism and the colonial mission. In the words of Gayatri Spivak, the European secular project has often been articulated *within* Christianity itself, understood as an inherently "secular religion" (2004, 105). "If the judeo-christian is seen as the religion of reason," Spivak writes, "de-transcendentalized into secularism, that is also a description of capturing and controlling the possibility of the transcendental as that which is worshiped, the characteristic of religion-as-culture" (105). In other words, Renan's uncritical version of secularism merely substitutes one object of worship with another, trading God for rationalism. Said's own fascination with Renan would seem to derive from Renan's redistribution of belief as a practice that is clearly opposed to Said's own project of "secular criticism," which is finally being understood as a profound engagement with religious belief and not simply as its negation. To describe this open-ended and properly postcolonial attempt to rethink secularism, Aamir Mufti has coined the term "critical secularism," which he describes as "a constant unsettling and an ongoing and never-ending effort at critique, rather than a once-and-for-all declaration of the overcoming of the religious, theological, or transcendental impulse" (2004, 3).

Renan's secular gesture—understood as a partially disavowed transcendental impulse—can be productively mapped onto the Islamic reformism represented by Afghani. An analysis of the celebrated 1883 debate between Afghani and Renan that took place in the *Journal des débats* demonstrates the *nahda* as an awakening in history, as a sudden recognition of coevalness accomplished both through the affirmation of an authentic subject of history and its defamiliarization. Such a proposition can also be inverted, suggesting that the affirmation of an authentic subject of history was viewed, in nineteenth-century nationalist discourses, as the ironic precondition for the possibility of a mutual recognition of coevalness. In the context of this particular debate, which took place at the height of French colonial expansion, and which centers on questions of religious, racial, and cultural identity as indices of decadence and progress, such a recognition is ultimately a guarantor not just of a future, but of the very right to exist in the present and *in the same time*.

The debate between Renan and Afghani consisted of the proceedings of a lecture Renan gave at the Sorbonne on March 29, 1883, published on March 30, Afghani's response of May 18, and Renan's rejoinder the following day, all published in the *Journal des débats*.[10] Renan's lecture, which he claims was inspired by a meeting with Afghani himself,[11] argues for the radical incompatibility between not just science and Islam, but also between science and "the Arab mind," and by extension the entire Semitic race. Afghani's response takes Renan to task for his erroneous and anti-Arab racism, while also agreeing with him that all religions, Islam included, stifle the rational spirit. The exchange has been seen as representing a rather small footnote to, and a reiteration of, Renan's views on Islam, Arabs, and science expounded in more detail in works like his *Histoire générale et systèmes comparés des langues sémitiques* (1845), *L'avenir de la science* (1848/1890), *Averroès et l'averroïsme* (1852), and *De l'origine du langage* (1859). His lecture, which according to the editor of the *Journal des débats*, "had a great impact," was one of the many public lectures that Renan gave throughout his long career, and simply served to reaffirm his position as the leading French Orientalist of his day.[12] For Afghani, on the other hand, his part in the debate has come to be seen as "one of the most striking of the many proofs that Afghani was far from being the orthodox believer he claimed to be before Muslim audiences" (Keddie 1968, 91). Never published in Arabic (on the advice of his Egyptian disciple, 'Abduh), Afghani's response has long been assumed by his non-European audience to be a defense of Islam, whereas, as both Kedourie and Keddie have previously argued, this is patently not the case.[13] While Renan's lecture more firmly ensconces him within his self-made fantasy of Indo-European spiritual health proven by Semitic decadence, Afghani's answer reveals the faultlines where Ottoman decline meets anti-imperialist critique.

To ground Renan's lofty remarks in the practical economics of colonialism, however, one only has to turn the page of the *Journal des débats*. In the very same issue in which Renan's lecture was first published, an address by Léon Say appeared that dramatically illustrates the military and political upshot of Renan's supposedly disinterested objectivity. Grandson of economist Jean-Baptiste Say, Léon Say was an antisocialist voice of French economic liberalism who served as finance minister in the Third Republic. Speaking to the Lyon Chamber of Commerce, Say decries the "deplorable error" of those Frenchmen who have lost interest in what lies beyond France's borders: "France is indeed great both internally and externally;

and if our commercial relations are diminished, France, too, is diminished." His call for "a very firm and clear-cut colonial policy" earned him "lengthy applause," while his plea for an energetic defense of France's North African interests merited the audience's "lively approval" (1883, 2). Say evokes the perennial fear of decline, equating France's economic fortune with the nation's stature as a whole in a manner that should, in theory, have offended Renan's admittedly idealistic and anti-mercantile sensibility. The point of referencing this banal speech delivered to French businessmen (just months before the French protectorate would be established in Tunisia) indicates the mundane ubiquity of the juxtaposition of Hegelian idealism alongside expansionist economic theories in the French 1880s. Like Benjamin's phantasmagoric vision of the Paris *passages* as the innards of the social body, the juxtaposition of Renan and Say suggests, however allegorically, that French colonial expansion provides Renan with the safe passage he needs to secure his own reflection in the secular dreamscape of history. Renan's imaginary dialectic of Indo-European authenticity and vitality emerges, like the dreams of the overfed bourgeois dreamer of Benjamin's allegory (see the Introduction), from the economic and political realities of capitalism and colonial occupation.

The debate reveals an important difference in the ways that nineteenth century Orientalism and the Islamic reformist element of the *nahda* configured the relationship between decadence and colonial modernity: While the Orientalist essentializes the Oriental and denies the East the possibility of correction or cure, except through European agents, the reformists insist on the right to awaken from what they surmise to be their own intellectual and political lethargy. For Renan and his broad readership, whatever decline may befall humanity can be overcome by retrospectively excising the diseased limb from the body of mankind, which then retains its healthy normalcy, even as the diseased part is given no recourse to a cure. For Afghani, and many writers of the *nahda*, the ascendancy of Europe reveals decadence as a cyclical phenomenon, while the current decadent position of Arabic or Islamic societies forces a recognition of their own complicity with this decadence, a search for its causes, and ways to ameliorate these perceived symptoms of decline. Renan reconstructs universal history to conform to his faith in European progress and vigor, and according to his "embryogenesis" of human origins; Afghani pieces together a series of arguments from a variety of sources, in reaction to specific acts of colonial aggression, arguments that change according to the audience he is addressing.

Afghani's experience of British imperial rule in India, which he first visited in early 1857, when he was nineteen, proved crucial to his anti-imperialist stance.[14] His 1882 lecture to young Indian Muslims is typical of nineteenth-century Islamic reformist discourse in its emphasis on the undeniably decadent state of Islamic societies, the importance of determining the causes of this decadence, the necessity of finding a cure for it, and the crucial role that educational reform must play in any such cure. "You spend no thought on this question of great importance," says Afghani, exhorting his audience to action, "incumbent on every intelligent man, which is: What is the cause of the poverty, indigence, helplessness, and distress of the Muslims, and is there a cure for this important phenomenon?" (1968, 120). In his answer to Renan, Afghani repeats this refrain after having refuted Renan's claims about the meaning of the word "Arab," admitting that "the problem [of decadence] exists nonetheless, and if it is difficult to determine the causes in a precise and irrefutable manner, it is even more difficult to suggest a remedy" (2003, 37). Renan does not concern himself at all with suggesting a remedy for Oriental decadence, only with diagnosing the disease, whereas Afghani's overarching concern is the search for a cure. Arabic/Islamic decadence for Renan comes to signal the death of an essentialized other as the revitalization of the self, but for Afghani the vital other reveals the necessity for radical self-transformation.

The double purpose that Islam serves for Renan, as a force that is as repressive as Christianity but also inherently inferior to it, demonstrates what is ultimately at stake for Renan in his Sorbonne lecture: a thoroughly European and Christian notion of the secular. Renan conceals the lecture's validation of an anti-Arab and anti-Islamic version of secularism behind the façade of a simple terminological disagreement with his fellow Orientalists. He bemoans "the lack of precision in the use of words that designate nations and races" and suggests that it is a grave error to think of racial or national groups as if they are "always identical to themselves" (10). His goal will therefore be to untangle the confusion caused by the terms "*science arabe, philosophie arabe, art arabe, science musulmane, civilisation musulmane*" (10). The assertion that racial or religious identity is socially constructed merely allows Renan to rebuild such categories in the image of his own philosophical convictions while also blurring categories behind a veil of scientific legitimacy.

The first knot Renan attempts to untangle for his admiring audience is that of "*science musulmane*," a combination of two terms whose facile juxtaposition, he tells us, has caused much confusion and which therefore requires a semantic segregation of sorts. The first "proof" in his argument about the incompatibility between Islam and science is, in fact, not scientific at all, but simply an assertion of Orientalist "common sense." Renan observes that

> all those with even a little knowledge of contemporary things can clearly see the current inferiority of Muslim countries, the decadence of States governed by Islam, the intellectual void of races that come by their culture and their education solely through that religion. All who have been in the East or in Africa are struck by the fatal limitations of the mind of the true believer, of that sort of iron girdle that encircles his head, making him absolutely closed to science, incapable of learning anything or of opening himself to any new idea. (2003, 10–11)

Renan's argument about the decadent state of Islamic knowledge is thus visually obvious for anyone who has visited a Muslim country. He extends the visual quality of Islamic decadence in his metaphor of the "iron girdle" of Islamic ignorance, which surely evoked for his learned audience the image of the turban. The passage carefully distinguishes between the essence of race and the accidents of religion, and even gives a developmental timeframe for the moment when religion makes its conquest on the unsuspecting child: "Beginning with his religious initiation, around the age of 10 or 12, the Muslim child, up until then somewhat awakened, all of a sudden becomes a fanatic, full of a foolish pride of possessing what he believes is the absolute truth" (2003, 11). Renan thus explains the current condition of races governed by Islam as resulting from the social pressure applied by Islamic dogma and the institutional sway of Islamic education. While any reader with a little knowledge of anti-Orientalist criticism is likely to note the way that this passage repeats the typical Orientalist gesture of homogenizing Islam into a unitary, monolithic force, it is also noteworthy that in doing so Renan reproduces the very error he has just denounced in others. He makes Islam identical to itself, both geographically and historically. Reiterating his argument concerning Ibn Rushd, Renan affirms that any transformation that occurs within Islam, including the period from about 775 CE until the middle of the thirteenth century, when it was, he admits, intellectually superior to the Christian West, happens *despite* Islam, not because of it. It is therefore incorrect, he concludes, to bind the descriptor *"musulmane"* to the substantive *"science."*

Despite his social-constructivist overtures, Renan ultimately relies on an essentialist ontology of race to make his point as he tries to de-Arabize "la science arabe." The terms "Arab" and "Islam" become nearly synonymous for Renan, as he argues that "to the degree that Islam was in the hands of the Arab race, meaning the first four Caliphs and under the Umayyads, no intellectual movement of a profane character was produced in its bosom" (2003, 13). The grandeur of what goes by the name of "Arab philosophy," Renan argues, is due almost entirely to Persian, Greek, Indian, and Christian influences, and has nothing to do with the Arab race per se. "The spirit of this new civilization [Baghdad under the Abbasids] was essentially mixed" (15), he asserts. As Renan's racial typology of the "degenerate Semitic" reinforces his anti-Islamic argument, he is able to refuse any and all claims to greatness that might be made on behalf of what has been called "Islamic civilization." "All these brilliant Caliphs, contemporaries of our Carlovingians—Mansour, Haroun al-Rashid, Mamoun—are scarcely Muslims. Externally, they practice the religion of which they were the leaders, the Popes, so to speak; but their spirit was elsewhere" (16). Instead of expanding his understanding of Islam to include the characteristics associated with the above figures (for example, an interest in Greek philosophy and science), Renan retains an orthodox conception of Islam that forces him to excommunicate everything and everyone that does not conform to it. The primary reason that "Arab science" is not "Arab" after all, but rather "Greco-Sassanid," for Renan, is that "the truly fecund element of it all came from Greece" (19). The hermeneutical circle of Renan's pseudo-constructivism closes when we remember that the test of intellectual fecundity is in the eyes, and requires little more than a cursory glance at the decadence of "Muslim countries," a decadence that must always be derived comparatively from Europe's ascendance.

All this merely serves as prelude to the chief reason that Islam is incompatible with science in Renan's view: it is the model of the nonsecular, of an institution that is incapable of the secularization required by the demands of scientific progress. Ultimately, Islam becomes for Renan nothing more than an abstract type for the triumph of dogma over reason, a kind of allegory of the restrictive function of all religion: "Islam is the indistinguishable union of the spiritual and the temporal, it is the reign of a dogma, it is the heaviest chain that humanity has ever borne" (26). The Arab Muslim, as an allegory for the religious censor, functions for Renan much the same way that the Jew will function in twentieth-century anti-Semitic rhetoric (from Maurice Barrès and Céline to Alfred Rosenberg and Hitler) as an allegory for all that is wrong with modernity. Structurally, Renan's philosophy requires Arabs to be degenerate and Islam to be decadent so that he may chart the progress of the healthy, ascendant, and normative branch of mankind through a homogeneous conception of historical time uncluttered by others, whose work in the "universal" project of human civilization would otherwise have to be acknowledged in the present.

Afghani's forceful response to Renan's philologically derived anti-Semitism, published in the *Journal des débats* in May 1883, reveals both his own heterodox views and partial agreement with Renan. Nikki Keddie notes that Afghani's answer is remarkable because "it seems more in line with twentieth-century ideas than Renan's original argument. It rejects Renan's racism and puts in its place an evolutionary or developmental view of peoples" (1968, 86). This is only partially true, however. Afghani wields the social-constructivist component of Renan's argument not as an empty display of the latest academic technique, as Renan seems to do, but as a vital tool that he uses to reimagine the Arab Muslim child, which Renan had made a centerpiece of his lecture, not as someone fated to fall into the sleep of fanaticism but as potentially awakening to his own authentic past. To Renan's visually mediated observation of Islamic decadence ("the iron girdle" constraining the Arab mind), Afghani responds with a worldly, subjective recognition of what it is like to be this very Muslim child, "yoked like an ox to the plow, to the dogma whose slave he is," and doomed to "walk eternally in the same furrow that had been traced in advance for him by the interpreters of the law" (1968, 40). "I know all that," Afghani confesses,

> but I also know that this Arab Muslim child, whose portrait M. Renan traces for us in such vigorous terms, and who, at a later age, becomes "a fanatic, full of a foolish pride of possessing what he believes is the absolute truth" belongs to a race that has marked its passage in the world, not only with fire and blood, but also with brilliant and fecund works which prove his taste for science, for all the sciences, philosophy included, with which, I must acknowledge, he was not able to live happily for long. (Keddie 1968, 40–41)

Afghani, the Persian Shi'ite posing as a Sunni from Afghanistan, responds to Renan from the position not just of the Muslim child but, more specifically, of the Arab Muslim child. Forced to work through Renan's politically violent acts of naming and unnaming (disguised as a simple clarification of academic terms), Afghani reaffirms Renan's emphasis on race over religion as a means of determining who may lay claim to the future, even if he does so in a more intellectually honest and convincing manner, and partially in the name of the other. Ultimately, Afghani makes his defense of the Muslim child outside an affirmation of Islam as a religion, but rather by asserting the Arab Muslim's "taste for science," as conceived by Renan's version of secular history. His reference to Arab history being built with "fire and blood" recalls Renan's celebrated Sorbonne lecture of the previous year, "Qu'est-ce qu'une nation?" with its well-known references to the "past glories" and "shared sacrifices" that enable a nation's future existence and the "desire to continue a common life" that must be renewed at each moment.[15] Afghani's genealogy of the Muslim fanatic replaces the intellectual vise of Islamic authenticity with an awakening to a racially defined, secularized version of European nationalist authenticity. Especially striking is the difference between the ways that Afghani and Renan conceive of the relationship between religion and politics in an Islamic context. It is precisely in this sense that the Islamic reformism of Afghani can be said to be a genealogical interruption that was conceived as a continuity of tradition, an awakening of an authentic subject of history within the dream palaces constructed by European narratives of secular history and nationalism. The case of Afghani reveals how the juxtaposition of selected elements of "medieval" Islamic philosophy and elements of "modern" European Enlightenment discourse denatured both the idea of Islam as a positive set of beliefs and practices and the idea of Enlightenment as a motor of human progress. Instead, we are left with history experienced as a shock that disrupts the continuous narratives of Franco-European progress and Arab-Islamic decadence.

Nahda *as Nomad Thought*

Inasmuch as the *nahda* can be seen as a non-unified set of responses to the narrative of secularization and Enlightenment viewed as distinctly European possessions, the *nahda* shares unexpected traits with Nietzsche's response to these same narratives, exemplified in his parodic critique of Renan. Having already briefly touched on some of the ways that one Islamicist element of the *nahda*, represented by Afghani, responded to the narrative of European progress, one may expand the understanding of *nahda* developed thus far, and to think of it, beyond many of the claims made on its behalf, as on par with the kind of exilic, cosmopolitan, "nomad thought" that Gilles Deleuze finds operative in the Nietzschean text.[16] While Renan's secularism reaffirms and redistributes the internal truth of his European audience into a nationalist faith in progress, the scattered voices in favor of secularism in the Near East during the *nahda* repeatedly implicate themselves in their own decadence and transgress the limit between the text and life.

In "Nietzsche Contra Renan," Gary Shapiro brilliantly demonstrates how Nietzsche "formulates some of his most distinctive thoughts" as "a critique and parody" of Renan, and more specifically he builds a case for how Nietzsche's concept of genealogy emerges, in part, as an alternative to the philosophy of history then current in Renan's writing. Shapiro contrasts Renan's "faith in continuous narrative . . . organicist aesthetics, and . . . belief in the convergence of religion, science, and art" (1982, 195) to Nietzsche's sense of history as something that "proceeds through the categories of scandal, rupture, and shock" (203). The ways in which Nietzsche represents an almost perfect inversion of Renan are numerous, and also a deliberate stylistic maneuver on Nietzsche's part: Renan, the French Germanophile, contrasts his own Celtic-Catholic health with Semitic degeneration in order to deny the idea of decadence a place in the philosophy of history; Nietzsche, the German Francophile, places the Celts in the position that Renan had put Jews in his attempt to exhaust the potential of the concept of decadence.[17] Nietzsche's critical and parodic use of Renan allows us to rethink the very paradigm of intellectual "influence": Instead of refuting or modifying Renan's claims about history, religion, and human origins, Nietzsche's texts enact the disjunctures of the continuous history that Renan makes the centerpiece of his philosophy of scientific progress. Viewed in such a light, even what has so often been understood as Nietzsche's anti-Semitism can be grasped as a parody of Renan's clearly anti-Semitic thought. Most relevant to the argument at hand is Nietzsche's radical negation of the kind of secularism Renan professed, which amounted to little more than a return of the religion that Renan had repressed since his departure from the seminary.[18]

Nietzsche's obsessive revisions of the concept of decadence, which multiplied toward the end of his productive career, take on added significance when they are understood as a response to Renan's expressed desire to excommunicate the concept from the philosophy of history. While Renan's fascination with the spectacular failure of the stunted Semitic plant betrays him as a decadent historian, Nietzsche's explosion of the idea of decadence into multiple and contradicting concepts reveals the critical force of such a polysemous term.[19] Whereas Renan narrates the progress of science as it travels the historical networks of comparative philology to ultimately find a home in *himself*, Nietzsche deploys the "decadence" of his anti-philosophy outward against the world in multiple directions. In the famous section from *The Gay Science* (1882), "We who are homeless," he commends his own "homeless" thought to the people of Europe's very real nomadic communities living in uncertainty and hardship (the text implies that he means Jews, in particular). Nietzsche's use of the first person plural invites these other nomads to join the new virtual community of the homeless that his text articulates: "We feel disfavor for all ideals that might lead one to feel at home even in this fragile, broken time of transition. . . . We 'conserve' nothing; neither do we want to return to any past periods; we are not by any means 'liberal'; we do not work for 'progress'" (1974, 338). This radical version of decadence displaces the binary pair (progress/decadence) that typically constitutes measurements of social health, while it also denounces the "mendacious racial self-admiration" that was serving to authenticate measurements of German national vitality. Said's notion of "traveling theory" and his practice of "secular criticism"—as a constant engagement against uncritical narratives of geographical and cultural belonging—follow a similar impulse to that of Nietzsche, but broadened to account for the mass displacements of people around the globe during the twentieth century.[20]

Two Syrian intellectuals, the Muslim reformer Abd al-Rahman al-Kawakibi (1854–1902) and the Syrian Christian writer Farah Antun (1874–1922), developed two very different approaches to secularization that reveal the Arabic *nahda* as the kind of unsettled and unsettling articulation of political consciousness awakening within the Ottoman Empire. Al-Kawakibi's *Umm al-qura* (The Mother of Cities, i.e., Mecca) (1899) recounts a series of imagined meetings of Muslim scholars from across the Ottoman East and provides a detailed list of no fewer than eighty-four reasons for the current state of the decadence—literally the "lassitude" or "stagnancy" (*al-futur*)—of the Islamic *ummah*. The text argues for the establishment of an Arab caliphate in Mecca but also proposes a peculiar brand of pan-Arab, anti-Ottoman secularism, where the caliph would function as a purely spiritual leader with no political power. In the text's appendix, Al-Kawakibi enumerates twenty-six reasons why "the Arabs of the Peninsula" should be the ones to lead the "religious awakening" (*al-nahda al-diniya*) of Islam, asserting their linguistic, cultural, and moral excellence.[21] Al-Kawakibi claims to elaborate upon this point "in order to avoid political or racial fanaticism" (*li-ajli raf' al-ta'assub al-siyasi aw al-jinsi*) (1899, 155). Such an assertion of Arab superiority seems clearly to represent the dialectical countermove to Renan's anti-Arab racism, merely replacing one set of racial assumptions with another within the same structural logic. However, this apparent influence of European racial theory and nationalist thought occurs in the specific context of al-Kawakibi's Egyptian exile, at a moment when the critical attention of many Syrian and Egyptian intellectuals, as Joseph Rahme has argued, was turning away from the external threat of European colonial expansion and toward the "internal" threat of Ottoman tyranny. Rahme emphasizes the significance of al-Kawakibi to this transition, claiming that "by shifting the focus from the external to the internal other [the Ottoman sultanate], who had been hitherto the unquestioned defender of the *ummah*, al-Kawakibi's reformist ideas contributed to and shaped the fragmentation and erosion of a precarious Ottoman collective identity."[22] *Umm al-qura* thus marks the recognition of an Islamic "enemy within" and deploys a radical mélange of Arabism, nationalism, and secularism in order to propose an equally radical cure. The fact that the meeting of *ulama'* his book claims to describe never actually occurred, combined with the near certainty that the text was indeed a piece of "Khedival propaganda" designed to further the Egyptian Khedive Abbas's political ambitions,[23] reveals the Arab national community at this early stage as a pure act of the political imagination. While al-Kawakibi may be understood as borrowing content from European ideas of nationalism, it is in fact more accurate to see him as an exiled Ottoman subject armed with Arab and Islamic history, who comes to political consciousness within the utopian discourses of progress that he received through his mentors, al-Afghani, Muhammad 'Abduh, and even the British poet, horse-breeder, and Arabophile Wilfrid Scawen Blunt. Instead of reaffirming the vital agency of the West as the active force that awakens a merely reactive and slumbering East, we can align the awakening of the *nahda* with the disruptive and "decadent" philosophy of Nietzsche, not as a matter of Nietzsche's influence but rather as an assertion of the mobilization of a politicized imagination within both the "West" and the "East" that disrupts the continuous dream narratives recited in each location, but at different speeds. Instead of hailing the modern, secular West as a model for a medieval, spiritual East, we can place all parties together in the moment of a critique of the present. As Abdallah Laroui writes in *La crise des intellectuels arabes*, "Within the West-object is hidden an anti-West that accompanies it like a shadow. The West interrogates itself at the same moment that the others interrogate it."[24] The irony is that al-Kawakibi replaces one dream narrative with another, even if the seams of disruption still show.

The case of Antun reveals how a direct engagement with Renan's Orientalist version of secularism translates in the context of the Arabic *nahda* when articulated from the minority position of Orthodox Christianity.

What al-Kawakibi saw as Ottoman tyranny, Antun considered a necessary guarantor of Syrian unity and the best hope for a secular society in the region. In contrast to al-Kawakibi's Arab-nationalist identification, Antun tended to identify himself as a Syrian and to attach a "slightly pejorative meaning" to the term "Arab."[25] While Antun translated sections from Nietzsche's *Zarathustra* and Renan's *La vie de Jésus* and *Les apôtres* into Arabic, he misread Nietzsche as "the patron saint of European materialism, industrialism, and aggression" (Reid 1975, 81). His reading of Renan's *Averroès et l'averroïsme* would spawn the most celebrated chapter of Antun's career, which emerged from a series of articles he published in his newspaper, *al-Jami'a*, on the subject of Ibn Rushd and secularism in Islamic philosophy, and the subsequent debate with Muhammad 'Abduh, all of which were collected as *Ibn Rushd wa falsafatuhu* (Ibn Rushd and His Philosophy) and published in 1902.[26] While Antun claims in the book's preface that his work is in fact a "summary of Renan and Ibn Rushd" (1982 [1902], 33), the use that he ultimately makes of the Cordovan philosopher is quite different from the function Renan had assigned to him. Renan wields the failure of Ibn Rushd as a warning against the French clergy but also shows how even the greatest of the "Arab philosophers" was inferior to Europe's original Greek philosophical heritage, thus proving, to his mind, the consubstantiality of the temporal and the religious in Islam. Antun, on the other hand, transforms Ibn Rushd into the archetypical secular thinker in order to reveal secularism at the heart of Arabic philosophical thought and warns about the "danger of mixing the world with religion" (*madarr mazj al-duniya wa al-din*) at the dawn of the twentieth century (1981 [1902], 31).[27]

By making Ibn Rushd into a rationalist, in a distinctly nineteenth-century sense of the term—that is, one whose philosophy conflicted explicitly with religion—Antun replays Renan's fundamental error. Roger Arnaldez attributes Renan's misreading to the latter's Christian understanding of the secular. Arnaldez compares Renan to the European medieval Averroist philosophers who also misunderstood this split in Ibn Rushd. Recent Ibn Rushd scholarship demonstrates, to the contrary, that Ibn Rushd's philosophical program was deeply motivated by Islam, the necessity of correctly interpreting the *Qur'an*, and the search for practical solutions in *fiqh* (Islamic jurisprudence). Both Renan and Antun transform the historical Ibn Rushd into a symbol of the eternal struggle between religion and reason, Renan's version proving the decadence of the Islamic and Arabic world, Antun's version serving as a radical assertion of minority rights. Whereas Renan writes in order to master what he considers to be the stunted branch of Semitic subhumanity, Antun dedicates his book to "the new shoots in the East" (*al-nabt al-jadid*)—the rapidly multiplying "men of reason" who form the imagined community of his readership (1982 [1902], 31).

The fact that Antun first encountered Ibn Rushd in Renan's French misreading, which he condensed and translated into Arabic, represents only a small trajectory in the overall circuit that Antun's secular ideas had to traverse in his quest for readers. Without delving into the Borgesian complexity of the forking pathways that brought Averroes's commentaries of Aristotle to his Christian European disciples in the first place, nor the labyrinthine avenues of scholarship that Renan followed to produce his own study, we can assert the irony of Ibn Rushd ultimately finding the "issue" that Renan had denied him in contemporary Arabic thought precisely through the conduit of Renan's own text, if in the form of rebuttals and critiques. The difference between censorship policies in Egypt during the 1890s and early 1900s and the rest of the Ottoman Empire complicates the picture even further. In order for Antun, from his Egyptian exile, to reach readers in Syria, his newspaper avoided Ottoman censors by traveling via French post and being distributed by secret agents. The short-circuiting networks of overlapping empires become clear in the fact that Antun had to send *Ibn Rushd wa falsafatuhu* via Marseille in order to send it to a French Orientalist in Istanbul.[28]

Nineteenth-century Islamic reformism, or the literary "Arab Awakening," represented neither a more or less successful imitation of various European discourses nor a complete break with the Arabic or Islamic past; rather, these "Arabic" discourses became caught in their own self-conscious awakening—viewed as a gradual process where the familiarity of what is called Islamic "tradition" (*turath*) or the Arabic literary tradition became denatured, defamiliarized, and abstracted. Such a reading allows us to understand *nahda* neither as a completed event nor simply as an ongoing process, but rather as a process of awakening to an Arab or Islamic self that becomes stalled within Orientalist epistemological and discursive structures. In other words, in the *nahda*, the process of historical transformation tended to get misunderstood as ontology, as the realization of a fixed, timeless reality. Nahda-as-awakening, in the sense developed here, represents only a partially successful disruption of the continuity of the authentic self, since this disruption is also imagined as a continuity of repetition and return.

In contrast, Renan's French discourse of Orientalism, which is always also a theory of decadence, either conceives of the European self as the agent of regeneration for the degenerate Oriental other, or conceives of the Oriental other's decadence as a kind of seminal force that can be channeled to revive the sterile European self, as seen in more sympathetic forms of Orientalism than Renan's. In both cases, the Orient is constructed intertextually, through the essentially closed system of Orientalist discourse. Even when the *nahda* adopts Orientalist tropes, ideas, and methodologies, it uses them in a way that is disruptive to notions of European authenticity and to Ottoman hegemony. The ironic result of these mutual acts of awakening has been, as demonstrated here, the assertion of an authentic subject of *national* history, which has marked all nationalist claims of the nineteenth century and beyond. The tangled narratives of progress and decadence emerge from the sudden juxtaposition of these different formations and reformations of "dreaming collectives," each awakening within passages created by others.

The decay that Orientalism makes constitutive of colonial modernity can be seen as an effect of both capitalism as "a machine that functions by breaking down" (in Deleuze and Guattari's words), and as a consequence of a political philosophy of history built upon the notion of an authentic national subject. One major mode of this decay is revealed in the vicissitudes of the "Semitic object" of Orientalist knowledge, which began as a hypothesis derived from comparative philology, but which becomes increasingly malleable as the French colonial empire continues to engineer and reengineer the Semitic object for its own nationalist purposes and manage the populations deemed Semitic inhabiting its colonies. What began as philology would soon morph into racism, policy, and literature. Yet even as the Semitic is molded, fractured, and redesigned, a new kind of philological work is being done in Arabic, as exemplified by the writing of Lebanese writer Ahmed Faris al-Shidyaq, the subject of the next chapter.

CHAPTER 2

Al-Shidyaq's Decadent Carnival

If the rubric of reformism served as one important register for articulating the decadence of nineteenth-century colonial modernity in both French and Arabic, this discourse also necessarily betrayed its own limits in the very institutional *deformations* it sought to enact. Renan's philosophical *re*formations and Nietzsche's performative *de*formations of European thought represent the two sides of this coin of decadence. Specifically, both philologists make language enact the symptoms of historical and social transformation. They formulate two divergent ways of conceiving of language's relationship to the human body. Whereas Renan transforms human language into the philological substratum that would prove the relative value of different racial types, Nietzsche uses the idiosyncrasies of the human body to deploy what he calls language's "mobile army" against the fixity of typological thinking.[1] In this sense, the Nietzschean text can be said to perform the "degeneration" of the multiple genres it attacks: historical narrative, nationalist discourse, and cultural reform understood as a prerequisite for human progress.

This chapter traces the shifting contours of the philological symptom of Semitic decadence, aiming toward a horizon somewhere beyond the stalled consciousness of both *nahda* and colonial secularism. Focusing on the major fictional text of nineteenth-century Lebanese writer, Ahmed Faris al-Shidyaq (1804–1887), *al-Saq 'ala al-saq fi ma huwa al-Faryaq* (here rendered as "Crossing Legs over Faryaq") will allow us to view the literary force field of colonial symptomology at the breaking point.[2] *Al-Saq 'ala al-saq* allows us to imagine an alternative *nahda* that configures a very different kind of continuity than those envisioned by the Arab reformers of the nineteenth century. What al-Shidyaq's irresolvable book offers is an utterly untimely outbreak of philological decadence, coinciding precisely with the dawn of the *nahda*, or "Arab renaissance." It is not a clean break with the past but a decidedly *filthy* one, a radicalization of decadence, akin in several important ways to the one Nietzsche will enact later in the century, but occurring here first within Arabic, as an activation of the recalcitrant agent both within and beyond Renan's foreclosed "Semitic object." In this, it does the work of Said's secular-philological humanism, challenging and dismantling Orientalist assumptions regarding language, biology, and the social. Al-Shidyaq points toward the larger project of this book, namely a working through of the political theology of race that remains embedded in the notion of the human, in Christian-imperialist secularism, and in the unfinished work of radical philological criticism.

Al-Shidyaq's novel crosses the carnivalesque tradition in Arabic literature with elements of a more European Menippean or carnivalesque literature in a way that pries open certain assumptions inherent in the Bakhtinian-Kristevan approach to language in the novel.[3] *Al-Saq 'ala al-saq*, published in Paris in 1855, was hailed by Henri Pérès, who taught Arabic at the Faculté des Lettres in Algiers, as "the first manifestation of the Arab literary renaissance." In typical Orientalist fashion, Pérès attributed the book's aesthetic successes to the author's travels in England and France, and especially to his reading of Rabelais and other European authors. Beyond the question of influence, al-Shidyaq's text enacts the "awakening" of the *nahda* by creating a truly carnivalesque brand of Arabic, showing how the maladies of overly rigid genre and dogma "degenerate" in the face of the excesses of language and laughter. To think the "Rabelaisian" or the carnivalesque in the comparative manner undertaken here allows us to think *the human* beyond both the linguistic anti-Semitism at the heart of French Orientalism and the claims of linguistic and national authenticity common to all nationalist revivals. To read decadence as regenerative carnival in a comparative manner that reaches beyond the specificity of the European renaissance context that grounds Bakhtin's own theorization of the concept is also a way of dislodging our understanding of the novelistic genre itself from its seemingly inevitable origins in European humanism. Finally, I demonstrate not only how the book's Arabic content is transfigured by the form of the novel, but also how *al-Saq 'ala al-saq* radically affirms of the existence of *indigenous Arabic forms*.⁴

Al-Shidyaq's sole novel, *al-Saq 'ala saq*, is the *enfant terrible* of the nineteenth-century "Arab Renaissance." Its nearly eight hundred pages brim with frank discussions related to religion, sex, politics, and bodily functions. Since its publication, the text has divided Arabophone readers into two main groups: those who are outraged by the book's lascivious language and themes and its unrelenting criticism of Near Eastern society, and those who, often guardedly, praise its liberating inventiveness as well as its masterful command of Arabic vocabulary and style.⁵ It is a foundational text of the *nahda* that ironically cannot be read in the *nahda*. The book has only recently been brought into a sustained discussion of what goes by the name of "world literature."⁶ *Al-Saq 'ala al-saq* stands as an event that has proven unassimilable to both the protonationalisms of the *nahda* and the reorganization of world cultures by Orientalism. In the words of Kamran Rastegar, al-Shidyaq's "literary imagination" is "irresolvable within nationalist-novelist readings of the literary history of the period" (2005, 2). His own approach to the Arabic language differs radically from that espoused by the prominent figure of the literary *nahda*, Butrus al-Bustani (1819–1883), whose 1859 lecture "Discourse on the Literature of the Arabs" (Khutba fi adab al-'arab) configures the "renaissance" of Arabic language as a kind of philological housecleaning, which would attenuate the oppressiveness of too much tradition and too many words. Al-Bustani seeks to excise all the "dead words which protrude out from the dictionaries of the Arabic language, and which do nothing other than to bear down upon the Arab mentality [*al-dhihn al-'arabi*]."⁷ On the contrary, al-Shidyaq's text sets into form an interpretation of how writing in the present might open "a space of hospitality"⁸ to the past, letting it arrive and disrupt the present, forging ambivalent links to a lived relation with the past. Abdelkébir Khatibi describes just such a "bond of separation" found within one language's difference from itself but also in the interference between different languages (Khatibi 2010, 1006). In Khatibi's words, such an author experiences his birth "into writing where the writer reestablishes his at once divided and re-welded identity through and in language, that indestructible bond of separation" (1007). My reading of *al-Saq 'ala al-saq* aims to reveal a *nahda* that was impelled not by admiration and imitation of Europe (many critics attribute al-Shidyaq's book to the influence of François Rabelais or Laurence Sterne), nor by a pure break with Arabic literary tradition, but rather by the constant eruption of the past in the present and the repeated claims for an Arabic that would function as a force of social transformation, at once singular and collective, generative and ambivalent.

Al-Shidyaq uses an omniscient narrator to relate episodes in the life of book's comic antihero, al-Faryaq (whose name is produced by condensing the author's first and last names). The narrative mirrors al-Shidyaq's autobiography, starting with his youth in Mount Lebanon, and continuing with his travels in Egypt, Malta, Tunisia, England, and France. The second half of the book introduces the reader to his wife, al-Faryaqiya, who travels with him to Europe and proves to be an astute social critic and formidable conversational partner. It is difficult to imagine that the author would do anything other than laugh at the confusion of critics who continue to struggle to classify the text in terms of its proper genre, since so many parts of the book deliberately exhaust a given genre through a combination of virtuosic imitation of other texts and the lexical excesses of its playful erudition. The short list of genres travestied include the *maqama* (which will be discussed in more detail), works of grammar (*nahw*), the dictionary format (*qamus*), travelogue (*rihla*), autobiography (*sira dhatiya*), and many kinds of poetry, from invective (*hija'*) and panegyric (*madih*) to love poetry and elegy (*ritha'*), often in surprising combinations within the same poem.[9] In *al-Saq 'ala al-saq*, as in *Ulysses*, according to Joyce, "each successive episode dealing with some province of artistic culture (rhetoric or music or dialectic), leaves behind it a burnt up field."[10]

The most obvious example of the "degeneration" in the book is al-Shidyaq's treatment of the Arabic genre of the *maqama*, usually rendered in English as "Session" or "Assembly," a short narrative in rhymed prose, often on a picaresque theme, and which was made famous in the tenth century by al-Hamadhani. Among the profuse satirical elements included in the four *maqamat* that constitute the thirteenth chapter in each of *al-Saq 'ala al-saq*'s four books, let me cite the particularly arbitrary reasoning the narrator provides to his reader concerning why he must write a *maqama* at such a place in the book: "The chapter carries a number between 12 and 14" (129). Such a comment, expressed in the elaborate rhymed prose of the *maqama*, reveals not just the arbitrary nature of the generic boundaries that the narrative legs of the novel continuously cross and recross, but also an unresolved tension between stylistic clarity and ornateness that obtains throughout the text.

While al-Shidyaq the novelist has attained a certain iconoclastic status in Arabic literary history, many scholars still regard him primarily as a linguist who helped modernize the Arabic language. Sabry Hafez, for instance, emphasizes the importance of al-Shidyaq's linguistic work of the 1880s, which he says "offers modern solutions to many linguistic problems in an attempt to widen the expressive and syntactic scope of the Arabic language in order to respond to the needs of a rapidly changing society" (1993, 47). Hafez underlines the high value of the "communicative function of language" for al-Shidyaq, but he also recognizes "his great admiration for the literary aspects of the language and his awareness of the vital interaction between language, history, and social reality" (47). Hafez's account of al-Shidyaq indicates a larger trend in the reception of the novel: Its undeniable inventiveness and linguistic depth have endowed it with symbolic value as a milestone in the *nahda*, even as these same factors have prompted attempts to hygienically cleanse and correct the book of its diseases and idiosyncrasies.[11] While there is much in the novel to support Hafez's view, whatever "modernizing" function *al-Saq* can be said to perform occurs in conjunction with the text's parodies, pastiches, satires, rants, elegies, obscenities, and its general celebration of linguistic excess, which is made particularly visible in the many instances of enumeration, and in the long lists of rare synonyms complete with brief definitions, all of which may extend over several pages. Such textual features have less to do with any salutary effects that European culture may have produced on al-Shidyaq, or the possible influence of Sterne or Rabelais, I would argue, than with the common perception that had been growing among educated Arabs of the Ottoman Empire during the nineteenth century concerning the decadence or lassitude of Arabic culture and society—*al-inhitat*, or *al-nuks*—which is felt most poignantly by al-Shidyaq as a pathology in language. In *Iterations of Loss*, Jeffrey Sacks provides a highly nuanced reading of how the novel inscribes the expression of loss in Arabic. To read *al-Saq 'ala al-saq*, Sacks writes, "is to read the compulsive insomniac relation to time to which language, in al-Shidyaq, points" (2015, 94). Sacks's analysis thus moves beyond questions of influence, awakening, the linguistic modernization of Arabic, prompting a reflection on the "relation to time" generated by language itself. It is in the text's ambivalent carnivalization of both soporific decadence and recursive *nahda* that *al-Saq 'ala al-saq* produces its "insomniac relation to time."

The very use of rhymed prose (*saj'*) throughout the book, and particularly in the novel's four *maqamat*, reveals al-Shidyaq's ambivalence regarding the use of ornate language, an ambivalence that has often confused the book's early critics. Marun 'Abbud's generally celebratory *Saqr Lubnan* faults al-Shidyaq for not having been able to break completely with a stagnant Arabic literary tradition, and for having succumbed to the "literary disease" of *saj'* in order to put his linguistic prowess on display (1950, 101). Pérès asserted that the *maqamat* in the novel are only a *"trompe l'oeil* in which the narrative is grotesquely cloaked," and that al-Shidyaq only used them "to rid himself of this outmoded genre" (1934–35, 249). Sulaiman Jubran (1989) points out that outside of the four *maqamat*, al-Shidyaq "slips" into rhymed prose when speaking of women or in moments of anger or longing, attributing the erratic combination of old and new to the "transitional" period in which he wrote. What remains to be explored is the significance of this ambivalence: what it means for a reading of the novel and its role in the *nahda*. My assertion is that the ambivalence regarding *saj'* and other forms of stylistic "ornament" in the novel is the very motor of the text, linking the generative force of al-Shidyaq's Arabic to the degeneration of forms effected in the text. *Saj'* permits al-Shidyaq to intervene into the knotted temporalities of tradition and modernity.

Close attention to the contextual layers of the framing of the narrative is required in order to understand the meaning of a given *maqama*, and those contained in *al-Saq* are no exception. In order to explicate this chapter in al-Shidyaq's novel, a brief summary is therefore necessary. The first *saj'* chapter opens with a comment that explains the arbitrary reasoning for including a *maqamat* precisely between the twelfth and fourteenth chapters of each book, as mentioned, and prepares the reader for the switch into the framed narrative in rhymed prose. Immediately after this introduction, al-Shidyaq opens the *maqama* with a formula that follows the method of replacing and converting letters seen in Faryaq's name: He combines phonemes from the famed narrators of both al-Hamadhani's 'Isa ibn Hisham and al-Hariri's al-Harith ibn Hammam—giving us al-Haris ibn Hitham— while also replacing the standard verb *haddatha* "he related" or "he reported" with *haddasa*, which is an intensified form for the verb "he conjectured" (141). Al-Shidyaq later produced a lengthy study of a related phonetic technique in *The Secret Nights Concerning Metathesis and Replacement, Sirr al-layal fi al-qalb wa al-ibdal*, which attempted to demonstrate how the conversion or replacement from one sound to a similar sound in a given word—from *dal to ta'*, for example—does not always change the word's meaning.[12] While the text's apparent thesis is that certain phonemes are attached to specific meanings, Peled suggests that al-Shidyaq's linguistic truth-claims (like those of Rabelais) are often occasions for playing with language, for revealing the arbitrary genealogies of words, sounds, and meanings. Along with the long lists of semi-synonyms scattered throughout the novel, the name of the protagonist and of the narrator of the *maqamat* reveal al-Shidyaq's explosion of the possibilities of the Arabic phoneme as his text straddles the limit between sense and nonsense. In the context of the *maqama*, such an attitude toward language suggests that *saj'* itself is ambivalent: As rhymed prose tends to replace sense with sound, it carries a negative cultural value for al-Shidyaq, but since rhymed prose can also be made to betray its own limitations, it becomes something generative, what Kristeva has called "*une négation qui postule*," a postulating negation (1970 90).

In chapter thirteen of *al-Saq*, al-Haris relates (or "conjectures" about) a night when he "seems to be the only person awake on earth" (141). He comes across a book by a relative of the famous Andalusian Ibn Hazm entitled *The Parallel between Two Situations and Two Instruments, Kitab muwazanat al-halatayn wa murazanat al-alatayn*, which lists the good and the bad elements of life in two long columns and concludes that the positive outweighs the negative, a conclusion the narrator finds suspect. In his desire to find a new perspective on the problem, al-Haris seeks the opinions of a prelate (*mutran*), who grows sleepy at the first sight of a text not written in *saj'* (143). After a schoolteacher proposes that al-Haris literally weigh the pages of the book, a jurisconsult (*faqih min jillat al-qawm*) long-windedly decrees that the number of letters in each column must be counted, which, along with the rhetorical style of each list, would determine the truth of the matter (143–44). Al-Shidyaq's text then has a poet suggest weighing the panegyrics versus the elegies in his latest collection of poems, and the Emir's secretary proposes balancing the times he has pleased his patron against those he has irritated him. Realizing that those he has spoken with "have progressively lost their intelligence as their social rank has increased," the narrator decides to seek the advice of someone young and undistinguished. Finally, he meets the youthful al-Faryaq, bone-thin and poor, hunched over the manuscripts he copies in order to earn his living (as al-Shidyaq did in his own life). Faryaq responds to his question by scribbling down his improvised answer in verse, which ends with the following lines:

> For those informed, our earthly world
>   is naught but lasting grief and ruin:
> The slave will die still fettered by
>   the same chains he was born in.

After reading this pessimistic response, al-Haris cries out, "blessed be the age that begot the likes of you!" (145), and curses those who have kept Faryaq in poverty, vowing to meditate further upon his words.

While al-Haris takes al-Faryaq's words for the truth, al-Shidyaq clearly indicates that the latter's pessimism is contingent on his social position, as were the answers of the others who were supposedly also trained in the use of correct language. This final poetic answer is further contextualized by an observation by al-Haris, who notes that he can already see "the beginnings of his future transformation" (*fi tala'tihi mabadi' al-maskh*) in the face of young al-Faryaq (144). The text of the *maqama* equates the narrator's wakeful state of consciousness with his dissatisfaction with facile, overly optimistic answers and his desire to seek out multiple responses from people of different social rank. The pessimistic content of al-Faryaq's answer proves less important than his position as a speaker: a young Arab Christian engaged in the act of copying by hand liturgical manuscripts, whose face betrays his transformation from copyist into the creator of the printed novel that both emerges from scribal culture and consumes it. What seemed to the young al-Faryaq to be the shackles of tradition have become, in the hands of the skilled novelist, links in what Bakhtin describes as the ambivalent chain of becoming, conceived as a disruptive force for social transformation.

One way that al-Shidyaq forges this ambivalent chain is through seemingly impossible lists of synonyms linked together through phonetic and semantic resonance and dissonance. These word chains far exceed in sheer quantity the enumerations in Rabelais and those, which we will examine later, in Céline. The printing of these fantastic lexical catalogues in the durable form of a book serves to preserve a language whose corruption the author strove to reverse.[13] These lists, however, also deliberately imitate the errors of the unskilled scribes that al-Shidyaq saw as being the true agents of Arabic decadence; they insert letters in unexpected places and perform the metathesis that he praised as being one of the singular aspects of the Arabic language. A passage where al-Faryaq describes the tension between Turks and Arabs in Alexandria reveals the precise social and political context from which the novel's ambivalence emerges—the marginalization of both Arabic and Arabs in the Ottoman Empire, even within the relative autonomy of Egypt:

> Regarding the people [of Alexandria], the Turks arrogantly wield authority over the Arabs, and the Arab isn't free to even glance at the face of a Turk, just as he isn't free to glance at another man's wife. If, by chance, a Turk and an Arab happen to cross each other's paths, the Arab will perform his duty and walk on the left side of the Turk, modestly [muhtashiman], submissively [khashi'an], head lowered [nakisan],

debased [mutahaqiran], cringing [mutasaghiran], diminishing [mutada'ilan], withering [qaffan]. (216)

The text goes on to include *fifty* more synonyms to describe the miserable state of the Arabs under Turkish control. The list begins with relatively common Arabic words with triliteral roots and moves toward strings of words with quadriliteral roots, often a sign of a foreign word that has been naturalized in Arabic. The effect is a defamiliarization of Arabic that reveals the flux within language, as letters seem to shift position within words at random. The words used all signify decline and diminishment, even as they reveal the ascendance of the Arabic writer's medium. The text describes both the decadence of the Arab political subject and the Arabic language by displaying the lexical richness, phonetic flexibility, and expressive vigor of Arabic. Al-Shidyaq feminizes the subordinate position of the Arab and his language by claiming that they have become "modest" (*muhtashiman*, evoking both female modesty and the word for "pudenda"—*mahashim*) and "submissive" (*khashi'an*). The text's description of the Arab Ottoman subject walking with "head lowered," *nakisan*, transforms the triliteral root *nun-kaf-sin*, whose semantic range encompasses degeneration, decadence, old age, inferiority, relapse, and falling, into an act of awakening, arising, and *nahda*. The novel's ambivalent carnivalization of Arabic shows how the recognition and articulation of decadence is the moment of rupture that makes possible the assertion of the generative continuity of Ottoman Arabs through language.

Inasmuch as al-Shidyaq's text pathologizes language, it can be said to find its restorative for Arabic decadence in the ambivalence of such pathology pushed to its limit. Among the dozens of word lists, scenes, and references in the novel to illness and medicine, there are two of particular importance which occur precisely at the mid-point of the text (which al-Shidyaq's title to chapter 19 of Book II calls "the center," *al-markaz*, of the novel). In the first scene, al-Faryaq contracts a new affliction each time he takes on a new linguistic study: grammar gives him conjunctivitis; syntax and morphology give him "an intestinal crisis brought on by parasitical worms" (359); the study of rhetoric gives him a bad itch; and logic finally communicates cholera to our suffering hero. (Total submersion in dog excrement, as prescribed by one shaykh, only plunges al-Faryaq even further into the depths of abjection.) When al-Faryaq decides to take up the study of Arabic prosody, a plague epidemic strikes all of Egypt (365).

This plague is not communicated to him, however, until he witnesses the spectacle of a converted infidel who attempts to resurrect a dead man.

The jealous convert kneels down and places his mouth between the thighs of the dead man, praying, "as Elijah prayed for rain, after having killed the Prophets of Baal" (367). This display of false piety sends al-Faryaq into an agitated state of nervous rage, which precipitates his falling ill from the plague. Al-Shidyaq's description of al-Faryaq's illness is analogous to the ambivalent articulation of generation and corruption that marks the carnivalesque. "A bubo the size of a citron appeared in his armpit," he writes, describing the first sign of the bubonic plague. In the depths of abjection, al-Faryaq has an epiphany that tells him to find a wife and create a family:

> During his illness, Faryaq had time to reflect upon what had befallen him during his time alone, as a foreigner, with nobody to keep him company and without a doctor to care for him. He said to himself: "If I die in this state, who will take pleasure in my books, which I have spent many sleepless nights transcribing? Yes, death is difficult under any circumstances—it is detestable—but still more difficult is the death of a young foreigner like me, isolated in torment. Praise be to God! In this city congregate all the varieties of disease stained by the color of death. If God were to clear for me the way now blocked by death, I would not leave this world until after having refreshed my vision [*la ufariqu hadhihi al-dunya illa qarir al-'ayn*] with the sight of a son who could elegize me. Then there would be more to me than books amidst the ruins of this earthly world. How could I not, knowing what happened to Absalom, the son of our master, David, who built his own monument so that he would be remembered after his death, were he not to have a successor? Yes, I will get married, and if I do not have a child, I will still build a tomb, as there is no lack of bricks in Egypt. O God, our God, prepare me for the task. Grant me your aid, O Generous One, O Merciful One, O Master of Mercy." (368–69)

While Paul Starkey cites this very chapter as representing the intimate, realist, and autobiographical element in the novel—as opposed to more ludic, abstract, or allegorical sections—the final chapters of Book Two should be read as *grotesque realism* (discussed later in relation to Bakhtin). While these chapters do provide an autobiographical account of the time al-Shidyaq spent in Egypt (1825–34), studying Arabic literature, logic, theology, and prosody, and where he met his wife, they also narrate an event in the history of Arabic literature: namely, the ambivalent *nahda* of *al-Saq*. The cholera epidemic of 1831, during which as many as one-third of all Egyptian children were said to have died in a single year, serves as the very real referent of the plague from which al-Faryaq miraculously recovers. The text stages its affirmation of the Arabic language in Cairo, one of the great centers of Arabic learning, but also a city infamous since medieval times for being a repository of disease. This affirmation of the language and the body emerges from an epidemic of physiological and linguistic pathologies that ultimately escalates into a pandemic. Cairo is the city where gather "all the varieties of disease stained with death," both literally and on the level of the ailments that al-Faryaq contracts while studying the language.[14]

The text fuses the realism of al-Faryaq's feelings about exile, melancholia, and mortality with questions about the capacity of the Arabic language to adequately convey such sentiments. At the center of his crisis rests an acute anxiety that links al-Faryaq's own handwritten manuscripts to the fear of death. Better than readers who might take pleasure in his writing would be a son, he decides, who could at least generate the text of an elegy for a dead father. However, al-Faryaq's decision to get married is not only made so that he will have a son, which his plan to build his own monument (as the biblical Absalom did) makes clear. Since Egypt has "no lack of bricks," he vows to build this tomb for himself. Again, the ephemerality of manuscript is brought into relief against the possibility of something more durable, in this case a self-built structure—the printed novel itself—which could house the vast spectral legions of Arabic vocabulary included in *al-Saq*.

After this meditation on writing and death, al-Faryaq skeptically questions the role his decaying body has played in his decision to procreate, self-consciously criticizing himself for having succumbed to the weakened state of mind brought on by his illness. To al-Faryaq's self-criticism, the narrator drolly adds, "Just as it occurred to the philosopher Bion and to a host of others sages and philosophers" (369), further contextualizing his apparently unique moral crisis as anything but unique. It is at this precise moment in the text, when al-Faryaq's body has become grotesque with plague symptoms, as he contemplates marriage and its discontents, that the healing hand of the author cures his creation of its disease:

> It was then that the Almighty God reached Faryaq with his mercy, graciously granting him the cure for his illness. So he arose from his bed as if rising from the tomb, and went over to his *tanbur*, and began to play and sing. Leave him there in that state—don't disturb him. Lift up the hems of your garments as I am doing, so we may jump over the flames burning before us and in what is to come.

The instant al-Faryaq is cured, he turns to music and instantly falls in love with his future wife, whose entrance in the novel is foreshadowed by the flames mentioned in the passage just cited. Thus ends the second of the novel's four books, with love and desire emerging from the maladies born by language study and religious tartuffery. To the failed showy resurrection attempted by the willful convert, al-Shidyaq juxtaposes the resurrection of al-Faryaq, which occurs, almost unintentionally, at the moment he is most skeptical and self-conscious. Al-Faryaq's renewal, which serves as the "pivot" upon which the text turns, is not accomplished by the medicine of European enlightenment, but rather through the deus ex machina hidden within the protagonist's meditation on the relation between bodily illness and desire. But this resurrection, this awakening, is not the arbitrary act of the divine, but rather the deliberate act of the human author of the novel healing his creation from the disease of language through an intensification of the language of disease. The upshot of all this is that al-Faryaq enters into dialogue with another human being, al-Faryaqiya, just as the first half of the novel, dealing mostly with Egypt and the Levant, enters into dialogue with the second half of the novel, mostly concerning London, Oxford, and Paris.

Al-Saq's carnivalesque degenerations and rebirths reveal the disintegrating margins that mark the limits of Orientalism's decadent discourse. Eschewing the question of the influence of European literary history on al-Shidyaq, I have instead read his work through the binary opposition of decadence and rebirth, and the ways that Arabic has been made to perform perceived states of social, cultural, and political morbidity and/or vitality. Part of what is meant by the term "decadence" in the context of this book is the familiar and normative constellation of ideas related to the rise and fall of different social entities, from a relatively specific milieu (such as the Lebanese Christian community in al-Shidyaq) to the vaster units of nation, empire, and planet. The more operative sense of "decadence" for our current purposes, however, is a more historically specific and specialized meaning that may be located in a variety of sites, from the "decadent" art and literature of the French 1880s and '90s, to Nietzsche's antiphilosophy, and now, in al-Shidyaq. The meaning of "decadence" for Nietzsche, as for the legions of his (mostly French) readers—from Georges Bataille to Gilles Deleuze to Michael Hardt—is less a self-contained meaning than it is the will to disrupt established regimes of authority through an insistence on ambivalence and the capacity to generate *other* meanings. Al-Shidyaq's writing functions precisely by such a generative ambivalence. In this sense, "decadence" is closely linked to Bakhtin's notion of carnival as the articulation of a profound ambivalence of generation and corruption; decadence is degeneration *as* generation and vice versa. It is not through the Francocentric lens inherent in the idea of Rabelais-as-influence that al-Shidyaq (and, later, in Chapter 3, Céline) should be examined, but rather from the point of view of textual performances and theoretical articulations of ambivalence, which, in the context of French Orientalist anti-Semitism, ultimately indicates the blind spot in the purview of what Bakhtin called carnival's "universal laughter," and which also emphasizes the cruelty performed within carnivalesque theater.

While it might be tempting to read al-Shidyaq with Bakhtin, it is advisable not to force the book into a "Western" or European paradigm of *Weltliteratur* just as much as one should avoid using a text "outside" the tradition he discusses to discredit Bakhtin. Yet Bakhtin can help elucidate how the frenetic power of *al-Saq 'ala al-saq* makes visible the limits of colonial decadence understood as the narration of an authentic subject of history. By theorizing literary history as a function that slides from carnival toward its decadence, Bakhtin helps open up al-Shidyaq's book to a reading that both confirms Bakhtin's arguments about genre and cuts against the Eurocentric assumptions governing them. The "decadence" of Bakhtin's carnival, exemplified in the works of Rabelais, occurs when one of three constitutive factors (the popular, the universal, or the ambivalent) weakens; that is, when one of these factors falls out of equilibrium with the others, we see the degeneration of the specific realm of carnival expression that Bakhtin terms "grotesque realism." The degeneration of the ambivalence expressed in grotesque realism is the result not of a simple break with the past, imagined as edenic golden age, but rather of the *disruption of a lived relation with the past*, a relation experienced as something that, for Bakhtin, must be continuously forged in the crucible of ambivalence. What is more, his theory of disruption rethinks the alienation of modern industrial capitalism as theorized by Marx; by placing the genesis of European folk imagination in the precapitalist society of the middle ages, Bakhtin emphasizes linguistic and generic structures without quite explaining the relation of such structures to their more properly material conditions and causes. The severing of generation and corruption witnessed in the degeneration of carnival becomes both a castration and a violently aborted pregnancy, with a gesture toward that figure so revered by the French *décadents*, the castrated *woman*. Fear of castration violence might be said to preempt any fear of carnival violence for Bakhtin, but only if this castration is understood as the deprivation of a transgendered and collective historical subject from control over its own "reproductive rights."[15]

Al-Shidyaq's promiscuous intertextuality, appropriating and redeploying styles, genres, and registers from across not only Arabic but also French and English literary history, ultimately disturbs the genealogy of Bakhtin's account of the carnivalesque and its role as a kind of proof of the European renaissance. The performative philological experiments of al-Shidyaq's book explode any notion of a dormant Semitic symptom incapable of reproducing itself, and instead improvise the timbres of Arabic futures constantly emerging within words, roots, and phonetic arrangements of sound. At the same time reading the book through Bakhtin's understanding of carnival ambivalence opens up *al-Saq 'ala al-saq* to reveal the text as much more than a failed novel, as many critics have claimed it to be, impeded by stubborn vestiges of the "decadent" era of Arabic literature and scribal culture. Certainly, the book does not simply testify to al-Shidyaq's role as a reformer of the Arabic language, cleansing it of the burdensome ornamentation that had accrued to it over the centuries, and crafting a more streamlined and functional tool for communication in the modern world. Rather, *Al-Saq 'ala al-saq*, read through a refocused Bakhtinian lens, helps us see how the genealogical interruption of modernity made energies available to a writer such as al-Shidyaq, living along the seams of multiple societies, languages, and writing through the transition from scribal to print culture.[16]

Al-Shidyaq carnivalizes Arabic and invents modes of a secularizing, cosmopolitan critique, written from the position of a religious minority member (before his conversion to Islam) living on the margins of the Ottoman Empire in a mostly preindustrial society. His work attempts to preserve and publish a language threatened by corruption in the age of the emergence of print media in the Arab world, at the dawn of a period that has come to be seen as a cultural "renaissance." The aim of this chapter, however, has not been to prove how he is symptomatic of any nation, community, or literary period, but rather to show how al-Shidyaq's text enacts the breakdown of language as symptomatic of social health by pushing language to its limits, and to thereby elucidate a mechanism in literary language that ironically resists symptomatic readings. It is my hope that such a reading illustrates al-Shidyaq's specific value on the broad spectrum of the carnivalesque, while also redefining this fraught aesthetic category. The distinctive use of carnival made by al-Shidyaq will come into sharper contrast in the next chapter, where I explore the frantic pop-Orientalist anti-Semitic style characteristic of both the Dreyfus affair in the 1890s and Céline's pamphlets of the 1930s. An interesting subtext in Bakhtin anticipates this distinction of two ways of "doing" carnival, namely in the opposition between the amoral and ambivalent nature of carnival "experience" as opposed to the ethical and liberatory use-value made possible by its textualization. Reading Céline, in his French colonial context, alongside al-Shidyaq, will vividly illuminate the differences demarcating these two limits of literary carnivalization, revealing the colonial text fraying at both ends.

This does not mean that these points are linked in any kind of causal relationship; al-Shidyaq's Arabic *nahda* and Céline's anti-Semitic decadence bring to light the limits of a narrative which is also not the *same* narrative. To read al-Shidyaq with Céline is a way of reading an early sally in the *nahda* alongside shots fired belatedly in the culture wars that were the French fin de siècle. If the Introduction and Chapter 1 read these two discourses as mutually inverted articulations of "national" awakening, each bought at the expense of the other's decadence, the disjointed comparison of al-Shidyaq and Céline in this chapter and the next examines two historically asymptotic text-events, carefully considering the specific context of each, while also insisting on the prerogative of global comparativism to let theory travel not just across space but also through time.[17] Such a juxtaposition allows us to dislocate the deterritorializing impulse that goes by the name of poststructuralist thought from its all-too European center, which I attempted to do in Chapter 1 by revisiting the *nahda* as a prefiguration of Deleuzean "nomad thought."[18]

Al-Shidyaq and Céline offer two divergent ways of yoking language to the human body as an ideological gesture. But what kinds of bodies are these texts, and what kinds of symptoms do they betray? Both authors anthropomorphize language in order to make it perform as a human body performs, and to make it suffer as a human body suffers. Yet both texts remake language not in the *image* of the body, but rather out of the profound ambivalence generated by the grotesquely human body. For al-Shidyaq, writing on the boundaries of multiple languages (Classical Arabic, Modern Arabic, Syriac, Turkish, French, and English), the embodied national language becomes something infinitely plastic, and ultimately fearless, as the Rabelaisian text was for Bakhtin. This fearless body differs from the half-exhumed corpses of the past that would soon begin to characterize certain nationalist ideas of Arab authenticity, just as al-Faryaq's miraculous resurrection differs from the failed attempt to revive the dead man in the scene discussed earlier. In this sense, *al-Saq 'ala al-saq* reveals the unmanageable force within Said's "Semitic object" doing things with language that render ludicrous the core philological prognosis declared by Orientalist philology, which decreed the branch of Semitic languages, and the human beings that spoke them, as decadent, as extrusions to be pruned from the healthy Indo-European family tree. Despite his very different "style" of writing and utter lack of faith in human progress, Céline's "ideas" represent a rebirth of Renanian anti-Semitism translated into the simulacrum of popular argotic speech for a post-Dreyfus French public. Both Céline and Renan evoke the apocalyptic fear of linguistic contagion while asserting the authenticity of the hysterical body of the French language. Even if one takes the supposedly apolitical poststructuralist stance of considering decadence as a kind of disruption in meaning and identity, as a production of difference and multiplicity—and many critics of Céline have considered him happily decadent in this ambivalent sense—we can assert that in its ultimate regression toward authenticity and ideological purity, the Célinian text demonstrates a degeneration of this "decadent" power. Reading Céline through the lens of the Dreyfus affair in Algeria will demonstrate how the laughter of Céline's text is not the "universal laughter" supposed by Bakhtin to be the articulation of the Rabelaisian carnival, and will instead take us far from Bakhtin's ideal carnival, where "all men become conscious participants in [the] one world of laughter" (1968 [1965], 188). While al-Shidyaq allows us to reorient carnival away from its supposed origin in medieval European laughter, much of which was of course aimed at the Jew and the other, Céline's text will perform what can only be called a truly decadent carnival.

CHAPTER 3

From Dreyfus in the Colony to Céline's Anti-Semitic Style

This chapter begins with the Dreyfus affair (1894–1906) and its afterlives in France and Algeria in order to identify and critique the political, rhetorical, and social mechanisms that fracture the Semitic object of knowledge fabricated by European Orientalism. Here we speak of decadence in a formal sense, as a breakdown, a disintegration of formerly integrated elements. Just as Arabic and Hebrew, along with Arab and Jew, had been thrown together in the creation of the notion of the Semitic and the figure of the Semite, so, too, will they be cleaved apart—by Christian hands drafting laws, running for office, and writing anti-Jewish pamphlets. This disintegration of the Semite into Jew and Arab is an underexplored consequence of Orientalism, and demonstrates the circuits through which the experiments carried out in the colony come home to the metropole to produce an affective minoritization of the majority French population. The politics of Semitism in fin-de-siècle Algeria provide a prism that will allow us to cross the full spectrum of linguistic carnivalization, taking us from al-Shidyaq's explosion of *nahda* discourse (the focus of Chapter 2) all the way to Céline's abjection of French—through the figure of the Jew. The chapter thus elaborates the affective stylistics of the disintegrating Semitic object, demonstrating how specific textual strategies of the carnivalesque and burlesque—grafting, plagiarism, ventriloquism—perform a frenzied identification with the figure of the Jewish Semite.

Disintegrating Semitism

Philological Semitism, as Joseph Massad reminds us, "has always been Anti-Semitism" (2015, 318), and this chapter argues for the importance of posing "the Semitic Question" in the context of Algeria. I am of course harkening to the "Jewish Question" that emerged in the late eighteenth century regarding the cultural and social status of Jews in modern Europe. By reframing this inquiry as "Semitic," I mean to revive the philological origins of the distinction between Semite and Indo-European, but most important, between Arab and Jew. I will then look at the Dreyfus affair in Algeria as a key moment when the so-called "Semitic object" of knowledge fractures. This exploration reveals the outlines of two divergent impulses within philology itself: a colonial, predictive, and ontologizing philology, versus a postcolonial mode of philological work that would be historical, worldly, and open to the future as unwritten. If al-Shidyaq opens up the possibility of postcolonial philological textuality, Céline illustrates a limit of Orientalist symptomology, recast as literary pop-philological anti-Semitism.

It is telling that the word "Semitism" was invented by an Orientalist (coined in 1781 by German Orientalist August Schlözer), whereas "anti-Semitism" was first disseminated by a journalist (in 1879, by the Viennese Wilhelm Marr).[1] For here we have the hundred-year lag between the "scientific" discovery of a philological *description* of linguistic commonalities and its explicit transformation into a normative *prescription* regarding the users of these languages as inferior and stunted. Perhaps the most pressing issue at the heart of the Semitic Questions is this: when and how did the Semite—against whom the word "anti-Semitism" was directed—become exclusively Jewish? What vicissitudes precipitated the splitting of the Semite into Arab and Jew? Gil Anidjar claims that the Nazis effected the final cleaving of the so-called "Semitic object," whereas Massad points to Zionism.[2] While one could argue the relative merits of either assertion, it is instructive here to return to philology. I will argue that Orientalist philology itself crafted the possibility of the partition between Jews and Arabs and that a divergently critical and anti-Orientalist philology is thus required to understand this move and get beyond it. Even as the creation of the Semitic object by Orientalist philology was an act of suturing together vast swaths of history and wildly diverse social formations, this philology was also invested in typologies and distinctions *within* the homogenized categories it invented. Edward Said himself characterized the views of Ernest Renan on this important point in a way that might mislead the incautious reader. "No modern Semite," Said wrote in *Orientalism*, "however much he may have believed himself to be modern, could ever outdistance the organizing claims on him of his origins" (1978, 234). The fact is, however, that Renan and other philologist rather confidently claimed that certain Semites appeared to have gained more distance from those claims than others, thus creating important differences within the category of the Semite. In 1847, when Renan was but twenty-four years old, he affirmed with certainty that Jews were superior to Arabs and Muslims, claiming that an "Israelite" could become "a modern man" if he had ample exposure to the Indo-European races, whose languages, Renan tells us, reveal a genius for internal diversity and the capacity for self-renewal and regeneration. In her article "Re-Membering Semitism," Gil Hochberg astutely speculates that "while Judaism introduced for Renan and his fellow Christian philologists a serious problem, given that it represented the religious origins of Christianity (and the religion of Jesus Christ himself), Islam represented the threat of a return to the very Semitism Christianity labored to rid itself of" (2016, 206). That is to say, that for Renan, Judaism was at least positioned in the "correct" historical slot, meaning *prior* to Christianity, and it therefore was useful in proving the teleology of progress that Renan wanted philology to demonstrate. Even as Renan created the Semite as other to the Indo-European, he engineered a crack in the Semitic object of knowledge, ensuring that the precise nature of the relationship between Jews and Arabs would remain in Christian European hands.

Said famously called Orientalism "the strange, secret sharer of Western anti-Semitism," affirming that the two "resemble each other very closely" (Said 1978, 28). Indeed, the shared history of imperialist representation and appropriations of Jewish, Muslim, and Arab cultures was among the missed opportunities for critical engagement Said identified in "Orientalism Reconsidered" (1985). Readers, he pointed out, had failed to note a crucial "conjuncture," namely

> that hostility to Islam in the modern Christian West has historically gone hand in hand with, has stemmed from the same source, has been nourished at the same stream as anti-Semitism, and that a critique of the orthodoxies, dogmas, and disciplinary procedures of Orientalism contribute to an enlargement of our understanding of the cultural mechanisms of anti-Semitism. (Said 1985, 100)

Certainly a core thesis of Said's perpetually disruptive book concerns the invention and manipulation of what he called "the Semitic object" of Western knowledge production. Gil Anidjar reinforced this disappointment, affirming that this conjuncture of Jews, Arabs, and Muslims as substitutable objects of discourse and thought in an Orientalist mode "should have become an entire field of study" (2008, 122). In trying to understand the absence of a discussion of Orientalism from contemporary debates about anti-Jewish anti-Semitism and Islamophobia, I am prompted to reopen this foreclosed field and to trace the "disintegration" of this discursive assemblage, an apparatus that I have begun outlining in earlier chapters. The overarching argument of this book is that Orientalism—as "a style of having power" over the East—functions by breaking down; it performatively embeds its diagnoses of biological degeneration, social backwardness, philological stuntedness, and historical belatedness in the subjects it only claims to describe (the so-called Orient and so-called Orientals), thereby *creating* the conditions it only claims to be observing, analyzing, and interpreting. In tracing the genealogy of the "Semitic object" back to its emergence in French in the nineteenth century, one in fact traces nothing less than the colonial engineering of enmity between Jews and Arabs: a kind of reverse engineering of an object designed to fail. Yet the Semitic in "anti-Semitism" is misleading, as it has come to refer specifically to Jews, even as the "anti-Semitism" continues to remind us of its early nineteenth century origins denoting a generalized denigration of all peoples termed "Semitic." Nonetheless, the linked histories of Jews, Arabs, and Muslims, as well as the totalizing discourses created about them in Europe, can and should, I would argue, be discussed in relationship to Orientalism. In thinking critically about the waves of the Semitization and de-Semitization of Arabs and Jews,[3] it becomes an ever more pressing task to detail, in a historically attentive manner, the disintegration of the concept of Semite that had been created to contain, manipulate, and control Jews, Arabs, and Muslims *en bloc*. My claim is that the Dreyfus affair, specifically as it played out in Algeria, represents a crucial moment when the Semitic object suffers an irreparable crack, and that the subsequent process of the disintegration of the Semitic is inextricably bound up with the accusations of the so-called decadence of the Oriental. In this chapter, I hope to travel along some of the hairlines of this fracture. Whereas the introduction and first chapter explore the philological register of Orientalist anti-Semitism broadly defined, and the second chapter offers anti-Orientalist Arabic philology, this chapter will focus on the juncture where colonial politics, economic activity, and highly stylized literary anti-Semitism converge to reconfigure the relationship between Jews and Muslims as both relate to the figure of the Semite.

It should be no secret to even the most casual observer of colonial history that European colonialism entailed the exportation of racist ideology on a planetary scale. Yet Dreyfus in the colony demonstrates the fluid volatility of racial fictions and the collateral damage of colonized peoples who are not only subjected to these fictions, but coerced to assimilate, internalize, and perform them, both as a question of survival, and as a precondition or price to be paid for their entry into (colonial) modernity. These racial fictions are then shipped back to the metropole, where the paranoid fantasies of a specifically anti-Jewish anti-Semitic conspiracy will circulate, mutate, and intensify, only to be broadcast back to the Arab world, such as what would occur during the rise of Nazism, when thousands of hours of anti-Semitic propaganda in Arabic were quite literally broadcast throughout North Africa by the Nazis, and millions of printed leaflets were distributed there.[4] It is safe to say that ever since at least 1948, each rise in anti-Semitism has been accompanied by a rise in Orientalist racism, what we now almost comfortably call "Islamophobia." The fate of the so-called Semitic object rides on the near-impossibility of aligning Western Anti-Semitism and Islamophobic racism under the banner of Orientalism and anti-Orientalist critique.

If the Semitic object was fabricated in the high-tech philological lab of scholars like Franz Bopp and Ernest Renan, it broke apart as a result of the most banal workings of commerce and money. Careful accounting of the production of the Semitic and its subsequent disintegration are necessary to counter what Hochberg calls the "naturalization" of enmity between Jews and Arabs that regulates so much of the discourse about the Israeli-Palestinian conflict (2016, 194). Hochberg's excellent work on the Semitic question outlines the shifting values and associations linking Jews, Arabs, and Muslims to the Semitic since the nineteenth century. She argues for something like a self-conscious revival of an awareness of the common enemy Jews and Arabs have in the Christian West that erected the term in first place. Of particular interest is her analysis of the "Judeo-Christian," a concept that was first devised to accuse the Catholic Church of having retained too many "Jewish, pagan, and oriental influences" (195), but which radically changed meaning after World War II, as Europe hoped to swiftly forget its own anti-Semitic history. While the hyphen linking "Judeo" and "Christian" in this formulation would seem to signify shared history, this *trait d'union* in fact functions as an operator that wills an active forgetting of hundreds of years of anti-Jewish thoughts and deeds in the

Christian West that culminated with the holocaust (195–98). This chapter, then, zeroes in on the role of French Algerian commercial conflicts and colonial politics during the Dreyfus affair, focusing on the period from 1897 to 1899, in order to remember Orientalism as the master signifying practice that both crafted the Semitic object and brought about its rupture.

Dreyfus in the Colony

It is striking the degree to which French colonial policy in the second half of the nineteenth century in Algeria matches up with Renan's claims about the capacity of Jews to assimilate to modern European society, however mediated by "Indo-European culture" it may have been. The series of legal maneuvers beginning in 1865 that dictated the different legal statuses of Algerian Jews and Muslims, most famously, in the Décret Crémieux of 1870, which automatically naturalized all Algerian Jews as French citizens, can be understood as an embedding of Orientalism within the legal code, as the distinction made in the laws between Jew and Muslim were civilizational in nature. Orientalist knowledge thus legitimated the grouping together of Jews and Muslims as potential objects to be assimilated into the French nation, and then with the stroke of a pen, created a fissure between them, generating animosities from all sides, as French pieds-noirs, Muslims, and European foreigners came to develop resentment against Algerian Jews who had been singled out and granted automatic citizenship.

Such were the conditions in France's most prized colony when the French Jewish naval captain Alfred Dreyfus was wrongly convicted of treason against the French state in 1894. The subsequent *affaire* cleaved French society between the Catholic right and the secular left, creating lasting enmities in social, political, and intellectual life, but it was in Algeria, perhaps more than anywhere else, that the Jewish Question necessarily had to confront the Semitic Question. While Napoleon III's Second Empire used statecraft to sculpt the Semitic population of Algeria from above and abroad, granting rights as facilely as it stripped them away, local politicians in Algiers and Oran were quickly learning the political uses of vulgarized Semitism to gain political advantage among the minority French and European populations caught in the grips of anti-Dreyfusard paranoia. Combined with the sequence of national decrees regarding citizenship and rights and the rise of the anti-Jewish press, the Dreyfus affair in Algeria demonstrates how the legal and political apparatus of France allowed the metropole to fine-tune Orientalism: by tapping into, amplifying, and strategically redirecting existing fears and local conflicts regarding Semites.

The case of Algeria provides an extraordinary instance of the way that enmity between Jews and Muslims was engineered through the everyday workings of colonialism's banal exceptionalism. Without devoting excessive space to the well-known history of Algerian Jews and the French colonial government, it is worth reviewing the sequence of political decisions that helped configure the specific conditions obtaining between French *colons*, indigenous Jews and Muslims, and the substantial population of "foreign" Europeans in the Algeria from the 1860s onward. The management of indigenous populations in Algeria was accomplished, in part, through a series of laws that specified which rights of French citizenship would be granted to which group of people. Citizenship rights were first made available to both the "*indigène musulmane*" and the "*indigene israélite*" in a Senate *consulte* decreed in 1865 and applied in 1866. This law was primarily formal, as Muslims, for example, could not make up more than a third of municipal governing bodies. The three million indigenous Muslims and thirty thousand indigenous Jews of Algeria were grouped together even as they were legally identified as distinct from one another; they were also granted the same status as the 250,000 non-French Europeans who had lived in the country for three or more years. To receive full French citizenship, however, meant renouncing most of the fundamental tenets of social cohesion that regulated the common life of Muslims in Algeria, requiring them to reject Islamic law governing areas such as marriage, inheritance, personal status, and property rights. The result was that fewer than three thousand Muslims over the course of the next century would apply for and be granted French citizenship under the conditions offered (Brett 1988, 456–57).

Even this limited set of "rights" would be curtailed with subsequent decrees. The Décret Crémieux (Décret 136) of 1870 automatically naturalized all Algerian Jews as French citizens, while a subsequent decree (Décret 137) reaffirmed the subject status of "indigenous Muslims." This also meant that the larger population of European residents remained disenfranchised, unable to profit from the rich spoils of Algeria's broadly corrupt colonial government. The manipulation of colonial populations through unequal treatment intensified with the establishment (1874) and updating (1881) of the Code de l'Indigénat (the Indigenous Code), which dictated harsh punishments for Muslims who were caught assembling unlawfully or demonstrating disrespect toward white French *colons*.

Widespread economic crisis also played a key role in the relationships between the various religious, national, and ethnic constituencies in Algeria at the time, so when Dreyfus was convicted of treason in 1894, much of Algeria had already been rehearsing anti-Jewish rhetoric for some time. The Dreyfus affair is, of course, one of the most documented and discussed events in modern European history. It pitted Dreyfusards against anti-Dreyfusards in ways that often did not simply reflect the explicit anti-Semitism of the participants, or conventional political affiliations, but rather brought to light an entire network of previously unspoken attitudes and alliances. Emile Zola's famous letter from 1898, "J'accuse," which explicitly called out the French army's role in actively covering up the truth of Dreyfus's innocence, is but one moment in the national drama instigated by the affair. Despite the fact that Algeria was the site of the only fatalities that can be said to have stemmed from events animated by it, little work has been done on the particularities of the Dreyfus affair as it played out in Algeria. In what follows, I will therefore be returning to the colonial archive in order to locate the epicenter that can be said to have cracked the Semite in two.

While conflict between Jews and Muslims had of course existed in Algeria well before the nineteenth century, the rise of specifically European anti-Jewish anti-Semitism—what I am tempted to call colonial fin-de-siècle Orientalism—was felt by Algerian Jews of the period to be a radically new development (as I will demonstrate later). For this reason, one should read accounts of "homegrown" anti-Jewish attitudes among Muslims in the Maghreb with a high degree of circumspection. Take, for example, historian Stephen Wilson's highly regarded *Ideology and Experience: Anti-Semitism in France at the Time of the Dreyfus Affair* (1982), which remains among the most authoritative and comprehensive monographs on the subject written in English. The author cites a passage from André Gide's journal from 1896 as proof of existing anti-Semitism in the Maghreb. Even a brief analysis of the passage cited by Wilson reveals that the example of Arab anti-Semitism that Wilson thinks he has identified is, in fact, a recent import from a France being shaken by the Dreyfus affair. In the text, Gide mentions that he has just introduced Athman Ben Salah, his young Tunisian servant, turned lover and poet, to the *1001 Nights*, presumably through the celebrated translation of Antoine Galland that first appeared in 1704. Gide continues in this vein, pointing out how things that one might assume to be part of Athman's experience have all been mediated by Orientalists and Europeans:

Athman has found some collection or other of "Lives of Famous Men" and now, on the subject of camels, quotes Buffon or Cuvier, never talks of friendship without naming Henry IV and Sully, of courage without Bayard, and of the Big Dipper without Galileo . . .

He writes to Degas upon sending him a walking-stick made of a palm stem: "What I like about you is that you do not like the Jews and that you read *Libre Parole* and that, like me, you consider Poussin a great French painter." (Gide 1955, 61)

What this passage illustrates is how "anti-Semitism" becomes just another item in a list of subjects (friendship, courage, camels, and constellations), which, like the *1001 Nights*, had been introduced to Athman already framed by Orientalist modalities of knowledge. In other words, this passage does not serve as proof of existing anti-Semitism among Maghrebi Muslims, as Wilson claims, but rather as evidence of its importation into the colony.

Reading Gide's journal while scrutinizing a painting of Gide and Athman from four years later provides visual confirmation of this argument. In Jacques-Émile Blanche's canvas from 1901, *André Gide et ses amis au café maure de l'Exposition Universelle*, Gide and his friends are depicted enjoying the transplanted exotica of an "authentic" Moorish café at the Exposition in Paris.[5] The left edge of the frame cuts in two the figure of a Maghrebi child serving tea, while on the right, Gide, dressed in black suit, cape, and hat, holds a cigarette and gazes implacably at the viewer. Through a window, one can glimpse scenes recreating foreign lands in the various pavilions around the Trocadero. Most importantly, Athman himself is framed in this faux-Orientalia decor, which, was in fact, not even that of the Exposition, but primarily consisted of items that Gide had brought from his home to add authenticity to the simulacrum that was the Café Maure. This painting, juxtaposed with the passage from Gide's journal written in Biskra, Algeria, four years prior, immerses us in the all-enveloping panorama of Orientalist representation and repackaging of the Arab and Maghrebi cultural past and present. They offer us a privileged perspective on the dirty import/export business of fin-de-siècle colonialism—that is, on the political economy of racism in France and the colonies during the Dreyfus affair.

Gide's journal confronts the reader with two distinct manifestations of the same phenomenon: first, a general anti-Jewish sentiment expressed in Athman's letter to Degas ("what I like about you is that you do not like the Jews"), and second, a specific reference to the systemically anti-Semitic press in France.[6] Athman also likes that Degas, an outspoken anti-Semite and anti-Dreyfusard, was a reader of *La libre parole*, the anti-Jewish newspaper founded by Edouard Drumont, who had written the comprehensive, two-volume best-seller, *La France juive* (Jewish France), published in 1886, which blamed the Jews for France's ills. That Athman associates Drumont's anti-Jewish newspaper with his own dislike for Jews reveals one way that modern European anti-Jewish racism was brought by the French to the Muslim populations of the Maghreb: through print media. Degas himself played a key role in the production and reproduction of the figure of the Semitic Jew. His 1879 painting, *A la bourse*, depicts a group of conspiring bankers, evoking common fears of Jewish bankers preying on capitalism. The image takes recourse to the visual repertoire of anti-Jewish anti-Semitism in an explicit enough fashion that *La libre parole* would be able to rehash the image twenty years later. An 1899 cover from Drumont's newspaper reworks the visual vocabulary of anti-Semitism that Degas himself had tapped into, while adding a commentary to Bernard Lazare's recently published Dreyfusard book, *Une erreur judiciaire*. And just as *La libre parole* was able to influence the attitudes of the young Athman Ben Salah, so would both Drumont himself, as well as his model of an anti-Jewish press, be imported to Algeria: Drumont was elected a deputy (Representative of the Lower House) of Algiers in the 1898 elections, and dozens of anti-Jewish newspapers sprang up in the country during the 1890s, particularly in the wake of the trial of Captain Dreyfus.

It is in the context of the legal decisions of the French government regarding the status of Jews and Muslims in Algeria, an ongoing economic crisis, and the spread of the anti-Jewish press in the colony that the Dreyfus affair will come to a head in Algeria in the last years of the nineteenth century. Major riots broke out in Oran in 1897, and then in January, 1898, in response to the publication of Zola's "J'accuse," riots and pogroms spread across the country. Wilson tallies the damage thus:

> Zola's open letter indicted the Army General Staff for anti-Semitism and cover-up, and prompted reactionary riots across France, the most violent of which occurred in French colonial Algiers. There, the burning of Zola in effigy sparked a riot in which 158 shops were destroyed, six Jews were assaulted (two fatally), and 9 rioters, 47 police, and a large but unknown number of Jews were seriously injured. (1982, 119)

Police records in Oran, where anti-Jewish rioting had first occurred in 1897, reveal that while some Spaniards and Muslims joined the French in these riots, both of these groups were recruited by the French anti-Semites, who paid them fifty francs to ransack the Jewish quarter and yell "*A bas les juifs! Mort aux juifs!*" The detective work of one secret police agent from

Algiers turned up the numbers of the specific franc notes that had been used to pay the rioters (Dermenjian 1985, 79). Amidst the violence and chaos of these riots, there were numerous reports of scared Jewish citizens finding refuge for themselves and their belongings in the homes of Muslim friends and neighbors. The anti-Jewish crisis in Algeria was largely a question of "political anti-Semitism" (Dermejian 1986, 236), that is, of regional and municipal politicians seeking political office and using anti-Semitic rhetoric to get votes. Such is the evidence pointing to just some of the ways that French Algerians implanted anti-Semitism in the colony.

Crisis of Signs, or Anti-Semitic Style

The anti-Jewish riots seemed to energize Drumont-style newspapers such as the weekly published in Algiers, *La lutte antijuive*, which had a run of thirty-seven issues beginning on February 2, 1898. The paper printed a list of crimes for which Jews had been convicted, covered local politics and business news, reported on the Dreyfus affair, and ran items urging French and other European women alike to boycott Jewish-owned businesses. One issue included a list of the initials of those women who had not heeded the boycott and had been spotted entering Jewish establishments. Within this imported model of mass-mediated anti-Semitism, one also finds strikingly literal examples of imported anti-Semitism announced in the advertisements. Ads for "*cigarettes antijuives*" and "*absinthe antijuive*" appear throughout the paper alongside pleas to boycott Jewish businesses. The moral crusade against absinthe corresponded to the period of the Dreyfus affair, when absinthe become symbolic of the decadence of France driven by Jewish businesses. After the half-Jewish Picard brothers had bought a controlling interest in Pernod Fils in 1894, Drumont declared absinthe "a tool of the Jews" (Adams 195). His friend Alphonse Daudet blamed the debauchery of French soldiers on their habit of drinking absinthe, which they had picked up while fighting in Tunisia and Algeria (Adams 49), and he would later declare: "I am for wine and against absinthe, as I am for tradition and against revolution" (Adams 195). The marketing of absinthe began adding the words *Patrie* and *Égalité* on the label, along with the French tricolor. A maker in the Doubs valley, Montbeliard, started making Absinthe Anti-Juive, and this was the brand advertised and sold not just in the anti-Semitic and anti-Jewish newspapers published in metropolitan France but also in *La lutte antijuive*, among other likeminded Algerian papers.

This newspaper also imported the stylistics of the Dreyfus affair, publishing in three installments what it announced would be a full-length serial novel, or *feuilleton*. *Les mystères d'Alger*, which changed its name to *Les mystères d'el-Djazaïr* before its first installment, tells the cloak-and-dagger tale of a French Algerian man who seems to have disappeared one night during a stroll, but who turns out to have gone to a secret meeting with a shady government minister's underling. In the February 4, 1898, edition of *La lutte antijuive*, the forthcoming serial novel was announced in a way that seems designed to appeal to readers' anti-Jewish paranoia, their fascination with the mystery of the Oriental Jew, and their desire for sentimental fiction:

> This novel has been written especially for *La Lutte*.
>
> It's a thrilling story full of revelations about the scandals that have recently shaken our population.
>
> All the events remain unexplained, the scandals hushed up, the crimes unpunished, the shameful jiggery-pokery [*tripotage*], in a word, all the . . . Jewish *mysteries* have found their place in this work and make it the most dramatic novel of our time.
>
> The scandalous scenes that are currently unfolding in the highest places give it a timeliness of the highest interest.
>
> All those who live or have lived in our city will want to read LES MYSTÈRES D'ALGER, which, alongside the revelations about which we have just spoken, offers us a study of local mores captured from life and a truly moving sentimental plot.

The announcement claims the novel's unremarkable melodramatic style as somehow a creation of the political and economic crises of the day, all of which are dubbed "Jewish *mysteries*," which the novel will present as a grand conspiracy to wrest power from the French in Algeria. This mystery will "find its place in this novel"—a formulation that suggests that in a world where cover-ups are the rule, in a media landscape of "fake news," only fiction can manage to supposedly point in the direction of the hidden truth. Part of the melodramatic style consists of the Semitic typology of the descriptions, in which the Semitic traits of the characters are unmistakable—and, so, too, the author's anti-Semitic perspective. We are led to believe that something like a grand conspiracy is being hatched, in which the French government, under Napoleon III, is laying the groundwork for Jewish control of Algiers. Readers would have been reminded of the Senate *consulte* of 1865 mentioned earlier, which was promulgated by Napoleon the III the following year, and opened up French citizenship to Jews and Muslims. Like the anti-Jewish press in Algeria, the pogroms, boycotts, and electoral successes of anti-Jewish politicians such as Drumont, who was voted out of office in 1902, this novel did not last, disappearing after three short installments. But it points to the importance of style as a function of belief in the racial fictions being disseminated in the colony.

Zola himself foregrounded the low, melodramatic, *roman-feuilleton* style of the intrigue that constituted the *affaire Dreyfus* in his famous letter *J'accuse*. According to Zola, the acts of one of the key players responsible for the government cover-up, Paty de Clam, were "haunted by fictional intrigues, stooping to the devices of dime store novels, stolen documents, anonymous letters, meetings in deserted locations, mysterious women at night smuggling crushing proofs" (hanté d'intrigues romanesques, se complaisant aux moyens des romans-feuilletons, les papiers volés, les lettres anonymes, les rendez-vous dans les endroits déserts, les femmes mystérieuses, qui colportent, de nuit, des preuves accablantes). What all these examples of imported anti-Semitism demonstrate is not simply the ambivalence or undecidability of racial signifiers that one might seek in, say, a deconstructionist reading, but rather the fictional construct of Orientalist knowledge itself, and ways that the racial fictions construed by such knowledge could be written and rewritten to suit the needs of those in power.

The Dreyfus affair went beyond the social, political, or economic spheres as it conjured a full-fledged crisis of signs that radically transformed the acts of reading, writing, and interpretation of the French public. And while Céline's anti-Semitic pamphlets remain the best-known instances of the literary afterlife of this crisis, it is in Algeria where the drama of reading and interpretation becomes most acute. Several factors come into play in this crisis, starting with the creation of specialized news sources, published and marketed specifically either to Dreyfusard readers or to anti-Dreyfusards, both of whom had come to mistrust print media for different reasons. Maurice Barrès articulated the anti-Dreyfusard mindset that claimed to be immune to facts, and which could instead read all it needed to know in the race of Dreyfus himself. "I don't need anyone to tell me why Dreyfus betrayed," Barrès wrote in 1902, three years after the Captain's pardon and release from prison. "Psychologically, it suffices for me to know that he betrayed. The interval is filled in. That Dreyfus is capable of betraying, I conclude from his race."[7] Such a statement declares *race* as the only text with a stable system of signs, and suggests that other media exist only to confirm the messages of race. Despite the somewhat better future for the Jew predicted by Renan and attempted with the Décret Crémiuex, this, then, is one possible end game of colonial philology: the cessation of careful reading and the foreclosure of all possible futures other than the one that philology claimed to have found in the past of so-called Semites: dependence, arrested development, and *decadence*.

The collapse of the perceived distinction between truth and fiction indicated by Zola pushed writers and readers in a variety of directions in search of a style. On one side, we see the emergence of a new market for the latest up-to-the-minute news, for more reporting. On the other side, there was an explosion of editorial forms and formats, as well as the birth of the "intellectual." Zola's letter in *L'Aurore* was more than the mere publication of his opinion; it was also an act that announced the advent of the politically engaged public intellectual in its modern form.[8] Caricature, burlesque, and other pseudo-comic styles rose up to counter the kind of doubling-down of a Zola who risked his freedom and reputation to broadcast what he understood as the truth. A rather extraordinary example of these two competing styles, of sincerity versus burlesque, can be seen by comparatively reading a short pamphlet defending Jews written by a C. Fany, and a somewhat longer anti-Jewish text, written by an author who went by the name of Hugolin.[9] Fany's *Le juif algérien* was published on April 22, 1898, in Algiers, while Hugolin's text appeared in 1899, also in Algiers. It is significant that Fany frames his defense of the Algerian Jew within the logic of Orientalism, progress, and assimilation. Countering the allegation that the Jews are resistant to civilization, Fany affirms that "one is obligated to concede that his march toward the realization of our dreams, of the mixing together of races, has been more rapid than amongst any other people" (3). In fin-de-siècle Algeria, Fany is likely speaking, at least in part, of other European foreigners when he compares the Jew's accelerated rate of assimilation to that of "other people," but the more obvious example would, of course, be Algerian Muslims. In his appeal to the principle of civilizational status, Fany echoes Renan himself when he distinguishes the Jews as being well ahead of the Muslim in the race to escape decadence and decline. His analysis of "the troubles for which our beautiful city has become the theater" (7) concludes that it is jealously that is driving the anti-Jewish movement in Algeria, a movement that he says one could not even have predicted a few years prior. In his defense of the Jewish people, Fany asserts that anti-Jewish sentiment arises from jealousy of the Jews' sobriety, their lack of backwardness or *retard*, their fine powers of observation, and their ability to live within their means. The pamphlet ends with a reappropriation of the phrase that Fany claims has been wrongly usurped by the anti-Jewish groups: *"La France aux français!"*—France for the French (7). This is where the principle of national affiliation prompts the author of this ten-page pamphlet to appeal to other French-born citizens against the European foreigners such as Paul Bidaine, a Belgian leader of the anti-Jewish movement in Algiers.

Whereas Fany presents his case directly in a tone of measured sincerity, enumerating the positive qualities of the Jews and psychologically analyzing the anti-Jewish movement, Hugolin provides a burlesque of precisely this kind of Jewish voice in Algerian politics. If Orientalism, in Said's words, is a "style of having power," then a close reading, a *philological* reading of an anti-Jewish pamphlet will give us the opportunity to read this style philologically, as opposed to doing a merely symptomatic reading of Orientalist philology and anti-Semitism. The text in question, signed only with the pseudonym Hugolin, contains both the "thesis" and the stylistic ventriloquism of the Jewish voice in its very title: *Burlesque Petition Addressed to the Two Chambers and to the Ministers by the Jews of Algeria, Who Claim That a War of Religion Is Being Waged Against Them Because They Are Being Kept from Assassination and Theft.* Essentially, the text mocks the claim that Jews are inherently "assimilable," and it does so by appropriating the voice of the Jew making an appeal to the state apparatus. The title is the only place where the text slips into the third person, where the carnivalized first-person plural agency of the petition reveals itself as the "they" of the Semitic object of Hugolin's rant. "We are Jews," the text begins, "and this title fills us with genuine pride, for Jewry is the finest essence of humanity, the highest aristocracy in the world."[10]

The author anticipates the same strategies that Céline will deploy in his anti-Semitic pamphlets of the 1930s. The text plagiarizes recently published anti-Jewish screeds and places philological corruption at the center of his rant, ultimately creating precisely the same kind of hysterical identification with the Jew that we will discuss later in this chapter in Céline. The *Pétition burlesque* thus operates by means of textual cannibalism, as if to illustrate a contemporary phrase that Fany references in relation to the ravenous state of anti-Jewish politicians in Algiers: "*généralement, on veut manger du juif*"—one wants to eat the Jew. One mode of this cannibalism is the recasting of the tradition of anti-Jewish polemics that cited the Talmud and Midrash to claim that Jews consider non-Jews less than human and that Judaism requires Jews to kill non-Jews, among numerous similar allegations. Instead of simply repeating these sorts of crude misreadings of rabbinic tradition, which had been a strategy of Christian attacks on Jews since the twelfth century, Hugolin goes one step further: He places the outlandish rhetoric of these polemics in the mouth of a fictional Jewish spokesperson for the Jewish community attempting an earnest self-defense of his coreligionists:[11]

> We sometimes kill goyim: that is true.
> We steal from them every day: that is truer still.
> We mangle [*tripatouillons*] universal suffrage and we endeavor to get corrupted men elected in order to become masters of politics: this is incontestable. (6)

The French word rendered above by "mangle"—*tripatouiller*, "*nous tripatouillons*"—is a blend of two terms from informal spoken French: *tripoter* (to finger, to fiddle with, or to masturbate, in its pronominal form) and *patouiller* (to fumble with, to handle clumsily, to get bogged down in). The use of this portmanteau word renders, in precise fashion, the *Pétition*'s own rhetorical and stylistic approach: it mangles both the previous anti-Semitic polemics that Hugolin plagiarizes and the rabbinic texts these polemics claimed to be based on. Yet the text affirms that it is the Jews who mangle the principle of universal suffrage; that is, they misunderstand, misrepresent, and mishandle their newly acquired right to vote and run for office, just as a poor actor would mangle—*tripatouiller*—the words of a Racine or a Molière.

The mocking inclusion of Semitic words throughout the text reveals the symptomatic force of language in the colonial anti-Semitic imagination as expressed in the burlesque. To describe the flesh of Jewish women who are "disposed to prostitute themselves," the text cites the opinion of "our persecutors," meaning, of course, the anti-Jewish politicians responsible for the text we are reading, and interjects the term *djiffa'* in italics—Algerian Arabic for "carrion" (4). *Goym*, *souccoth*, and *peçah* are some of the Hebrew words that receive similar treatment, where italics and context mark these terms as both alien and pejorative, with the aim of creating a strong sense of the impurity of the Algerian Jew's French. Let us dwell just a moment longer on the lone Arabic word included in the pamphlet: *djiffa*. The word's trilateral root boasts a semantic range including *shun, repel, loathe, and cast forth foam, scum, or refuse*, and a nominal form, *djiffa'*, which had come to mean "carrion" in Algerian Arabic, but also "bastard." Several nineteenth-century French sources attest to the word's use as a way that Muslims referred to non-Muslims, including Jews, specifically in the locution *djiffa' bin djiffa'*, or "Carrion Son of Carrion."[12] The use of this term in the context described earlier, a burlesque ridiculing the very act of colonized Jews appealing to the state that had thrust naturalization upon them thirty years prior, allows the anonymous author of the text to engraft the abstract moral lesson of Semitic philology—namely, that both the Semitic and the Semite are not merely *decadent* but indeed are already *dead*, precluding any further development—onto the transliterated words themselves. Like certain Arabic loan words that have become semi-naturalized in French—*fatma* or *moukère* (woman), for example—these terms with Semitic origins are made to function as tumorous symptoms of corruption and disease pushing up against what would be the otherwise healthy skin of the French text, "*encysted* in the language," as Laurent Dubreuil has written in the context of Céline's *Mort à crédit* (2013, 104). The derisive inclusion of Arabic and Hebrew words can be called anti-Semitic in the properly philological sense of the term in 1899; that is, they both isolate and generalize the Semitic and also set the different kinds of Semites against one another.

In detailing the ways that European anti-Jewish anti-Semitism was imported to the colony and embedded within Muslim society, I am in no way trying to diminish or excuse racism coming from Arabs or Muslims directed at Jews, nor that coming from Jews aimed at Arabs or Muslims. Instead, I hope to bring into focus a turning point in the shifting configurations of Orientalist modes of power functioning on intersecting planes (juridical, political, commercial, representational) that still animate what Hochberg rightly affirms as "one of 'the best kept secrets,' namely the overlapping between anti-Semitism and Islamophobia" (2016, 211). On the juridical plane, we see the Décret Crémiux emerge as something like a singular solution to the problems of colonial nationalism, the minority question, and Crémieux's own grappling with the Jewish Question in these contexts.[13] The ad-hoc nature of the different legal statuses of French, Europeans, Jews, and Muslims in Algeria gives rise to strange alliances, paranoia, and an elevated sensitivity to accusations of treason. (Charges of separatism by the metropole made the French *colons* eager to find scapegoats that would take the focus away from them.) Politically, the Jewish Question in Algeria had to confront the Semitic Question. Whereas French Jews seeking acceptance and rights had long appealed to the spirit of Republican universalism, in the colony leading Jewish figures sought this same end by appealing to the French pieds-noirs as fellow *minorities*. Simon Kanoui, the main Jewish political player in Oran at the end of the nineteenth century, testified in 1900 before a government commission that the Jews had no choice but to vote for moderate candidates supported by the administration, knowing that "in Algeria more than anyplace else" Jews could simply not live peacefully "without the principle of authority and without the support of the government, given the four million Arabs surrounding them" (Dermenjian 1986, 35).

It is the merging of commerce and representation, however, where we can most clearly see the disintegration of the Semitic object, which sends its shards into the twentieth century and beyond. The mass-mediatization of Jews, Arabs, and Muslims as plastic, manipulable figures of Orientalist desire and antipathy gains momentum during the Dreyfus affair, transforming race into a marketable, fungible fetish. The racialization of not only Arabness, as witnessed in the rise of Arab nationalism, but also of Jewishness are both crucial consequences of the political minefield of the Affair. For Bernard Lazare (whose *Une erreur judiciaire* was featured on the cover of Drumont's *La libre parole*, discussed before) the Dreyfus affair revealed the unattainability of assimilation and prompted a neo-Zionist affirmation of the exceptional nature of the precariousness of being Jewish in the system of nation-states. Yet in a twist that illustrates the vicious circle of Semitic racialization, Lazare's affirmation of the Jew's irreducible difference would be welcomed by none other than the engineer of the anti-Jewish movement itself, Drumont.[14]

Céline and the End of Carnival

These multiple trajectories of the disintegration of "the Semitic object" will impact the emerging rhetorical forms of twentieth century Orientalism as it splits into anti-Semitism and Islamophobia conceived as unrelated discursive-affective fields. Out of the split between these two kinds of Semites will spring the entire legacy of "anti-Semitism" within Arab, Muslim, and Jewish societies in Algeria and well beyond. Anti-Semitism in France and the rest of Europe will continue to intensify, as the experience of Dreyfus in the colony is exported back to the metropole. This is where the polarity of racial ambivalence *flips*, so to speak, switches over to instill a lasting fantasy of minoritization among the metropolitan majority population. That is, what we witness as the Dreyfus affair gets shipped to the colony and then sent back, transformed, to the metropole is something like the importation of the experience of the colonized subject as a constitutive element of the citizen in the age of the decline of what Arendt has termed "traditional nationalism" (1973, 3). This chapter closes with a reading of one of Céline's anti-Semitic pamphlets, *Bagatelles pour un massacre* (Trinkets for a Slaughter, 1937), which offers perhaps the most striking instance in French cultural history of a collision between identification with the figure of the Jew, minoritization of the majority population, and what we can call pop-philological anti-Semitism. Even though Alice Kaplan has identified the multiple sources that Céline redeployed in his pamphlets as a "veritable anti-Semitic international" (1995, 44), rereading Céline through the specific lens of the Dreyfus affair in Algeria demonstrates how the paranoia and perceived victimization of French colonials served as a crucial relay in the circuit of faux-minoritization of the French metropolitan majority population that his texts ultimately produce. Like that of Hugolin, Céline's writing cannibalizes the Jew whom it would devour, plagiarizing and ventriloquizing the hated minority, blurring the lines between the burlesque, the carnivalesque, and the abject.

Céline's own remark that the persecution he himself suffered for his anti-Semitism and collaborationism—dismissal from his clinical post, assassination plots by the Resistance, arrest, trial, Danish exile, and seventeen months in prison—amounted to "a Dreyfus Affair, in reverse"[15] further obliges a contextualization of Céline's writing from the 1930s within discourses of pathology, paranoia, and social degeneration, which reached a critical point at the end of the nineteenth century.[16] *Bagatelles pour un massacre*, the first of three virulently stylized anti-Semitic pamphlets, celebrates what Céline calls "vulgar style," and begins with the narrator confessing to his own unwilling capitulation to the sincere, elevated style: after much resistance, "poor Ferdinand" has become "strangled by emotion... by [his] own *refinement*" (1937, 12). Celine's proxy narrator tells us that style kills, strangles, and smothers. A few years later, after the war, Céline will try to justify his anti-Semitism by claiming that he is, in fact, simply a "man of style" instead of one with ideas or a message; such a claim indicates the voracity of the category of style for Celine, consuming as it does here any possible link between the aesthetic and the ethical, between literary creation and social contract. Julia Kristeva writes that the Célinian text is not about "the Death of God but a reassumption, *through style,* of what lies hidden by God," which for her is ultimately the horror of the godless authority of the superego (1982, 133). However, the exceedingly violent and blunt style, Céline's "frankness"—which he opposes to the dreaded "refined style"—is itself an ideological choice that draws on the centuries-old distinction between the racial purity of the Franks and the *métissage* of the Gallo-Romans. Andrea Loselle writes that "style, for Celine, must be organic; it must be slangy, emotive, and inventive without linguistic intermarriage (*babélisme*). Stylistic originality, then, is race specific, autochthonic, and not allogeneous, so that"—and here she quotes Alice Kaplan—"'what makes [Céline] avant-garde is the same thing that makes him national; this is precisely where his populism verges to the right' [1986, 118]" (1995, 187). Loselle argues that Céline's frank style functions as a racially marked oral transgression of the refined style of written law, which Céline links to the figure of the Jew as well as to the Académie Française (190).

Throughout, Céline's vulgar take on linguistic Darwinism is infused with the language of decadence, decline, and degeneration. Whereas academic Orientalist philology advanced a set of truth claims about the inherently decadent status of Semitic languages and peoples, Céline's texts *perform* the decadent state of the Jew in a pop-philological style, purportedly devoid of any message, or whose message has become completely absorbed by style. Yet Célinian style does not operate in a vacuum, but rather functions dialectically with established notions of decadence and rebirth, generation and corruption, language and social vitality. As such, it offers grounds for comparison with the ambivalence of *nahda* discourse, especially that which occurs in al-Shidyaq (see Chapter 2). Al-Shidyaq and Céline's texts both fall well within the purview of the Bakhtinian carnivalesque, and both authors play with the idea of texts as bodies that suffer, laugh, convulse, and consume. Céline's pamphlets, however, perform the hysterical dance of a convulsive civilization, whose language can only ever be fertilized by its own waste, even as it opens to the horrors of global contagion. Céline's writing embodies racism as a form of linguistic denial that secretes a degenerative historicity, offering us a self-fertilizing cul-de-sac of language as symptom. His strange and horrific brand of anti-Semitism ultimately indicates the occlusion in Bakhtinian carnival's "universal laughter" and emphasizes the cruelty performed within carnivalesque theater.

Céline's kinship to Renaissance discourse, Rabelais, and the carnivalesque were duly noted in a 1938 review by Léon Daudet, an ardent Céline supporter, well-known anti-Dreyfusard, and fellow anti-Semitic pamphleteer, who spoke of the novel in terms of its

> Rabelaisian vigor [*verdeur*], in a language to my mind superb, stuffed with argot, peppered with irony, sordid and over-the-top, acidic, juicy, here filthy, there baroque. . . . But make no mistake: this book is AN ACT that will one day perhaps have fearful consequences. *Bagatelles pour un massacre* is a carnivorous book that appears beneath a stormy sky illuminated by flashes of lightening.[17]

Daudet accounts for the novel's chaotic and volatile style as a camouflage for its effective reality as performative language. Whereas Céline's own claim denies any epistemological link between his style and his "message," Daudet, it seems, would make of Céline the kind of writer who (following Nietzsche) "philosophizes with a hammer," albeit with a hammer forged from Renaissance steel.

Céline diverges rather bluntly from the optimism of a Bakhtin looking back at a high point in European literary history. While the pamphlets dance on the limits of a certain Rabelaisian renaissance inventiveness, Céline can be more accurately located at the crossroads of fin-de-siècle decadence and a certain neo-Romantic notion of "century-sickness." Albert Chesneau writes that "the path that Céline shows us is one of infertile stress, generalized trauma, failure. From a purely literary perspective, one sees the culmination of the *mal du siècle*, carried to its absolute limit" (1971, 150). Nicholas Hewitt charts the complex role played by the *belle époque* in Céline's interwar writings, and argues that he "perceives himself as caught in a cycle of historical repetition," a view of history opposed to the faith in historical progression so prevalent in the nineteenth century (1987, 12). In her excellent book *Dance Pathologies*, Felicia McCarren traces the nineteenth-century semiotics of the pathologized body, which, she claims, Céline inherits from the likes of Kraft-Ebbing and Charcot. Part of this inheritance is a specifically fin-de-siècle obsession with hysteria as an individual manifestation of social ills such as syphilis, prostitution, alcoholism, and immigration. "Reading the social body for signs of 'health,' reading class and color as signs of its sickness, Céline uses a symptomology familiar from the 19th century, one in which dance figures significantly as a model" (1998, 190).

The style of the pamphlets, which critics have called both hysterical and psychotic,[18] exploits a very fin-de-siècle racist paranoia based on age-old fears of population decline, which becomes grafted onto a model of linguistic decay and extinction.[19] In *Les beaux draps*, Céline writes: "We'll disappear body and soul from this territory like the Gauls, those mad heroes, our great duped forebears in futility, the worst cuckolds of Christianity. They did not leave us twenty words of their own language. As for us, if the word 'shit' lasts, that would be a pretty feat" (79). Here Céline declares the French language decadent from the beginning, or at least in as much as Gaulish purity was corrupted by Roman-Christian influence. Céline's restorative then, will be to reinsert his "*merde*" as compost into the language—a form of "self-pollution'—in order to augment it and to purify it from within.

This singular approach to language purification informs much of Céline's work, but it becomes particularly frantic beginning with *Bagatelles pour un massacre*. Céline's ferocious rant begins by identifying a list of exemplars of this refined style he detests so much, and coins a list of short phrases in the infinitive to slander this style in his popular, "frank," and transgressive style. He confesses that he has, after much resistance, become

> a verifiably refined person, refined by right, by custom, official, sposed to write at least like M. Gide . . . M. Vanderem, M. Benda, M. Duhamel, Mme. Colette, Mme. Femina, Mme. Valéry, the "Théâtres Français" . . . to swoon over the nuance . . . Mallarmé, Bergson, Alain . . . to anal-yze the adjective . . . to goncourtize . . . shit! to assholify the gnat, to freneticize Insignificance . . .

> Un raffiné valable, raffiné de droit, de coutume, officiel, d'habitude doit écrire au moins comme M. Gide, M. Vanderem, M. Benda, M. Duhamel, Mme. Colette, Mme. Femina, Mme. Valéry, les « Théâtres Français » . . . pâmer sur la nuance . . . Mallarmé, Bergson, Alain . . . troufignoliser l'adjectif . . . goncourtiser . . . merde! enculagailler la moumouche, frénétiser l'Insignifiance. (1937, 11)

An ironic emblem of his newly come-by refinement, the neologism functions as a double-bind fastened both around Céline's own neck and around the neck of his rival and model, the "Jewish" intellectual. In this it evokes the anti-Jewish press in metropolitan France and Algeria, and it functions much as the kind of double-bind that Derrida describes in an essay on Freudian resistance, where resistance to analysis becomes a paradoxical knot or scar that the analyst attempts to "solve" or loosen. The catch, Derrida tells us, is that "a double bind cannot be fully analyzed: one can only unbind one of its knots by pulling on the other to make it tighter" (1937, 36). Céline's own severe resistance to both "*raffinement*" and to criticism place him squarely in Derrida's own analyst's chair. Among the various types of Freudian resistance, Derrida hits upon one particular brand that illustrates Célinian "style" particularly well: "the repetition compulsion, hyperbolic resistance of nonresistance, [which] is in itself *analytic*; it is that whose resistance psychoanalysis today represents, in the surest form of its ruse: disguised as nonresistance" (24).[20] While Derrida's literary model, Bartleby (a scribe like al-Faryaq, whose reiterated "I'd prefer not to" exemplifies this type of resistance) seems to be the stylistic opposite of Céline, both present their message as a nonmessage. *Bagatelles pour un massacre* is indeed the text of a medical analyst who reads the symptoms of social pathology in the individual, and whose diagnosis claims to be a nondiagnosis; not a message or an idea, but mere "style."[21]

Evoking the neologisms in Hugolin's anti-Semitic *Burlesque*, Céline's coinages scorn the very kind of sterile French he claims to hate, and are achieved by "grafting" a form of "*cul*" ("ass" or "anus") or "*con*" ("cunt" or "bastard")—or other related terms—onto another word, which may or may not be itself a corruption. One of the ingenuities of such language is that it criticizes one kind of hybridization with another. Céline uses specifically Latinate words that have lost their sound-substance (a sign of linguistic longevity); neither *con* nor *cul* quite betray their Latin roots *cuniculum* or *culus*. By reextending these words (within other words), he comically reveals the process of linguistic decay in an attempt to reverse it, thereby distorting the schema of naturalized language laid out by those first Renaissance defenders of the French language, such as Joachim Du Bellay. This type of *pullulement* relates to the *"verdeur rabelaisienne"* of which Daudet spoke: the evolving connotations of both *pullulment* and even *verdeur* indicate modes in which biology becomes ideologized.

Two masochistic pleasures in particular power the Celinian text: name-calling (Céline is *"un sous-Zola sans essor"*) and appropriation of another's discourse in order to ridicule and destroy it.[22] In the passage that follows, Céline ventriloquizes the voice of a critic accusing his work of a series of major faults, all of which the critic expresses in a burlesque of "refined" style:

> Monsieur Céline disgusts us, tires us out without surprising us ... A sub-Zola sans the soar ... a plagiarist of newsstand graffiti [...] his style is nauseating, a perversion.... Readers! Readers! Be careful not to buy a single book from this dirty pig! ... To buy a book from M. Céline at a moment when so many of our authors, the great ones, nervous and loyal talents, the honor of our language (the greatest of all ... would be to stab, at a moment of such gravity for all of our arts, our French Belles-Lettres! (the most beautiful of all!)
>
> Monsieur Céline nous dégoûte, nous fatigue, sans nous étonner ... Un sous-Zola sans essor ... un plagiaire des graffiti d'édicule ... son style est un écœurement, une perversion.... Lecteurs! Lecteurs!.... Gardez-vous bien d'acheter un seul livre de ce sale cochon! ... Acheter un livre de M. Céline au moment où tant de nos auteurs, de grands, nerveux et loyaux talents, honneur de notre langue (la plus grande de toutes).... Ce serait poignarder dans un moment si grave pour tous nos arts, nos Belles-Lettres Françaises! (les plus belles de toutes!).
> (1937, 14)

As Alice Kaplan has amply demonstrated, many of the celebrated stylistic effects of the pamphlets are less the result of Céline's own textual inventiveness than of creative acts of plagiarism (Kaplan 1986). The leap from

Hugolin's anti-Semitic tract from 1899 to Céline in 1937 is a short one, yet Céline takes the *Burlesque* a step further by having his imaginary critic accuse "Monsieur Céline" of plagiarism; more specifically, of plagiarizing "*graffiti d'édicule*," "newsstand graffiti," the place where one would have bought both the journals and pamphlets, such as Hugolin's *Burlesque*, that Céline's text consumes and regurgitates. Tellingly, Céline does not place a single neologism in the mouths of his critics. These he reserves for his own critique of a style of French that he considers deformed and corrupt, albeit in an inverse relation to more traditional notions of formlessness, contamination, and language purity.

Two of Céline's neologistic expressions, "*troufignoliser l'adjectif*" and "*frénétiser l'Insignifiance*," taken together, can even be said to form the problematic *ars poetica* of his pop-philological anti-Semitic style. Both expressions are used to describe the activity of the "refined" writer. "*Troufignoliser l'adjectif*" is precisely what Céline's prose does (both literally and figuratively): it places an analytical ("*fignoliser*"—to scrutinize minutely) void ("*trou*" or "*troufignon*," asshole) in what he considers to be the "*adjectif*" or the secondary, nonessential, descriptive term, the "*bagatelle*." "*Frénétiser l'Insignifiance*" is to drum nonsense up into a frenzy that approximates physical sensation, which suggests the important link between Céline's style and nineteenth century notions of clinical hysteria. By means of her analysis of dance aesthetics and pathology rhetoric, McCarren elaborates a thesis linking Céline's poetics to a hysterical identification with the dancer's body. She then takes her analysis further, distinguishing between a feminized, Mallarméan *vide* as the locus of the artist and of creation for Céline, and the derogatory term "*con*," as the epithet he hoists upon his readers, who end up feeling "tout con" (1998, 208). Céline's identification with the hysterical object of his disgust, which is both an appropriation of discourse and a double-bind, is apparent in each of his grafted, hybrid, "voided" neologisms. McCarren continues: "Those who are 'con'—the rival writers and critical readers—remain impotent while Céline flourishes in the 'vide.' He uses the 'vide' to make others 'con'; his talent is the art of 'déconner.'" Just as the dancer "transforms what is potentially 'con' into an idealized 'vide,'" so does Céline's writing, in its hysterical identification with the pathologized body of the Jewish Semite, create "form without losing the passion of the unformed." Ultimately, Céline's writing performs a hysterical identification with the pathologized body, gendered feminine, but also marked as Jewish. "Such passion," McCarren writes, "is the hysterical 'idea' at the core of Célinian 'style'" (209). This style is not just an expression of the horror of the superego's authority (Kristeva), but reveals the impersonal force of disintegration at the heart of Orientalist anti-Semitic philology.

While the preceding description would serve to describe much of Céline's writing from *Mort à crédit* on, the style of the pamphlets is based on a semiotics of anti-Semitism wherein virtually any word may come to signify "Jew" or "Jewishness." The principal *adjectif* in *Bagatelles pour un massacre* is, of course, "juif," which Céline will "freneticize" and "analyze" throughout the course of the text, until it attains a state of polysemous hysteria, which nonetheless still signifies. Among the earliest critics to have commented on this specific characteristic of Céline's anti-Semitism is Georges Zérapha, in his article "Le Cauchemar du hibou: A Propos de Bagatelles pour un massacre de L.-F. Céline" in *La conscience des juifs*, in 1938:

> Here we touch upon the proof of the metaphysical character of anti-Semitism in general, and of Céline in particular. The corrupter, the dominator is not the actual Jew, who, depending on his particular affinities, always benefits from exceptional favors from anti-Semites; the accursed one is the Symbolic Jew, the Jewish entity.[23]

Such a critique anticipates Sartre's writing on anti-Semitism as a both a Manichean metaphysics and a "sadistic attraction," which often leads "sworn enemies of Israel to surround [themselves] with Jewish friends" (1948, 47). Céline fits this description quite well, as both textual and biographical information affirm this same conclusion: that Céline had Jewish acquaintances with whom he was on good terms, but that he had no problem attacking the "symbolic Jew."[24] The relative comfort provided by the stylized abstractness of anti-Semitism is what has led critics to downplay or ignore this aspect of Céline's work.[25] Efforts to transform his oeuvre into an exemplar of postmodern indeterminacy have also tended to reproduce Céline's own language, so that it becomes possible to claim, for example, that the "immoderation" of Céline's pamphlets is a result of a "syntactic necessity."[26] Whatever "necessity" may have driven Céline, *Bagatelles pour un massacre* uses the Jew to act as allegory for the symbolic function of language itself. From the false safety of his feminized, protective void, Céline stuffs his argot down the maw of his allegorized Jew. The "style" of the pamphlets ultimately fuses the academic discourse of Orientalism—"the strange, secret sharer of Western anti-Semitism" (Said 1978, 28)—with its popular articulation as a kind *la haine pour la haine*: hate for hate's sake.

Conclusion: Toward a Postcolonial Philology

Two divergent impulses within philology are revealed in the chasm between al-Shidyaq's carnivalized *nahda* and Céline's carnivalesque disintegration of the Semitic symptom: first, an Orientalist philology that functions as a human evaluation machine that would power the closed loop of the imperialist imagination, a machine that turns culture into biology and biology into teleology—that is, that fabricates destiny as historically determined and scientifically legitimated. It ontologizes the desire that language would articulate and destabilize. In the words of Werner Hamacher, "philology becomes the methodical procedure for the securing of epistemic orders," furthering their hegemony, and it does so, in Hamacher's account "against itself," meaning against a distinctly *other* impulse of philology. Hamacher proposes that this other philology would be "the name for a future of language *other* than the intended one" (39). An anti-Orientalist philology would follow Aamir Mufti's call for "a better close reading" of the Orientalist archive that would be both "radically historical" and attentive to the lived realities of language use, of the worldliness of language. The Semitic Question in Algeria demonstrates the ways that the French imperial state manipulated subjects in a way that was germane with the evaluations supposedly "proven" by philological research, and also how politicians in the colony vulgarized philological Semitism for their own political and commercial interests. And yet the plastic and volatile categories of Semitism require close attention to what Sheldon Pollock calls the "vertiginous contingency" that would be the purview of what I would call a radically historical world philology: a kind of reading that would question the persistent forms of filiation and identification forged through Orientalist modalities of knowledge production, and thereby allow the creation of new politics and unheard of affiliations.

The limits of literary carnival that al-Shidyaq and Céline illustrate provide an instructive contrast between those who have been Orientalized and those doing the Orientalizing, between two philological impulses. On one hand, we have al-Shidyaq (as a singular exemplar of *nahda* discourse) improvising an unrehearsed relationship to an Arabic language threatened by Ottoman rule and European power. On the other hand, we witness Céline "renewing" French by plagiarizing reactionary colonial clichés about the Semitic minority. What Lloyd calls the "unequally distributed relation to damage and survival" (107) that marks colonial modernity comes into full force in the juxtaposition of these two writers, both of whom configure damage and decay in wildly divergent ways. As we will see in the second half of this book, the articulations of majority and minority positions will take on new accents and cadences in the era of decolonization and independence, even as the specter of decadence will continue to haunt the emergence of national cultures, as well as attempts to assess and remedy past damages and losses.

PART II

Working Through Postcolonial Decadence

CHAPTER 4

Resurrecting Colonial Decadence in Independent Algeria

Orientalist decadence in its colonial mode, as the first part of this book has shown, measured and accounted for losses within a matrix whose scope was civilizational, racial, and comparative. This second part explores the ways that loss becomes configured differently in a postcolonial context. The critique of postcolonial decadence outlined in subsequent chapters will be organized around (and sometimes against) the entity of the nation-state and national culture. The voices of what Abdellah Laroui has called "the second nahda" will engage in a concerted working through of the concept of decadence itself, inquiring into the very tools that Orientalism had used to assess social health or morbidity, to establish trajectories of historical ascendency or decline, and which consequently centered critique and knowledge production in Europe and "the West." This inquiry will necessarily entail a confrontation with the losses and traumas of colonialism, engendering a self-critique of the complicity of both the postcolonial critic and the postcolonial nation-state with the discourse of Orientalist decadence, and, ultimately, a traversal of the colonial fantasy at the heart of the process of Orientalization. The "way out" of decadence will thus be indistinguishable from the *crossing through* of Orientalism's adjudications and diagnoses of "the Orient," conceived as a kind of *Malade Imaginaire*.

The discourse of colonial decadence was predicated upon the authenticity of a colonial subject claiming to occupy a position outside the historical spaces whose vitalistic expansion he narrated. The stylistic disparity between Renan and Céline reveals Orientalism's seemingly infinite adaptability, its capacity to "mutate" by adopting supposedly progressive or pseudo-revolutionary methods and vocabulary—the ruse of social constructivism in Renan, or Céline's hysterical identification with the hated minority, expressed in "the language of the people." The pioneers of the "Arab Awakening" (*ruwwad al-nahda*), among whom I include the Islamic modernists and reformists such as al-Afghani and Muhammad 'Abduh, reworked this language of cultural, racial, or religious authenticity into the local vernacular with the stated aim of liberation from various forms of foreign domination. The limits of this discourse of colonial decadence become visible, in strikingly divergent ways, in the carnivalesque ambivalence of al-Shidyaq and Céline, whose pamphlets both generate and degenerate the idea of a "pure" physiological identity. The disintegration of colonial modernity also materializes in the writing of an anticolonial figure like Aimé Césaire, whose earliest poetry both pathologizes and Africanizes the French language, crafting neologisms by grafting together heterogeneous and deracinated linguistic elements, all in the service of bringing to life the authentic body of *négritude*.

In describing the passage from colonial decadence to what I am calling postcolonial decadence, I will be narrating a constellation of discursive moves, all of which link up with the fate of Orientalism as a decadent engine of colonial modernity. Decadence takes on two senses in this context: Orientalist discourse becomes both a self-contained and flexible technology that disintegrates as it functions; and Orientalism is also an epistemological machine that generates statements about decadence, performatively accomplishing the words it utters. The discursive fragmentation becomes apparent in the genealogy of French anti-Semitism in the Arab world as one of the lasting legacies of the colonizing mission. Whereas in Renan's writings up through the 1880s, the term "Semitic" integrated both Arab and Jewish peoples, the turn of the century, exemplified by the cleavages of Dreyfus affair, witnessed the disintegration of the Semitic, where Arabs and Jews begin to use what are essentially Orientalist (and originally "anti-Semitic") arguments against each other.[1] These discourses played themselves out in the context of independent Algeria, where the question of language returns with the full vengeance of postcolonial *ressentiment*.

That adaptation—or mutation—functions in uneasy proximity to the "mutation" that Frantz Fanon famously celebrated as spreading throughout the collective nervous system of revolutionary Algeria; beside the radical transformation of the human organism (as part of the social organism) effected by the anticolonial struggle exists the mutation of Orientalist propositions about the relationship between the body and language—what Derrida has ironically theorized in *Le monolinguisme de l'autre* as appropriations of the inappropriable, where language serves as a "prosthesis of origins" (1996, 24).[2] In other words, there is a certain structural complicity between these two modes of transformational politics, between discourses born out of both anticolonial revolt and colonial command. In postcolonial Algeria, the mutations of these fields of meaning are often related in a nonoppositional way; each discourse of power partially constitutes the other, even as each adapts to the other's adaptations. This is the very problem of "National Culture" that Fanon foresaw in *The Wretched of the Earth*, where he links negritude to the "Arab renaissance" to warn against the danger of black and Arab societies becoming precisely what colonial discourse intended them to be:

> Thus we see the cultural problem as it sometimes exists in colonized countries runs the risk of giving rise to serious ambiguities. The lack of culture of Negroes, as proclaimed by colonialism, and the inherent barbarity of the Arabs ought logically to lead to the exaltation of cultural manifestations which are not simply national but continental, and extremely racial. In Africa, the movement of men of culture is a movement toward the Negro-African culture or the Arab-Moslem culture. It is not specifically toward a national culture.
> (1963 [1961], 217)

Fanon both cautions readers about the "ambiguities" of postcolonial national cultures founded on broad notions of racial identity and warns that trying to pass over the "national period" would be a mistake, since international consciousness must, in his account, first be nurtured in a strong national consciousness (247). His famous conclusion to this treatise, however, ultimately affirms the "newness" required of this national consciousness as opposed to what he calls the sickening monstrosity of colonial mimicry (313, 315).

Attitudes toward the languages of postcolonial Algeria, and the violence that has marked Algerian language politics, represent the "success" of the

Orientalist discourses that were disseminated in both the Maghreb and the Mashreq (or "Arab East") during the time of colonial rule, a success that is ultimately indissociable from the country's economic and political losses since liberation. It should be noted that this is not a way of suggesting that there is nothing outside the discourse of European power, or that Algerian violence is a purely European creation; on the contrary, Orientalism functions as an epistemological technology that *structures* local content and organizes attitudes and ideas about Arabness that had long been current within Arabic literature and society, developing outside of European colonialism and predating it by centuries. Local content, in turn, itself becomes transformed in the structural molds enforced by Orientalism, as did the very term "Arab" as it came to be reworked in the colonial crucible serves to inform institutional structures in postcolonial society. At the very heart of this problem are the economic dependencies that predicate the forms of postcolonial political states. In order to explain these assertions, it is useful to recall the symbolic value of the Arabic language in the context of Arab nationalism in Egypt and the Levant and to attempt to hear the new accents placed on this changing value as it drifts westward to Algeria through the colonial era, the war against France, and into the independent state apparatus. The Algerian state policy of Arabization (*ta'rib*) instigated by President Ahmed Ben Bella in the 1960s derives much of its authority from the discourses of the reformist *nahda*, which in the Mashreq tends to be dated as far back as Napoleon's entry into Egypt in 1798, but which in Algerian historiography is usually given a belated birth in 1925, when *al-Muntaqid* ("The Critic"), the first Algerian Islamic reformist journal, was published in Constantine by 'Abd al-Hamid Ibn Badis (also "Ben Badis").[3]

What Fanon calls the "serious ambiguities" of the postcolonial "cultural problem" in the Algerian context can be traced back to the early formulations of Arab nationalism, which included important secularist elements.[4] The idea of pan-Arabism emerged as a dialectical countermove to the reductions and generalizations of European Orientalism (understood as the cultural wing of colonial military power). In trying to disprove their supposed barbarity, Arabic intellectuals were also inventing the very category of the modern Arab "nation," which would soon stretch from Iraq to Morocco. The modern meaning of the term "Arab," is, in part, a concoction of anti-Ottoman British foreign policy, but also the transcendental signifier that would motivate anticolonial revolt while also subsuming religious and other differences.[5] The point to be made here is that the nineteenth-century Arabic intellectual's encounter with Europe, and the construction of a pan-Arab identity, both occur in the intellectual climate of decadence, a fact that carries great significance for any attempt to understand colonial modernity and its disintegration.

Specifically, the agonistic relationship between French and Modern Standard Arabic (MSA or *al-lugha al-'arabiya al-mu'asira*) in Algeria needs to be understood within the patterns of affliction drawn by the crossed discourses of colonial decay.[6] The FLN's definition of the Algerian state as exclusively Arab and Muslim reiterates Ben Badis's famous motto, "Islam is our religion, Arabic is our language, Algeria is our country," which can be seen as a structural reiteration of much early Arab nationalist thought. The most obvious antagonist in this war of languages, French, fell victim to the monolingual and monological cultural ideal that had been pursued by French colonialism itself; along with French went the languages actually spoken by the majority of Algerians: the many varieties of "Berber" and the diversity of Algerian Arabic dialects, which were all repressed and officially marginalized by the centralized state.[7] The specific politics and policies of French colonial linguistic purification, which constitute one of the central strategies of Orientalism, thus remained the status quo in Algeria after 1962, even though the languages that were to be purified and purged had changed. Accusations of colonial decadence (Arabic language and culture as too ornate or not sufficiently rational) became reversed (French language and colonial culture as morally decadent). Global economic pressure combined with Algerian administrative policies would both contribute to the extreme violence that was to accompany these language wars. A telling example of external economic pressure occurred when France withdrew 28,000 French engineers and technicians from Algeria in response to Boumédienne's nationalization of the petroleum industry in February 1971.[8] This withdrawal of trained personnel in industry had its parallel in the French Ministry of Education's deliberate strategy of sending virtually untrained teachers to Algeria, one of the important factors that contributed to the steep decline in Algerian education during the 1970s. These examples reveal a fraction of the concrete damages inflicted on both the economic and cultural spheres by the former colonial power, putting the postcolonial state seeking autonomy in a bind, where the imaginary value of languages imposed through colonial rule and legitimated through Orientalist philology continues to structure life in the independent state.

Loss in Two Languages

Omar Carlier contextualizes what he euphemistically calls the "rise of incivility" in Algeria during the 1980s and 1990s by tracing the perilous course of Arab nationalist ideas from their early manifestations in Algeria through the twentieth century into the age of globalization:

> Beginning in the 1920s and 1930s, the ideas of nation and Nahda took hold, disseminated by the schools and by newspapers, and taught by schoolmasters and sheikhs at the instigation of the party and the *cercle*. They spread to rural areas with World War II, and acquired a sacred aura with the war for independence, reaching their peak in the 1960s. Yet, with the next generation, the nation (watan) was confronted with the globalization of consumer and spiritual goods, and with the reversal that pitted communist and Third-World "revolutionary" universalism, already on the point of collapse, against the Islamist reiteration of religious universalism. (2002, 94)

In explaining how "holy history turned against the regime that was exploiting it" (87) (i.e., the FLN), Carlier narrates the transition from French Algeria to independent Algeria as a tale of generational decline. The ideological "reversal" that allows for a transference from a Marxist to an Islamist articulation of universalism hints at an uncanny complicity between discourses that might otherwise be considered oppositional. These discursive structures parallel the political and economic structures inherited from the French by the postcolonial regimes, even as their new inhabitants fill them with new, or "local," content. The linguistic-economic divisions created by Ben Bella's French-Arabic bilingual policies of the 1960s, followed by Boumédienne's policy of more comprehensive Arabization as it was implemented between 1976 and 1981, bear this point out. The requirement that Modern Standard Arabic be the exclusive language used in government, education, and broadcasting did little to keep French from remaining the language of the Algerian business world. This created what R. A. Judy has termed a situation of "uneven Arabization" (1997, 131), which forged "the identification of Arabic culture with ideology but not the economy" (107), while creating "a population locked out of the secular economy and ripe for the reactionary agendas of the Islamist" (130).

What Carlier calls "the globalization of consumer and spiritual goods" indicates the register of postcolonial decadence as an attempt to collapse the distance between the ideological and economic spheres that Arabization had managed to widen and aggravate. The "sacred aura" of revolutionary national consciousness was shattered and then replaced by replicas of this consciousness, as the pressures of Cold War politics led to a splintering of both the communist and the Islamic tendencies evinced by Algeria's diverse anticolonial movements. All these trends come to a head when the FLN cancels the electoral victory of the Islamist Front Islamique du Salut (FIS), resulting in the precipitous disintegration of Algerian society during the Algerian Civil War of 1991–2002, where as many as 200,000 people died, the vast majority being civilians. The extreme animosities of this war, variously referred to as *les années noires* (the dark years), *la décennie de plomb* (the decade of lead), *la décennie de sang* (the decade of blood), or *la sale guerre* (the dirty war), have been illustrated by critics, historians, and theorists by the comments of the Algerian Arabic writer, al-Tahir Wattar (sometimes transliterated as "Ouettar") (1936–2010) regarding the assassination of the Algerian francophone writer Tahar Djaout (1954–93) by Islamist assailants in May 1993. During a program televised in May 1994 by the Franco-German station Arte, when asked whether Djaout's death was a loss for Algeria, Wattar responded that it was "a loss for his wife, a loss for his children, a loss for France, certainly," suggesting that Djaout's death was, in fact, not a loss for Algeria.[9] Lahouari Addi suggests that such a comment "makes transparent the hatred that exists between Algerians" (1995, 137), while for Omar Carlier, Wattar's "justification" of Djaout's murder indicates the "ethical collapse" that reigned during the 1990s (2002, 90).

But what does it mean to speak about national loss, and more specifically, what might be said to constitute a "loss" for Algeria? According to what calculus of the incalculable could such a question even be posed, much less answered? Finally, how might this calculus of loss be graphed onto the iterations of colonial and postcolonial *decadence* that continue to pre-program discursive, social, and political possibilities in the postcolonial world? I ask these questions particularly as they relate to language as a function of systems of literary exchange across local, national, and global economies. While there have been many critiques of Wattar's answer, no one, to my knowledge, has considered the question itself: "*Hal kanna maut Tahar Djaout khasara lil-djaza'ir?*" Was Tahar Djaout's death a loss for Algeria?

What conditions of possibility allow such a question to be asked in the first place? The question interpellates the respondent—here Wattar—presupposing that the loss of a writer may be measured against the grid of the nation, that a simple *la'* or *na'm*, no or yes, would in fact be possible. In the interest of rejecting the interpellating force of this question the following inquiry into the imbricated force fields of loss, literature, and the nation will proceed through the staging of a critical encounter between two novels. It is my hope that the specific modalities of literary thinking in these texts will take us beyond the neo-Orientalism that pits French versus Arabic in a facile opposition, and that these modalities will instead provide traction for a critique of the ways that the internal ideological forces set in motion by Orientalism collide and collude with the external violence of globalization.

Hafid Gafaïti's analysis of Wattar's response goes even further in its unpacking of the complexity of the Algerian context, suggesting that this comment by Wattar (who was ethnically Chaoui Berber) reveals an attitude that is similar to that of certain political movements formed by Kabyle Berber francophone elites (who have been known to disavow the diversity of Berber peoples, as well as their own ethnic African or the Middle Eastern ethnic heritage, and instead trace their ancestors to Europe). Gafaïti writes:

> The tribalist instincts of the Kabyle culturalists reflect a position that is no different from that of the Arabophone reactionary writer Tahar Ouettar, who declared . . . that the death of the poet Tahar Djaout, who was ethnically Kabyle (I personally would identify him simply as an Algerian and as a friend who is deeply missed) was a loss for his family but certainly not for his country. This kind of tribalism undermines the hope for a genuine multiculturalism. The Kabyles' struggle for recognition of their identity, language, and culture should not blind us to the fact that the ideological discourse that their movement defends is both a legitimate claim to Berberitude, one of the fundamental dimensions of Algerian identity, *and* a dangerous discourse of ethnic exclusion structurally identical to that of the enemies—the regime or the Muslim fundamentalists—they claim to fight. (2002, 40–41)

Gafaïti recognizes the ambivalence and structural similarity found in claims of cultural authenticity, equating Arabization's invented traditions with those of the Kabyle culturalist groups. While Wattar's "tribalist" position regarding Arabic is indeed "structurally" similar to that of the Kabylists, his defense of Arabic as the language of Algeria is even more complicated than Gafaïti's equation might suggest. Mere condemnations of Wattar's comments, whatever their individual merit, ultimately reinforce the cultural and linguistic antagonisms already mapped out between the multiple segments of the Algerian population. Instead of reading Algerian language politics through the categories of affect, ethics, or a historically decontextualized structuralism—as the preceding comments do—I propose revisiting this contested ground as the site where the vestiges of Orientalist philology and colonial policy meet the contradicting demands of the postcolonial nation-state in the era of globalization. This specific understanding of Orientalism contrasts with Gafaïti's rather vague notion of what he calls "the colonial subconscious" (2002, 43). Although he makes it clear that this destructive force, which he likens to both a kind of "monotheism" and of a "Jacobinism" informing both Arab and French forms of "colonialism" (203), the looseness and interchangeability of these metaphors reveals the need for a more historically attentive and theoretically rigorous reading of the Algerian language war within the civil war of the 1990s. The main thrust of Gafaïti's essay, which aims to get beyond the Manichean, and ultimately *Orientalist* divide that has framed the debate about the Algerian civil war as a struggle between "good" francophone secular rationalism and "bad" Arabic religious violence, is to be applauded. Yet the terminological slippage remains symptomatic of a lack of conceptual rigor in his analysis. The title of his essay reworks the title of Jacques Derrida's meditation on language in Algeria, *The Monolingualism of the Other*, while also borrowing some of its conclusions, such as Derrida's claim that "all culture is colonial" (1996, 39). Just as Gafaïti's argument fuses colonial and postcolonial attitudes under the headings "colonial" and "Jacobin," so, too, does Derrida's claim blur the historical specificities of Orientalist techniques of colonization and the worldwide reorganization of knowledge and cultural production that it accomplished. A close reading of Djaout and Wattar will demonstrate the danger of generalizing and dehistoricizing claims about colonialism, culture, and language.

Earthquakes, Deserts, and the Impossible Algerian Future

The novels by Djaout and Wattar provide rich materials for engaging the problematics of postcolonial decadence. Published thirteen years apart in Arabic and French, respectively, Wattar's *al-Zilzal* (1974) and Djaout's *L'invention du désert* (1987) are both experimental texts that narrate the conditions of possibility governing Algerian nationhood during the period of Arabization, industrial nationalization, and the rapid growth of political Islam. Wattar's novel contrasts its hypocritically puritanical main character, Shaykh 'Abd al-Majid Bu al-Arwah, with the diverse voices of the people which the Shaykh overhears on his itinerary through the city of Constantine. The text thus maps the destruction of monological colonial Algeria onto the renascent multiplicity of the modern independent state. *Al-Zilzal* is written using modern literary Arabic, and its primary intertextual references are decidedly Arabic and Islamic, a distinction which, in general, sets the Arabic novel apart from the Francophone novel in Algeria. Djaout's text interweaves a series of autobiographical narrative itineraries with a creative biography of Ibn Tumart, the Berber religious leader of the twelfth-century Almohad movement. The avoidance of both colonial and postcolonial Algerian historical referents in Djaout's novel reveals how this history serves as the unspoken trauma that motivates and structures the text's evocations of the desert as the virtual space of the postcolonial nation. Wattar's text works through and functions within the painful history of colonial collaboration in a way that parallels his own commitment to working within the state apparatus as a proponent of Arabization. Djaout's novel, on the other hand, emerges from the nightmare of colonial modernity to traverse the virtual spaces and "utopias of purity" afforded by the French language to an Algerian writer.

Al-Zilzal both draws on the Arabic literary tradition and unsettles it in significant ways. The character of Bu al-Arwah represents the religious elite during colonial rule, while also evoking the picaresque figure of the religious hypocrite found in the classics of Arabic literature such as the *maqamat* ("seances" or "sessions") of al-Hamadhani. Whereas the classical parodies of Islamic piety imply "the exemplarity of the ideal imam or shaykh—the Prophet Muhammad" (20), Bu al-Arwah's implied positive ideal is manifested through fragments of dialogue that merge into the stream of his own free indirect monologue. These anonymous voices break through the shell of his consciousness, as they are heard praising Algeria's modernization, criticizing the country's faults, and condemning American and Israeli policies. The novel clearly functions as a *roman à thèse*, as Lila Ibrahim-Ouali has pointed out, which contrasts the wealthy, isolated, paranoid, murderous, and incestuous shaykh with the poor urban multitude who represent the plurivocal force of the country's future, even as they lament the grief they suffer from the very crimes Bu al-Arwah has committed. By using the stock figure of the religious hypocrite, but replacing the implied ideal of Muhammad with that of the *vox populi*, Wattar champions the forward-looking vision of the Algerian state over a thoroughly colonized conception of Islam sunk deep in the past.[10]

This last aspect of Bu al-Arwah's character—as the representative of a past incarnation of Islam that would be both more pure and more just than its current incarnation—compels us to situate the novel's antihero in the context of another important leitmotif in modern Arabic literary history, that of the resurrection or time-travel narrative.[11] Wattar's text redirects the framing device of Muhammad al-Muwaylihi's *Hadith 'Isa ibn Hisham* (1898–1900), which borrowed the form of al-Hamadhani's *maqamat*, as well as the name of his narrator. In al-Muwaylihi's fiction, 'Isa ibn Hisham's macabre encounter with Muhammad 'Ali's long-deceased minister of war, Ahmad Pasha al-Manikali, frames the series of dialogues about the decadence of Egyptian social institutions under Lord Cromer (consul-general from 1883 to 1907) during the British occupation that make up the bulk of the text.[12] Since Bu al-Arwah is returning to Constantine after a sixteen-year absence (which would thus date from a few years prior to independence), Wattar's text produces a similar effect to that of al-Muwaylihi's, albeit without resorting to the specific narrative device employed by the latter. Like Ahmad Pasha, Bu al-Arwah wanders through an urban landscape that has changed radically under a new regime, all the while railing against the transformations he observes and appealing to God for help. Upon first arriving in Constantine, the shaykh remarks that from a certain angle, "everything seemed to him as it always had," from the French-engineered al-Qantara Bridge to the statue of Joan of Arc, but he soon realizes that "everything has changed," all the while invoking the name of Ibn Khaldun (26–27).[13] Wattar thus inverts the relationship between al-Muwaylihi's revenant shaykh and the critique of European rule: Whereas the Pasha returns from a time of Egyptian (and Arab) revitalization to critique the decadent colonial present, Bu al-Arwah returns from the decadent French colonial past to critique the Algerian (and Arab) present as it suffers the pangs of modernization and broad reform.

Both *al-Zilzal* and *L'invention du désert* revisit the decadent postcolonial city through the eyes of characters who represent the reemergence of a puritanical, "traditional" form of Islam; it is from their perspective that the contemporary world acutely signifies loss. By carefully mapping Bu al-Arwah's increasingly hallucinatory journey through Constantine, Wattar superimposes the shaykh's disintegrating consciousness—as an embodiment of the discourse of colonial decadence—onto the living networks of a city and people whose consciousness of decadence is decidedly postcolonial. Bu al-Arwah affirms the necessity of segregating society according to race, class, and gender; he curses pregnant women and the streets "flooded with people" (*fadat bi al-bashar*) (32/14); and he laments the new hybrid urban topography, where one end of a street is named after a martyr from the Algerian revolution (Ziriyut Yusuf), and the other end bears the name of a communist country, Yugoslavia (48/34). His desire for division, isolation, and purity leads him to express envy of the Berlin Wall: If such a wall were to be built in Constantine, the shaykh thinks to himself, it would help "assure the character of each district" (*yu'akkid shakhsiyyat kull jihah*) (52/37). The text thus situates Bu al-Arwah's critique of postcolonial Algerian society in the discourse of the reformist *nahda*, which theorized political emancipation as necessarily emerging from the authenticity of Islamic tradition or the Arab past. In this case, this past is also explicitly the time of French colonial rule. "It was so peaceful at the time of the French, very noticeably so," Bu al-Arwah declares at one point, contrasting the crowded and chaotic conditions of the city to his memories of a better time (27). The constant shuttling of his thoughts back and forth between the figures of Ben Badis, who promoted an Arab-Muslim view of Algerian liberation, and Ibn Khaldun, who demonstrated how the dialectic of tribal authenticity structured the cyclicity of dynastic power, reveal Bu al-Arwah as the embodiment of the reformist *nahda*, understood as a "duet played under the foreign dominator's watchful and somewhat ironic eye" (Laroui 1976 [1964], 85), meaning an apparently free exchange whose rules were primarily determined by only one party.

Wattar's text constructs its own form of critique by working through the ideas of the *nahda*'s decadent discourse. What emerges are precisely the critical attitudes that Abdallah Laroui defines as being constitutive of the "second Nahda," a movement he dates to the early 1960s, and which replaced the traditionalist attitude of the first *nahda* with a more rigorous historicism. The interweaving of Bu al-Arwah's thoughts with the voices of the multitude reveals what Laroui terms "a second-degree awareness," where "Arabs became aware of their thinking as ideological thinking," and began to reformulate questions regarding the nature of imperialism, revolution, and underdevelopment (90–91).[14] Wattar's characterization of the shaykh brings to life the ideology of the "Arab Awakening" in order to expose certain ambiguities within Arabism and Islamism, understood as movements that compromise historicism in the name of invented "traditions." An important element of Wattar's critique here relates to the self-misrecognition on the part of Algerians who identify themselves as "Arab" and disavow their Amazigh (Berber) or mixed heritage. Standing before the Great Mosque, Bu al-Arwah notices "something peculiar about the city":

> The faces are all different in Constantine. Facial features vary from one person to another, as do people's physiques. At the time of the occupation, people looked either European or Arab, but not now. Today, you can tell the difference between the Shawi Berber from Ain Baida or Ain M'lila, from Banta, Khanshala or Shalgoum al-Id. You can tell who is from Fajj M'zala, Milia or Collo, or from Skikda, Zenah and Azzaba. Their facial features, like their odours, reveal their true identities in loud screams that echo throughout the city. (29/10)

The perception of Algeria's ethnic homogeneity that was induced by colonial antagonism (one is either Arab *or* European), has, since independence, given way to what the shaykh perceives as a cacophony of tribal differences. The litany of affiliations recited in this passage reaffirms the diversity of Algerian society over and against the pan-Arab ideal imported from the Arab East as an ideological weapon against the French. By revealing Bu al-Arwah's lack of critical distance from his ethnoracial beliefs, the text displays an awareness of its own ideology qua ideology.

The novel does not stop at this affirmation of diversity, however. Rather, it reconstructs the multiplicity of the Algerian nation out of the fragments of the shattered fiction of an exclusively "Arab" Algeria. This reconstruction emerges from the gradual destruction of the shaykh's ability to identify the "true identity" (*al-nafs*) of a person based on his or her phenotypical variations. The more Bu al-Arwah attempts to shield himself from the assault of crowds, smells, sights, and voices, the more his defenses—both external and internal—break down. In descriptions of this psychic disintegration, Wattar vividly illustrates the neurophysiological degeneration of the colonial organism, whose perceptive faculties merge as the shaykh succumbs to the kind of synesthetic experience that exemplifies the discourse of French decadence from Baudelaire to Huysmans.[15] Bu al-Arwah perceives the dissolution of social barriers based on class and gender as signs of the impending apocalypse, and soon "the city's aromas and stenches blend together like the different accents, faces and sexes" (42). His confusion increases as he ventures deeper into the narrow streets of the old medina, until the shaykh senses that "the odours have started to lose their distinctiveness as everything blends together" (*bada'at al-rawa'ih tafqid mawjataha wa takhtalit*) (100/93).[16] What Bu al-Arwah experiences as a dystopic sensory disorder, Wattar proposes as the possibility of a pluralistic society, born amidst the ruins of the colonial order.

Wattar configures the decay of colonial consciousness, where "lowest and highest no longer remain" (*la yabqa hunaka asfal wa a'la*) (100/93), as the outcome of the tension generated by the shaykh's hypocrisy. Bu al-Arwah justifies his ideology of purity, class division, and the right to private property by claiming that all these things are guaranteed in the Qur'an (27, 115, 158), but the novel gradually reveals that both the shaykh's ideas and his mounting rage are merely disavowals of his own crimes and failings. We discover that his great-grandfather "opened the gates of the country" to the French (142); his grandfather assembled an army to slaughter those who refused to fight with the French against Tunisia and Morocco (143); and his father "was the only Algerian to possess land beside all the colonialists" (143). The shaykh's position as a man of religious and moral purity serves to cover up his incestuous and violently misogynist past; he and his father engage in intercourse with each other's wives, and the murder of his first wife, his brother's wife, and the death of his mother become fused in his mind as a joint act performed with his father (144–47). His father's second wife blames the deaths of children born in the household on 'Abd al-Majid Bu al-Arwah, declaring that "he will be the destruction of the house of Bu al-Arwah" (147). His own lack of progeny confirms his ideological role in the novel as a collaborator, representing both the promiscuity and ultimate sterility of colonial power in Algeria.

By mapping the shaykh's cognition of decadence (as something external) onto the reader's knowledge of Bu al-Arwah's (internal) history of collaboration and incest, *al-Zilzal* illustrates how the shaykh maps his perception of decadent social reality onto his own ambivalence toward women. Writing about the more measurable decline in employment during the 1980s, Carlier suggests how such a gendering of decline has victimized Algerian women in order to reassert the authority of Islam:

> The feeling of general decline in values easily leads many to see women as one of the causes, if not *the* cause, of all the rest, the ultimate threat. Loss of male authority, loss of female modesty—are not these the signs of an upside-down world, which ought to be set aright? The sign is eschatological, the response prophetic. The Islamic solution not only relies on a theologico-political discourse, it comes forth to reiterate an originary Word. (99)

Bu al-Arwah reads the social transformations of decolonization and independence as signs of the apocalyptic earthquake of doom, foretold in the Qur'an, that he repeatedly wishes upon the city of Constantine. The text reveals the way that Wattar's language itself genders this discourse of waning masculine authority perceived as apocalypse. The shaykh's own position as a teacher of religion and classical Arabic, as well as his internal recitation of classical and MSA texts should contrast linguistically to the voices of the poor that he overhears on the street (who would, in actuality, be speaking in dialect). Although Wattar puts a mostly formal and modern standard version of Arabic in the mouths of the urban populace, he gives the reader clues to indicate that these characters would be speaking dialectical Algerian Arabic or Berber in the world outside the novel. The opposition set forth here is that between Bu al-Arwah's "pure" and masculinized Arabic and the "impure" feminized language of the common people, which Wattar's text masculinizes.

While the series of oppositions between Bu al-Arwah and the voices of civil society makes clear the ideological position of the novel, certain elements of the text suggest an uncomfortable complicity between Wattar and his main character. Debbie Cox suggests that Wattar's reliance on the metaphor of sterility to critique Bu al-Arwah ultimately "validates masculine potency, a virile culture where women's role is one of reproducing the male line" (103), adding that "women's agency [in the novel] extends only as far as their ability to haunt Bu al-Arwah's conscience and thereby contribute to his downfall" (104). His reluctance to "feminize" the regenerative force of the Algerian people by allowing them to speak their "mother tongue," can be seen as the same kind of matricidal violence that Bu al-Arwah enacts, but which also distinguishes Arabization's attitude toward dialectical Algerian Arabic.[17] Viewed in retrospect, the shaykh's sentiment that the Egyptians should have killed Naguib Mahfouz for writing the controversial *Children of the Alley* (50) evokes Wattar's ambivalence about Djaout's murder. Finally, the biographical similarities shared by Wattar and his fictional shaykh suggest that *al-Zilzal* be read as both a confession and an exorcism of an Orientalism that has been internalized.[18] As a Marxist committed to working within the state apparatus, Wattar understood all too well the dangers of the FLN's exploitation of both Arab nationalist and Islamist discourses, which sought a "reactivation of a new father image" (Carlier 2002, 102), so often accomplished at the expense of violence against the mother and the deactivation of women's political agency. His text, however, perpetuates much of this gendering of Algerian nationalist virility, even as it betrays an awareness of this very issue.[19]

Al-Zilzal reveals the negotiations required by a writer inhabiting the shifting ground between the specificities of a pluralistic society and the totalizing demands of the postcolonial nation in the age of global capitalism. R. A. Judy's analysis of Wattar's *Tajribah fi al-'ishq* ("A Love Experience" or "An Experiment in Affect") (1989) inquires into the meaning of these kinds of textual negotiations. "What is the function," Judy asks, "of contemporary Arabic forms of expression whose principle task is to articulate a cultural identity that is both local and supranational (the singular Arab identity) in a global system whose language can translate everything and nothing of local value?" (1997, 104). For Judy, Wattar's writing

> articulates the difference between specificity and unity, according to which civil society is the force of cultural heterogeneity, and the state is the force of totalizing unity. His experimental form—which is structurally autonomous from Islamic discourse and genealogically autonomous from non-Arabic aesthetics—functions as an exchequer of culture, regulating the transference of meaning across increasingly disparate civil economies. (134)

Judy's answer emphasizes Wattar's role not as a translator of incommensurable (or "unfungible") discourses but rather posits the *regulatory* function of his text, which serves to index the unequal value of languages on the global market. Such an account of Wattar's project, viewed in the context of an Algeria attempting to fulfill the revolutionary goal of Arabization in a global economy that continues to exacerbate the social differences between users of different languages, compels a rereading of the question concerning the value of Djaout's death and national loss.

The question then, is how might a text like *al-Zilzal* "regulate the transference" of Algerian local value into the somewhat more global currency of *la francophonie* performed by Djaout's *L'invention du désert*? In other words, how can we deploy Judy's analysis of Wattar—as a writer whose literary value is neither merely national nor exchangeable in the "World Republic of Letters"—to read *francophonie* in the overdetermined context of Algeria? Since Judy's term "transference" conflates the economic and psychoanalytic registers (whose merging marks the tenor of the global political economy), let me begin by trying to forge some preliminary links between the psychotextual spaces that structure Djaout's text and the world literary market in which the text circulates. The claustrophobic space of Wattar's overcrowded Constantine correlates to the exclusively Arabic intertextual spaces traversed by Bu al-Arwah (Ben Badis, Ibn Khaldun, *al-Qur'an*). The same is true of the relationship between geography and intertextuality in Djaout's text, in which the narrator shuttles back and forth between France and Algeria, makes the pilgrimage to Mecca, and continues on to Aden (in addition, his narration of Ibn Tumart's rise to power crosses all of North Africa, from Egypt to Marrakesh). Correspondingly, the narrator finds himself fantasmatically fused with Ibn Tumart and Rimbaud, who both function as fellow exiles from the "utopia of purity" that haunts Djaout's text. Even this brief sketch of the textual mobilities available in these two works indicates the relative translation-value of the Algerian novel published in Algeria and the Francophone Algerian novel published by Seuil in Paris. I am suggesting that the very different intertextual chronotopes in these two novels can be understood as indicating something about the kinds of access afforded their idioms in the system of world literature. At least for these two works, the question of the loss-value of the Arabic-language writer is thus yoked to the means of *national* production and reproduction, whereas the value of the francophone writer remains a function of *world* literary evaluation.

In contrast to the precise temporal and geographical grounding of *al-Zilzal*, Djaout's novel explicitly foregrounds its vision of national belonging as a product born between several places, and even several temporalities. The text alternates between the narrations of multiple itineraries while shifting between the narrative present, recollections of childhood, and the twelfth-century Almohad movement. Djaout superimposes images of France, the Maghreb, and the Arabian Peninsula onto one another to illustrate how the communities we invent are never self-identical but are always being imagined in transit and from a distance. "The desert invented here," Bensmaïa writes in an analysis of the novel, "proves to be none other than the liminal figure of the nation's history as a space to be discovered" (2003, 76). This performative function of the novel contrasts with the more pedagogical function of Wattar's text: while *L'invention du désert* narrates the impossibility of a discourse that might be called "national," Wattar narrates Algerian actuality amidst the ruins of colonial violence.[20] These differences do not indicate authorial prerogative but rather mark out the different global networks accessible to French and Arabic worlds in Algeria in the 1970s and 1980s.

Djaout's novel opens multiple lines of flight in and out of the Maghreb even as it circumnavigates the very historical traumas that *al-Zilzal* seeks to expel from the hidden depths of the colonial past and bring to a reckoning. The coincidence of Djaout's birth in 1954 with the insurrection that marked the beginning of the War for Independence, which is nowhere mentioned explicitly in the text, provides the allegorical key to what his partially autobiographical text might in fact be claiming about Algerian history. In the place where one expects history, Djaout offers a meditation on time; instead of the specific history of the Almoravids, which he has been commissioned to write, he narrates the story of their conquerors, the Almohads. Yet, the unsaid is precisely what motivates and structures the merging chronotopes of the novel, which begins with the narration of a nightmare:

> An irreversible cataclysm forever bans me from the territories of childhood. An invisible yet swift boat carries me towards a world of decrepitude; I watch the years transformed into threatening animals rushing past me in the opposite direction. A distress much stronger than anguish and death wrings my breath from me. I can't even protest. I know that, in any case, it's useless to call for help in this universe where verdicts can't be appealed. The nightmare only lasts an instant, and then I wake up, paralyzed, sometimes my face soaked with tears,

with the feeling that something irreplaceable, as precious as life itself, somewhere has been shattered. (14–15)

Un cataclysme irréversible m'exclut à tout jamais des territoires de l'enfance. Une barque invisible mais véloce m'emporte vers un monde de décrépitude; je regarde les années matérialisées en bêtes menaçantes filer dans le sens inverse de mon parcours. Une détresse plus forte que l'angoisse et la mort m'étreint jusqu'à étouffement. Je ne peux même pas crier. Je sais que, de toute manière, il est utile d'appeler dans cet univers où les verdicts sont sans recours. Le cauchemar ne dure qu'un instant et je me réveille, transi, parfois le visage inondé de larmes, avec le sentiment que quelque chose d'irremplaçable, d'aussi précieux que la vie même, s'est brisé quelque part.

Djaout contextualizes this nightmare as being recurrent during the Parisian winters of his adult life (and not his youth in the Soummam), linking his awakening to time-as-catastrophe both to his temporal expulsion from the Eden of childhood and to his physical exile from his native land. This perception of the cataclysmic irreversibility of time also signals the traumatic rupture of colonial modernity in ways that prefigure later references to Djaout's own French education and that make the French of his text signify this rupture. The text thus equates the narrating subject's coming to consciousness of temporality and history not with the rebirth of the present in the guise of the past, but rather as an irrevocable, unmournable loss of an authentic self. Such a passage reverses the vision of the *nahda* as an awakening to the genuine Arab self, and instead offers history as terror, paralysis, and decay.

This nightmare appears in the text immediately before Djaout launches into his account of the history of the Almohad Berbers. "I must now tell their story," the second section of the text begins, suggesting that the trauma of colonial history has, in some way, necessitated the reanimation of Ibn Tumart (16). Djaout hints at his reason for rehearsing the life of the medieval shaykh as soon as the scene of narration shifts back to contemporary Paris: it must be told in order "to get free [*se débarasser*] of the Almoravid chronicle" (26).[21] History is not merely written by the conquerors here; rather, the history of conquest becomes the only lasting memory. Djaout likens the narrative of Ibn Tumart to something that "beats beneath the carapace of winter," and which he must "lug around" with him as he travels along the crossing lines of the Paris metro. The impossibility of liberation from temporality becomes apparent, however, as past and present, winter and summer, France and Algeria merge in the window of the train he is traveling in: "I traverse, behind the windows of the train, other cities grown more and more rigid from boredom and frost. The birds have deserted the planet. Travel. Traversal of things scarcely dreamt or felt. France hasn't known a winter like this since 1956" (26). The novel's narration of the puritanical and belligerent Almohads (as a proxy for both the Almoravids and contemporary Algerian history) emerges in the imagined global networks of the text as a deserted, utopic space that is always to be invented. Among the "things scarcely dreamt or felt" that Djaout's text traverses here is the winter of 1956, which marked the onset of "total war" in Algeria, punctuated by the Battle of Algiers in January 1957. Whereas Wattar's text enacts the decay of colonial discourse by explicitly working through the material that constituted it, Djaout's traversal of colonial fantasy traces the virtual circuits of travel that always circumscribe the primary signifier of historical trauma.

The two novels engage the discourse of colonial decadence through characters who represent the Maghrebian Islamic establishment during vastly different periods, and yet both texts aim their critique at the Algeria of the 1970s and '80s. Wattar's pathologizing of Bu al-Arwah—as a walking symptom of Orientalism internalized—is ultimately a much more severe indictment than Djaout's treatment of Ibn Tumart. In a passage that reveals the Mahdi of the Almohads as a figuration of the narrator's superego, Djaout's Ibn Tumart appears to the author in a dream and says, "It's because you are sterile that you want to murder. You want to suppress me simply so you won't have to talk about me" (49). Ibn Tumart is suddenly transported to contemporary Paris, where he strolls the Champs Élysées, becoming shocked by the "decadence" of French society. Echoing Bu al-Arwah's experience of the modern city, Ibn Tumart feels that "the world is upside-down, that modesty and shame have switched places" (52). The "timeless Imam" (*l'imam intemporel*) complains about the "swarming" (*grouillement*) of the multitude and the "aggressiveness of the body stripped naked by advertising, commerce, and spectacle" (51). Most surprisingly, perhaps, Djaout uses Ibn Tumart as a vessel through which he speaks of immigrant subjectivity. As the shaykh wanders through the heavily African neighborhoods of Barbès and la Goutte d'Or and sees the racist graffiti painted on the walls of the metro stations, the narrator's voice merges with that of Ibn Tumart: "To be an immigrant is not to live in a country that is not one's own, it is to live in a no-place, it is to live outside the territories" (*hors des territoires*) (53). The shaykh, the narrator's own internalized authority figure from the Maghrebian past, comes to feel "great pity for this pullulating humanity" (55), and the narrator ultimately expresses admiration for his vigilance (57).

Through this dream, the text reenters the nightmare of colonial modernity to reveal the menacing father of Islamic purity as a figure who also extends sympathy to those exiled by this trauma. Ibn Tumart's Oedipal claim on the narrator becomes attenuated as the narration of the dream transfers the terror and paralysis of the nightmare back onto the father. Paris serves as the multiethnic dream-city that makes this transference possible and whose strangeness induces the rapprochement between the narrator and the Mahdi. This apparent resolution of the father and the son is indeed the stuff of dreams, however. It is in the village of the narrator's childhood that the actual direction of Algeria finds its ultimate articulation in the text, not as resulting from paternal violence, but as the issue of filial love of the daughter. The final section of the text finds the narrator observing his own daughter as she plays in the village where he was raised. "She is the depository of my dreams and my explorations," Djaout writes. "She circulates in the wind, on the clipped, cold grass, filling her pockets with pinecones. She is the depository of my dreams and of my sense of discovery. She is the one who will prolong me in the joys and disappointments of inquisitive flesh. And she is my only consolation" (199). In a gesture that counters the terror of sterility articulated by both Bu al-Arwah and Ibn Tumart, the novel thus transmits the continuous project of national reinvention to Algerian women of the next generation. Djaout suggests that this project includes both the cosmopolitan dreams of Oedipal resolution and the nightmares of historical catastrophe. The end of the novel compels us to return to Wattar's statement that Djaout's death was a loss not for Algeria but only for his daughter. Djaout's text affirms that the postcolonial nation may emerge from the ruins of colonial modernity in a way that does not simply reproduce the patriarchal colonial family, but which imagines new genealogies of the future.

The two novels illustrate the recognition of complicity, of one's embeddedness within the problem, that is required to move beyond the trope of authenticity, a complicity that defines the discourse of postcolonial decadence and distinguishes it from the disavowals that characterize colonial consciousness. These texts demonstrate the exact strategies by which Orientalist notions of purity have become internalized within Algerian society and have fused with local versions of ideas that lend themselves to such a merging. The Arabic and French circuits through which each text travels reveal the internal and external structural ruins bequeathed by French Orientalism. These practitioners of Laraoui's "second nahda" enter into the decomposing skin of the authentic colonial subject, and through the very act of confessing complicity with decadence, they pry open a space for Algerian discourse. Wattar's gendering of this discourse reveals one of the crucial limits of his texts' capacity to "regulate the transference"—or translation—of "Algerian" meaning into the French language. Such a limit provides an important point of entry for a gender critique of Algerian national discourse, but it does not authorize a wholesale dismissal of the larger critical project articulated by *al-Zilzal*. Rather, Wattar's commitment to navigating the treacherous and deeply entrenched networks of Algerian history allows us to see the historical collapse that structures *L'invention du désert* as something other than a liberating narrative strategy for imagining a virtual transnational homeland (contrary to Bensmaïa's otherwise stimulating analysis of the novel). Wattar's Arabic text reveals the *temps informe* of Djaout's Francophone novel as an acute symptom of exile from the time of history understood as an instrument of collective self-consciousness and communal regeneration.

CHAPTER 5

Algerian Women and the Invention of Literary Mourning

Decadence and Orientalism are discourses constituted by a pathologized negativity, configured on a model of lack or loss, and this negativity has been gendered female in all the various manifestations discussed in this book. Yet every document of pathology, to rework once again Benjamin's famous formulation, is also a document of cure. Likewise, mourning, as a form of social labor, can perpetuate loss, but it can also cut into it as an unsettling force. As the previous chapters have revealed the recalcitrant agent within the object of Orientalism, this chapter reconsiders the traditional *object* of loss—the female, the feminine, women—in order to demonstrate how women writers in particular have refashioned the gendered economies of loss in future-oriented ways. This chapter does not aim to present a comprehensive account of gender politics in relation to decadence and Orientalism, but rather to outline literary strategies that challenge a broadly comparative set of moves that have feminized the negative in a wide range of discursive fields. Functioning in stark contrast to the feminization of Semites and Semitism (Renan, Drumont, Céline), of the void (in Céline), of the unconscious (in psychoanalysis), or of theological feminization of the sacred in Islam, as well as the nationalist masculinization of the public sphere (in Wattar et al.), the texts explored below actively experiment with and crack open the feminized configurations of Orientalist decadence and loss. In lieu of puritanical and neocolonial modes of national reproduction, the inventions of literary mourning discussed in this chapter produce local and transnational communities whose solidarity emerges through the very losses and wounds inflicted on the Orientalized woman.

In a stunning confession that sums up the way that the masculinist logic of female substitutability has structured certain ethnic, national, and religious attitudes toward Algerian life since independence, the male protagonist of Ahlam Mosteghanemi's 1993 Arabic novel *Dhakirat al-jasad* (*Memory in the Flesh*, retranslated and published in 2013 as *The Bridges of Constantine*) confesses that "a thousand other women took mother's place and I never grew up." If the previous chapter explored the ways that loss becomes nationalized, this chapter listens for the sustained critique of the ways that national losses become *gendered*. *Dhakirat al-jasad* does this by revealing an opposition between the singular, irreplaceable loss suffered by the male revolutionary martyr and the replaceable loss of the Algerian woman, exemplified by the protagonist's mother. Mosteghanemi's text works through the language of national loss in the specific language—Arabic—in which the novel locates the complexes and constraints of trauma, melancholy, and their remainders in bodily memory. In order to think about a range of literary configurations of mourning, the languages used to do this work, and the public and private injunctions addressed to women in particular, this chapter will consider works by Algerian women in which the language of literature is called upon to speak to unspeakable loss. The texts under consideration here—Yamina Méchakra's *La grotte éclatée* (1979), Mosteghanemi's *Memory in the Flesh*, Assia Djebar's *Le blanc de l'Algérie* (1995), and Hélène Cixous's *Si près* (2007)—have been selected because they each produce spontaneous, singular forms of female solidarity that may be said to arise both through language and outside of languages ("hors les langues" in Djebar's phrase). What is more, they do this despite institutional expectations relating to language, religion and the state that overdetermine the value of women's *memory work* (and *forgetting work*). In order to elaborate what constitutes such work, this chapter begins with theoretical approaches influenced by Freud and psychoanalysis (from Nicholas Abraham and Maria Torok to Jacques Derrida)[1] but steers away from them in order to foreground the primacy of the specific kind of mourning work that literature does and how this work relates to the social division of psychic labor in Algeria, in which women are enjoined to perform various kinds of public mourning. In particular, a comparative reading of the above texts demonstrates how these writers both implicitly and explicitly invent their own literary forms of mourning in relation to the gendered social practices of mourning the dead in Algeria.

Exploding the "Female Grotesque"

The texts that will be discussed were not chosen in order to narrate any kind of *development* of literary mourning in women's writing in or about Algeria, although they do provide historically specific instances in which women address the question of loss and reopen the traumatic past to a rearticulation in the present. Yamina Méchakra began writing *La grotte éclatée*, her novel about the Algerian War for Independence (1954–62), in 1973 and published it in 1979, seventeen years after the Evian Accords that marked the end of the war. She thus wrote it during the decade that saw massive projects that nationalized agriculture and industry, a period that also saw the publication of the first Algerian Arabic novels (by Tahir Wattar and Waciny Lâredj). Méchakra then published her book on the eve of the decade, the 1980s, that would witness the emergence of newly politicized Islamic movements. It is in this context that *La grotte éclatée* comes into existence, a novel that alternates between two impulses: On the one hand, it is a feminist critique of the roles that women are expected to perform in the process of national reproduction, while on the other hand, the text is also an unabashed celebration of the birth of the nation that marks the end of the text. One critic, Pamela Pears, has claimed that the book thus illustrates the "forced reconciliation" of "the conflicting societal expectations that came out of the war" (2004, 63), in which the radical transformation of gender roles accomplished during the revolution came into contact with what many saw as diminished possibilities for women in Algerian public life following the war. An alternate reading of what remains unreconciled in this this urgently poetic, fragmented, and experimental text would begin with the conceit that animates the writing throughout, namely the cave, *la grotte*, of the title, which at the level of the narrative serves as the hideout for a group of rebels and militants during the war, including the narrator.[2]

Méchakra describes the cave as a protective feminine space; indeed, it is a *grotte-matrice*, a cave-womb, both a space where the narrator gives birth to her son amid the bloodshed of war and the very womb in which the nation suffers its birth pangs. "Out of the entire world," the narrator says, "they only left us a cave that will never give birth to us!" (*De toute la terre*, *ils ne nous ont laissé qu'une grotte qui ne nous accouchera jamais!*) (27).[3] Her son Arris shares the name of the small town in the Aurès Mountains that is her ancestral home; it is also the name of the father, another maquisard.[4] The cave is blown up by the French one month after her son's birth, leaving her the only survivor. The exploding cave at the core of the novel presents readers not with a reconciliation between two poles, but rather with a vivid vision of what happens when mourning becomes inexpressible (psychically, affectively, because of censorship): Language collapses extremes, fractures along multiple fault lines, and then suddenly breaks apart. These extremes of birth and death suffered within Méchakra's cave are an exemplar of Abraham and Torok's reading of the melancholic subject's "incorporation" of the lost object of desire that leads to what they call its "encryptment." "Inexpressible mourning," they write, "erects a tomb inside the subject" (1994, 130). Quite literally, Méchakra's text entails a *grotesque encryptment* of the lost object within the interior feminized *grotte-matrice*, which both yields new life and can *never* give birth to the emerging Algerian national community.

More specifically, the space of encryptment in Méchakra's text describes the interlacing features of what Mary Russo has called the "female grotesque," an aesthetic that Russo traces from the grotesque's fifteenth-century origins following the discovery of the grottos of Nero's *domus arena*. She argues that the two parts that compose the grotesque—the "carnival grotesque" and the "uncanny grotesque" are closely related to two conventional ways of thinking about the female: first, a superficial, decorative *public* façade, and second, an individual, fantastic, and *private* interiority. Méchakra's *grotte-matrice* is the place of becoming-nation, but in a way that weds the uncanny, private, (and female) interior space of the grotto to the (male) public space of the nation, proposing something akin to what Judith Butler has, in another context, called "a melancholy of the public sphere" (2000, 81). Despite the apparent contradiction between the novel's simultaneous critique and celebration of the traumatic nature of nation-state formation, the lasting images of Méchakra's text radically reinvent both the militant and the creative potentials of women's memory work. In the overdetermined context that would posit the nation as female while discrediting the roles women played in securing it, the novel opens what Mary Russo calls "a room for chance" that "emerges within the very constrained spaces of normalization" (1995, 12). Following such a claim will allow us to think about how the subjugation of women within the larger matrix of colonial modernity creates the conditions for a transnational feminist critique of the trauma at the intersection of decadence and

Orientalism—in spite of everything. Russo opposes the female grotesque to the Kantian sublime, emphasizing instead the untheorized features of the material body. As we will see, the grotesque female bodies in Méchakra's novel exceed theorization much the same way, as these bodies themselves become spaces of risk and invention.

A striking description that the narrator gives of her own metonymic, fragmented body illustrates the way her external features change within the internal space of the cave: "I thought for a moment about the bald woman that I was, eyes made red by long sleepless nights, lips hardened, earrings hanging from her ears making her look like a genuine pirate from the mountains" (*Je songeai un instant à la femme chauve que j'étais, aux yeux rougis par les longues veilles, aux lèvres durcies, aux boucles qui pendaient à ses oreilles et la faisaient ressembler à un authentique pirate des montagnes*) (26). The text here witnesses the transformation of the narrating subject from female first person into a masculine third person whose transformation turns precisely on the ornamental accessories (the earrings) that mark the superficial female grotesque. The text describes another grotesque mutation of the convalescing maquisards assembled in the candlelit cave: "The fleshless profiles of my wounded men were dancing with the candle flames on the walls of the cave, taking on its form and becoming monstrous" (*Les profiles décharnés de mes blessés dansaient avec les flammes des bougies sur les parois de la grotte, en épousaient la forme et devenait monstrueux*) (21). The flickering silhouettes of the men mutilated in battle "marry" (*épousaient*) themselves to the form of the cave's anfractuosities, projecting a living anamorphosis of male suffering onto the interior surface of the "female" *grotte-matrice*. In this tenuous way does Méchakra's text pry open "a room for chance" in an "encrypted" space where men fight and women care for the wounded, an *invention* of mourning, a "coming across" (from the Latin *in venire*) that has the force of a "creation" or a discovery.

Unconscious Melancholia and Literary Substitution

Méchakra's invention of mourning is no mere involuntary return of a repressed, inexpressible traumatic event but rather the deliberate work of the author, first of remembering, and then of sabotaging the nationalist prescriptions dictating what women are to remember, how they are to remember it, and to what end. Incorporated memories likewise structure Ahlam Mosteghanemi's *Memory in the Flesh*, as the title suggests, this time in a reexamination of the continuing effects of the War for Independence narrated at a remove of thirty-one years from 1962.[5] The text performs its memory work through the first-person rendering of the thoughts of Khalid, a man who has lost his arm in the war before turning to painting to recover his lost relation to external reality, and who eventually falls in love with the younger daughter of his former commanding officer, Si Tahir, who has died in combat.[6]

Like Méchakra's female narrator, the male narrator of Mosteghanemi's novel collapses a constellation of desired objects, places, and people, transforming the woman he loves into the city of Constantine, into the painted canvas, and most notably into the nation itself. Both texts describe something like a transference of each narrator's love of the lost object of desire onto another person and ultimately onto the homeland. The difference between these two cases of substitution is that in Méchakra's novel, the same word signifies the land ("ARRIS" in all capital letters), as well as both the deceased father and the newborn son ("Arris"). The typographical discrepancy between ARRIS and Arris, explained in the novel's footnotes, indicates an attempt, albeit an ultimately unsuccessful one, to keep the name of the village distinct from the name shared by both father and son.

Whereas Méchakra's text attempts to distinguish between the private and the political, Mosteghanemi's male narrator collapses this distinction as he actively produces the substitutions of female lost objects that emerge in the wake of the death of his mother. Such emotive, masculinist rhetoric is the very stuff from which the novel is made. After joining a guerilla cell in the mountains near Constantine, he realizes that he is "probably the only one who left behind the fresh grave of a mother who died from sickness and a broken heart" (14).[7] The death of Khalid's mother occurred a year after the outbreak of war in November 1954, and he reflects on this strange coincidence:

> The old adage—the orphan is not the one who loses his father but the one who loses his mother—is absolutely true.
> I was an orphan, and I realized this profoundly all the time. Because the hunger for affection is a fearful and painful feeling that continues to tear you from the inside and stays with you until, one way or another, it finishes you off.
> Did I join the national revolution at the time as a subconscious way of seeking death, a beautiful death remote from those feelings of nausea that were gradually filling me with hatred for everything?
> The revolution was entering its second year and I was in my third month as an orphan. I cannot remember now exactly when the country took over the character of motherhood [malamih al-'umuma, 27]

and gave me an unexpected and strange affection and a compulsive
sense of belonging [al-intima' al-mutatarrif, 27]. (14–15)

The narrator thus describes his new attachment to the nation as a "compulsive" "affection" that redirects the love of his deceased mother into nationalistic feeling. Here begins the series of substitutions that will dovetail into the love story that constitutes the larger share of the novel, which presents the unconscious substitutions of its male protagonist within the distancing frame created by the author.

What is particularly striking is that just a few lines earlier, Khalid had affirmed the unique and irreplaceable nature of the male martyr, saying that "they were not mass-produced martyrs. Each one was a martyr in his own right" (*lam yakunu shuhada'* . . . *kana kullu wahid shahidan 'ala hida* [14/27]).[8] What is more, the narrator's father figure, friend, and resistance hero, Si Tahir, assumes the role of the mother in the narrator's mind, as Khalid envies "that sudden tear in his eye that elevated Mother to the role of martyr" (19). Si Tahir, the soon-to-be martyred male *mujahid* has the power to consecrate the loss of the narrator's mother in a vicarious act of mourning that endows the infinitely substitutable woman with the status of the singular, irreplaceable male martyr, who would thus enter that state beyond mourning: melancholia. Khalid wants "to lie as a corpse in his arms, to think that after my death there would be a tear in his eye" so that Si Tahir might "witness that I belonged to nobody else save this country, and that I was leaving behind nothing but the grave of a woman, my mother, and a younger brother for whom my father had already chosen a new mother" (19). Like Méchakra's invention of revolutionary mourning, Mosteghanemi's retelling of how Khalid's attachment to the nation formed during the revolution can also be understood as an encryptment, this time an encryptment of the dead mother that marries her death to the nation being born in a wholly melancholic manner. With the birth of Si Tahir's daughter, Ahlam, whom the narrator immediately calls "my daughter" (24), and the death of Si Tahir soon afterward, the cycle of substitutions will continue until Khalid's confession that will mark his recognition of this logic near the end of the novel. This logic proposes that women are assimilable and thus mournable, while men are not. The legacy of trauma that Mosteghanemi recounts in this novel is one of postcolonial melancholia, not in the cosmopolitan sense that Paul Gilroy outlines in his book by the same name,[9] but rather in the sense that the injunction to mourn those who died for Independence requires that there be no end to mourning and no assimilation of those lost; it is a working through that must never cease.

In this, it shares much with Ranjana Khanna's declaration that postcolonial studies is itself a melancholic discipline that must refuse any overly facile assimilation or working through of past trauma and instead vigilantly orient itself toward enactments of justice that would always be *to come*.[10]

Over the course of the effusive and poetic novel, Khalid continues this series of substitutions that began with the death of his mother. First, he replaces the arm he lost in the war with his new passion for painting. He then demonstrates that his love for Ahlam, the daughter of Si Tahir, functions according to this same law of substitution and replacement: "a painting is female too" (45) he admits early in the text. His paintings erase Ahlam and transform her into a city:

> You were not a woman. You were a city, a city teaming with diversely conflicting women, different in age and features . . . women who ranged in age from before the days of my mother to your own days.
> . . . I was witnessing your gradual transformation into a city that had haunted me since time began. I was witnessing your sudden change as day by day you took on the features of Constantine, its elevations and grottos and memories and secret caves. (92)

This passage is but one of many in which the replaceable woman is described in terms of the female grotesque, which weds the private uncanny interior to the public superficial exterior. At another moment, Khalid says that "we belong to nations that only wear their memory on occasion" but these feminized nations "quickly take it off just like a woman who takes off her jewelry" (76). Memory is superficial and fickle "like a woman," but it is also an internal and timeless haunting figured as the beloved woman who becomes transformed, through the act of artistic creation, into the grottos and secret caves in and around Constantine.

The author's choice of a male voice that details his own wartime exploits, which seeks to understand the mechanisms that dictate his desire and lack of desire, allows Mosteghanemi to critique the logic by which this character operates while also maintaining him as something of a hero. The turning point in the story comes on the eve of Ahlam's marriage to another man, when Khalid goes to visit his mother's grave. He goes to the cemetery where she is buried, but he has to "seek help from the custodian's records to find the pathway that would lead to the grave, and to you" (214). At this point, the cycle comes full circle, as the trauma of the mother's death and the imminent loss of the woman who would replace her produce a kind of short-circuit in the narration. It is at this precise moment that the narrator makes his shocking confession: "A thousand other women took Mother's place and I never grew up" (215) ['*awwadatuha bi-alf imra'a ukhra . . . wa lam akbur* (329)]. The Arabic verb that the text uses here, based on the intensive form of the trilateral root '*ayn-waw-dad* tells us that the narrator "substituted" or "exchanged" his mother for the other women. By writing these words (the text we are reading is also the novel within the novel that Khalid comes to write over the course of the story) he thus both actively occupies the grammatical position of the one doing the substituting and provides a theory of *ta'weed*, or "replacement," that indicates that the text has consciously entered into the place of this heretofore unconscious mechanism. And while it is a male character who performs the work of mourning within the frame of the narrative, it is the novel that both frames his work and reinvents mourning in literary form.

By insisting on the deliberate, conscious work that these texts perform, I do not mean to affirm any absolute distinction between the conscious and the unconscious as these categories might relate to literary work; even less am I attempting to validate a clear difference between mourning and melancholia, in the sense Freud gave to these terms in his enormously influential paper written in 1915.[11] And yet at the same time, it is worth remembering that these interpretive categories are useful for the analyst precisely to the degree that they help distinguish between different kinds of repetitions articulated by the subject who has suffered loss. It is safe to say that these categories appear to be operative in the writing done by the authors being studied here. "The psychoanalyst's gambit," Sam Durrant reminds us, is "to distinguish between 'involuntary' repetition and an active process of working through, between melancholia and mourning" (2004, 10). It is thus enervating to see the way that critics such as Khanna prescribe melancholia as the preferred position of the postcolonial critic concerned with justice. "While the work of mourning may relegate swallowed disposable bodies to the garbage can of modern nationalism," she writes, "the work of melancholia, critically attesting to the fact of the lie intrinsic to modern notions of sovereignty, is the only hope for the future" (2006). While I do not dispute the main thrust of Khanna's argument, which rightly takes a strong stance against the possibility of "successful" assimilation of the dead into a grand national narrative, it is valuable to examine this new normative advocacy of melancholia in light of the original function of these categories for Freud, namely as a means of distinguishing between conscious and unconscious repetitions. The current chapter is less an attempt to analyze these authors and their characters in order to identify and classify them as either more or less conscious, as indicating more or less "successful" instances of mourning (which would itself depend on which definition of "success" one uses) than it is an attempt to read the way that Méchakra, Mosteghanemi, Djebar, and Cixous themselves inflect the voices of their texts with accents and rhythms that indicate the degree to which these speakers, thinkers, and writers have consciously entered into the grammatical position of the words and phrases that had heretofore been speaking *them*.

Inventions of Mourning

Hélène Cixous's 2007 meditation on her relationship to her native Algeria, *Si près*, is a text that presents a textual shape and structure inversely symmetrical to that of *Memory in the Flesh*. Mosteghanemi's novel speaks in the first-person voice of the male *mujahid* whose trajectory inadvertently leads him to his mother's grave. The poetic, rhetorical, and psychic mechanisms of female substitution discussed before serve as the novel's *point d'arrivée*. Contrasted with this, we have Cixous's autobiographical text, which speaks in the first person voice of the Jewish woman, a *would-have-been mujahida* whose return to Algeria has been deferred for thirty-five years. The figurative and psychic mechanisms that separate her from her native land, which is also where her father is buried, serve as the *point de départ* of the text. Both books contain versions of the same scene, where having come to the threshold of the deferred or prohibited grave of the deceased parent, recourse to the written record of the caretaker of the cemetery is required to find the precise location of the tomb. Beginning, then, at this point of departure, *Si près* will elaborate an anguished series of syntactic inventions that reorder, rearrange, try out and try on, and that *come across as if discovering* the trauma that marks the narrator's exile from Algeria at the moment it comes to constitute a nation-state in its own right.

The text proceeds sporadically, through a kind of hypothetical articulation of what it would mean to return to Algeria and to the grave of the dead father buried there:

> For thirty-five years I have not wanted to go to Algeria, I say to myself, I never thought of going there, I always thought of not going there, I wanted rather not-to-go-to-Algeria, each time that I could go to Algeria in the end it didn't happen, there are some countries to which I end up not going, I have no role in this, on the one hand I have my reasons, on the other there are circumstances, as regards Algeria it's not that I wanted never again to go there, I wanted rather to go there for sure, better not to go there than to go there in the wrong way, I couldn't go there in just any old way, it's much too dangerous,

> I have always been careful to hold onto the hypothesis that admitted a trip to Algeria was probable, but I have always admitted simultaneously the opposite hypothesis: it could be that I will never get around to going to Algeria. (10)[12]

> Il y a maintenant trente-cinq ans que je ne veux pas aller en Algérie, me dis-je, je ne pensais jamais à y aller, je pensais toujours ne pas y aller, je voulais plutôt ne-pas-aller-en Algérie, chaque fois que je pouvais aller en Algérie cela ne se faisait finalement pas, il y a des pays où je finis toujours par ne pas aller, je ne fais rien pour cela, d'un côté j'ai mes raisons, de l'autre il y a les circonstances, pour l'Algérie ce n'est pas que je ne voulais plus jamais y aller, je voulais plutôt y aller à coup sûr, plutôt ne pas y aller que d'y aller de travers, je ne pouvais pas y aller n'importe comment, c'est beaucoup trop dangereux, j'ai toujours eu soin de garder l'hypothèse qui admet pour vraisemblable un voyage en Algérie, mais j'ai toujours admis simultanément l'hypothèse contraire : il se pourrait que je n'en vienne jamais à aller en Algérie. (21)

This passage weaves together the conscious propositions of the narrating subject and a dazzling array of verbal constructions and syntactical possibilities that would seem to perform the ambivalence and reticence of the narrator faced with the possibility of return to her native land. By trying out these multiple possibilities in literary form, Cixous is also recreating Algeria as textual utopia, as a "Jardin d'Essai," which names the real botanical garden in Algiers mentioned throughout the text, but also frames the essay being written as a kind of prelapsarian "Garden of Literary Essays" that would be a "Paradise on earth" (2009, 11). Each of the verbal structures enumerated in the text plays along the impossible seam that separates postcolonial Algeria from its exiles, its remainders: those unassimilable ones, like Cixous, whose citizenship status as an Algerian Jew had been subject to series of reversals beginning three years after her birth with the abolition in 1940 of the Crémieux Decree (which in 1870 had accorded citizenship to Algerian Jews).[13] Extending Khanna's argument in *Algeria Cuts* about the way that women trouble the frames of Algerian national representation, we can affirm that Cixous's *essais* dance along the lines that would demarcate the community of national belonging, those impossible ports of entry where the narrator, lost to her homeland, would be assimilated into the nation. This movement of the rejected part toward the whole can never be one of successful assimilation, however, but can only ever get *so close* and no closer. "What separates these two countries," Cixous writes, referring to France and Algeria, "is nothing, it's a cup of water . . . a notch of nothing" (127). The movement from "nothing" to "a notch of nothing" indicates the overall movement of the text, which by traveling toward its destination in increasingly precise language only finds unassailable distance in proximity.

The work of literary mourning performed by the text would thus seem to belong to the realm of melancholia, since the lost object can never be assimilated: The point of departure for Cixous is precisely the impossibility of arrival. Yet mourning and melancholia become fused here, radically changing their apparently oppositional relationship. The text deliberately manipulates the figures of language that facilitate this seemingly infinite deferral between two points: "The word Algiers had been called up only by metonymy, I was ready to swear it. I had not wanted to say that perhaps I would go to see my father, or else my father's tomb, that is, my father by metonymy, or else the metonymy of my father, the most unbelievable, mysterious substitutions get produced within us" (33). But is the father a metonym for Algeria, or vice versa? The impossibility of determining an *urgrund* from which to measure her rhetorical substitutions precludes the closing of the gap between what would be a private loss and a public one. Instead, the narrator is left with figures of language: metonymy, allegory, substitution, and invention:

> I recognize that for thirty-five years an *Allegory* has taken the place of Algeria in my head. And before the allegory was produced, I have no other memory except so profoundly planted in the folds of my flesh, so engraved in my personal grotto [*ma grotte personelle*] that, as soon as I say this sentence, I seem to be in the antiquity of a fiction I invent and whose invention I am. (46)

Yet again loss has been incorporated within the interior of the female grotesque, inseparable from the flesh as its living proof, but what has been lost is also indistinguishable from the figures of language that would secure the deferrals and substitutions of this loss. In Cixous's articulation of mourning or melancholia, assimilation is revealed as a catachresis, a perversion of language that holds out the hope of something undeliverable.[14] As the gap closes between the speaking subject and the doubled metonym/ allegory "Algeria/father," as Cixous approaches the prohibited lost homeland and the father's grave, language can only invent the public/private mise en scène of this rapprochement. *Si près* opens a space for experimentation within the overdetermined and highly constrained spaces of exilic memory and the trauma of nation-state formation. Like Abdelkébir Khatibi, Cixous creates a series of "testimonial exercises," in which she both experiments with the possibilities of witnessing and exercises her right to remember otherwise—or not at all.[15]

Languages of Mourning

It is with this understanding of the female grotesque as a space of experimentation that this chapter now turns toward the role that language plays in the invention of literary mourning in Assia Djebar's *Le blanc de l'Algérie* and Méchakra's *La grotte éclatée*. Difficult as it is to rehearse the tortured history of language politics in Algeria, it would nonetheless be impossible to ignore the ways in which this history marks out the conditions of possibility of each of these texts. *Le blanc de l'Algérie* is a text that mourns the murder of several of the author's friends during the civil war of the 1990s, but also draws lines of flight in and out of fratricidal violence that has periodically erupted in Algeria since the War for Independence. Published in 1995, barely one year after the most recent of the bloody events that the text recounts, *Le blanc de l'Algérie*, like many of Djebar's texts, meditates upon the meaning of its own use of the French language while alluding to the multilingual reality of the country. It is a text caught between its *langue*, the French language, and its aspiration toward a *langage*, a line of flight that her text terms "writing in search of a language outside of language" (*l'écriture en quête d'une langue hors des langues*) (245) in its final sentence.[16] Like Méchakra's exploding cave, Djebar's language would be something so internal that it would announce itself as a kind public melancholia. *Le blanc de l'Algérie* ends with the desire to "find the 'inside of speech,' which remains our one fertile homeland" (*retrouver le 'dedans de la parole' qui, seul, demeure notre patrie féconde*) (245).

Djebar's plea for a language that would allow for both a space of refuge and room for the invention of the self and the "patrie," written in the midst of the bloodshed that marked a catastrophic period for the Algerian experiment, demands to be read alongside a similar plea at the end of Méchakra's text. In a section that bears the title "19 mars 1962," the date of the ceasefire that marked the first full day of Algerian nationhood after the signing of the Evian Accords, *La grotte éclatée* describes a romantic, Herderian vision of a poet around whom "the refugees found refuge" (157). "He knew all the songs of the country," Méchakra writes, "the entire country, and each of us was relearning Algeria" (*Il connaissait toutes les chanson du pays, tout le pays et chacun de nous réapprenait l'Algérie*) (157). The section ends thus: "Tongues untied themselves and children learned and spoke a language previously forbidden" (*Les langues se délièrent et les enfants apprirent et parlèrent un langage hier interdit*) (157). At this point in the text, the problems of *la langue* become dissolved in the metonymical replacement of the physical *tongue*, while the children learn not one of the actual languages that were repressed and forbidden under the French, but rather a *langage*, associated here with inclusiveness and newly unimpeded possibilities of expression freed from restraints of the colonial system of censure. The fact that Méchakra publishes her novel after a decade of President Boumediene's Arabization, which saw the repression of dialectical Arabic and "Berber" languages spoken by Kabyle, Chaoui, and other linguistic communities, suggests that going back to the dawn of national possibility in Algeria is also a way for her to articulate a renewed hope of a *langage* in which all the songs of the country might be sung.

Her novel asks to be read as an experimental series of inventions in this new language. Yet multiple scenes clearly emphasize the traumatic, as opposed to the celebratory, nature of this kind of literary work. Huddled in the cave with her newborn son, the narrator thinks to herself that she "needed a new flag to plant on some future planet, where my children would have no memory of the dark centuries." "Invent a flag," she tells a companion (87). While recovering in the hospital after the explosion in the cave she tells the nurse that her scars are "invented" (98). The impetus for this remark is an old newspaper dating to 1945, the date of the massacres at Guelma and Setif. This traumatic event and the wake of violence that lead to the outbreak of war in 1954 are also "invented" (97) in the narrator's account. She continues: "My son: invented. The cave: invented. The orphanage: invented. Me: invented. You: invented. The war: invented" (98). The chapter ends with the confession, "I invented it all, like the newspapers did" (99). More than representing a denial of reality or an affirmation that fiction creates or intensifies experience, this insistence on invention deserves to be read as a voluntary act of the author remembering to do the literary work of forgetting. Like Cixous, who claims that her own book "is the work of forgetting" (*l'oeuvre de l'oubli*) (103/141), Méchakra replaces memory with invention, in the sense of something neither factual nor fictional, but rather as writing that may serve as a place of hospitality where one plays host not only to an endless working through of past trauma, but where one may experiment with the "inside of language" in order to open it up toward an unforeseeable future.

And yet despite the rhetorical and literary labor these texts perform on *langage*, *la langue* remains among the most potent remainders of postcolonial melancholia. For Mosteghanemi's male narrator, French is a language that only represents "great freedom" to the degree that it is "a language foreign to [his] traditions and psychological restraints" (104). It allows him to "say things without complexes, without restraint" (144). To the complex understanding of the relationship between repression, expression, and tradition in *Memory in the Flesh*, Djebar's advice to an acquaintance who insists on being psychoanalyzed in classical, literary Arabic—"Just be Algerian!" (*Soyez simplement algérien!*) (30–31)—might come across as somewhat simplistic. The overall story about language and its relation to loss that Djebar tells is much more nuanced, however. Referring to conversations she has with her friend M'hamed Boukhobza, assassinated in 1993, she confesses, "we speak French. Not like we did before. Not due to being cautious or for the sake of appearances, in order to veil our imperceptible embarrassment, or shared stiffness. There, on American soil, our pre-dawn French flows as simply, after all, as the maternal language that we all share should have flowed" (20). It is worth noting here that the published English translation of the book leaves out the conditional past tense of the original French, which specifies, "Our pre-dawn French flows out as simply, after all, as the maternal language we share should have" (*Notre français d'avant l'aube se déroule aussi simple, après tout, qu'*aurait dû être *la langue maternelle que nous partageons*) (my emphasis; 20).[17] What this use of verb tense hints at, in a way that scarcely covers its "embarrassment," is the violence done to expression by both French colonialism and Arabization, which imposed the more formal and literary Modern Standard Arabic at the expense of the popular dialectal languages of Algeria, in a way that has in some cases reinforced the use of the French language, functioning as a backup language of sorts. The simple poignancy available to Djebar in French thus also reveals a regret concerning the absence of the maternal language.

It is at this precise moment in the text where we clearly see the decadent Orientalism that has brought about the breakdown of precolonial linguistic traditions, understood as a function of the decay of colonial modernity, overdetermining any articulation of loss, thus pushing Djebar "outside of languages" in her "irresistible search for a liturgy" (12). In remembering her brother-in-law, the poet and playwright, Abdelkader Alloula, she writes of the specific qualities of his way of talking, noting the "briskness of your speech in each of the two languages" (*le frappé de ton verbe, dans chacune des deux langues*) and affirming that it was "the accent alone and its liveliness [which served] as the bridge between them." Summing up, Djebar adds, "I was listening to your inner rhythm" (*J'écoutais ton rhythme intérieur*) (26). In such passages, the reader is prompted to listen for the *dedans de la parole*, the sounds a singular body makes when speaking, where what gets remembered is the way this body turns itself inside out to articulate its relation to others. Djebar's writing opposes such an understanding of singular instances of *parole* to the unitary concept of *la langue*. The inventions that matter, that may serve as the only "fertile homeland," would then be those that operate between, within, and outside of languages, constantly transgressing linguistic boundaries.

While literature serves as one space for such inventions, it is by no means the only one. Throughout her career, Djebar crafted texts that take their cue from actually existing social practices—especially women's practices (of musical performance and mourning, most significantly)—but the literary is never seen as an end in itself. In a scene that gives an account of a ceremony honoring slain psychiatrist Mahfoud Boucebci, Djebar depicts an invention of social mourning that transgresses the borders of the text, fusing the two aspects of the female grotesque in a "melancholy of the public sphere." The story itself is framed as an oral account given by a female teacher and friend of the deceased whom she meets in an unspecified European capital.[18] The ceremony is attended by official representatives of various groups, the Minister of Universities, of Health, and "us women, those from feminist groups" (76). The event takes a radical turn when fifty people from the crowd, wearing jeans, tunics, and headscarves, decide to sit down and occupy the middle of the street: "So we sang, shouted, protested; sang especially: a kind of improvised concert . . . Not like yesterday's female mourners!" (76). They sing the national anthem, and then "other anthems in Arabic followed; two or three in Berber fused with exclamations in French, slogans for democracy, calls for Mahfoud, words of love . . . " (76). In texts such as the short story "Il n'y a pas d'exil" and *L'amour, la fantasia*, as well as her film, *La Nouba des femmes du Mont Chenoua*, Djebar weaves together the voices of women who vocally and musically mourn the dead into her own retelling and reimagining of emerging networks of women's solidarity and empowerment. The exclamation of the teacher telling this story, however, marks a stark contrast between the improvised street festival honoring the Algerian dead and the *pleureuses d'avant*, the "female mourners of yesteryear." The text thereby aligns its own multilingual liturgy of grief with the defiant demonstration of public mourning for Mahfoud, positioning both scenes (that in the text and that in the street) somewhere between the official masculine language of mourning and the traditional expectations of social mourning in Algeria, which place an undue burden on women, who are the ones hired to mourn, but who are also given license to act in ways that might otherwise be prohibited and considered improper or excessive.[19]

The account of this unexpected event continues with a description of the suspicion it arouses:

> the officials who were coming out looked at us with uncertainty. For we were inventing, with rage, a new ritual: after all, Mahfoud was the physician of madmen, and all of a sudden we who had fought, who had taken to the streets at the slightest public occasion, we were now becoming a little mad. And we needed his presence more than ever: that he be there, with his excesses, his joy, and his generosity. (76–77)

This scene can be read as fulfilling some of the promise of Méchakra's poet, who would sing the songs of "the entire country" both in languages that were real and those in the process of being born, invented. Read from our perspective, looking back at the protests of the Arab Spring, in which mourning the dead (from Mohamed Bouazizi in Tunisia to those killed by the military and the police throughout most of the Arab world) took wildly inventive and unprecedented forms, Djebar's text enters into a long genealogy of how women's mourning work has opened up spaces both in the text and in the world not simply for honoring the dead or refusing to forget them, but for *experimenting* with memory and forgetting. Such experiments may be grounded in local practice, but they can also have global repercussions.

Instead of founding a new community on trauma by claiming the lost object as *property*, the inventions of mourning in the texts examined in this chapter ask a question and follow multiple trajectories in pursuit of possible answers (Méchakra's "grotesque" experiments, Mosteghanemi's theory of substitution, Djebar's "dedans de la parole" [245] and Cixous's inventions of mourning). These texts *listen* at least as much as they *speak*: they listen to the voices of men and women who cannot forget and/or who feel compelled to remember. Yet while each author explicitly refers to psychoanalytic discourse, what has interested us here has been the *literary* modes of working through, of mourning that they activate. Reading Mosteghanemi, Méchakra, Cixous, and Djebar as pathological melancholic objects afflicted with inexpressible grief, beset by repetition, and haunted by endless chains of substitution would repeat the Orientalist gesture of feminizing loss; on the contrary, this chapter has sought to demonstrate how they each, in their singular ways, produce active forms of remembering and forgetting. This memory work places their texts in the position of the analyst of the psychoanalytic session more than that of the analysand. Méchakra, herself a practicing psychoanalyst, explodes the "female grotesque" and pries open a space that troubles the roles allotted to women mourning at the threshold of private grief that would be assigned a public meaning. In Khanna's words (2008), her text "cuts" through the gendered frames of nationalist representations of loss. *Memory in the Flesh* presents a narrative that is structured by the signifying chain that binds women to infinite substitutability within nationalist discourses of martyrdom, and then stages the event that breaks this chain when her narrator consciously enters into the discourse he seems doomed to merely reproduce. The syntactic variations of *Si près* provide another kind of break, opening a space where Cixous invents and reinvents possibilities of belonging and expressing loss within the overdetermined structures of the history of Algerian citizenship, particularly in relation to Algerian Jews. Finally, Djebar's *Le blanc de l'Algérie* prompts us to consider the importance of the institution of *literature*—as a location where the relationship between public and private, between language and loss may be articulated otherwise. Rather than adhering to the injunction announced by the ethics of postcolonial melancholia to remember the past without idealizing or consuming it, these texts gesture in the direction of an unconditional hospitality toward the transformational potential of loss. Such an approach is exemplified by Hélène Cixous, who when asked whether *Si près* was indeed her way of trying to claim Algeria as *hers*, turned the question around. "On the contrary," she declared, "this text is my way of asking, 'Am I yours?'"[20]

The inventions of solidarity and experiments with new cadences of belonging discussed in this chapter chart ways out of the impasse of Orientalist decadence. Their affirmations of a right to public melancholia and improvised modalities of kinship beyond the masculinist national "family" attest to the energies released in the decay of colonial modernity. As a counter-move to both the feminization of loss and the heavy losses suffered by women in particular, Orientalized women have been thrust into the avant-garde of those working through what Aching calls the "perilous yet creative possibilities for autonomous action and for sovereignty" (2011, 44), sifting through the fragments of colonial occupation and war, seeking out the half-forgotten graves of dead ancestors buried in overgrown cemeteries. The final chapter will examine a different cure for Orientalist decadence in the itinerary of Abdelwahab Meddeb's migrant texts, which traverse the perilous fantasies of Islamic puritanism, contemporary Euro-American Orientalism, and the remnants of colonial decadence left scattered on the postcolonial map.

CHAPTER 6

Virtual Secularization
Abdelwahab Meddeb's "Walking Cure" and the Immigrant Body in France

On August 12, 2006, Raed Jarrar, an architect and human rights activist of Iraqi and Palestinian descent, was prohibited from boarding a flight from JFK to Oakland because his Middle Eastern appearance and his T-shirt, which read "We will not be silent" in both English and Arabic (*lan nasmut*), made a number of passengers uncomfortable.[1] This relatively banal incident was reported in the news media and subsequently made into a minor cause célèbre, including *"lan nasmut"* T-shirts available for sale on Jarrar's website. This minor prefiguration of the "Muslim Travel Ban," initiated by Donald Trump in January 2017 and held up by the US Supreme Court in June 2018, brings into relief the countless, often unreported occurrences of racial profiling, surveillance, intimidation, detention, rendition, torture, and murder of those who resemble the undeclared enemy in the so-called War on Terror since September 11, 2001. The anxiety caused by Jarrar underscores the treacherous values attributed to "Arab" appearance and Arabic script in the repertoires of post-9/11 Orientalist fantasy. More specifically, the case suggests how this fantasy reacts to the conjunction of the Arabic language and the Arab body, whose very abjection would also indicate its power as an instrument of terror, necessitating the removal of this body from the networks of global travel. The danger attributed to the mobilized Arab body is at least equally pronounced in the context of contemporary France, where the fear of an Arab and Islamic conspiracy to take over the secular and universal ideals and institutions of the French Republic has been a national anxiety often expressed in the French media since the beginning of the "Islamic headscarves affair" in 1989 and revived in the wake of the string of attacks in French cities beginning with the Charlie Hebdo massacre in January 2015. This Orientalist fantasy reveals the ease with which the prewar paranoia of a global Jewish conspiracy has come to be rearticulated as "anti-Semitic" paranoia of *Arabs*.[2] The profound irony of anti-Jewish anti-Semitism among French Maghrebian youths serves as a constant reminder of the internal antagonisms generated, in part, by the disintegration of Orientalism's "Semitic object."[3] France's long history of Islamophobia has been reanimated in reactions to to the suburban riots of October and November 2005, and, more recently, to the terrorist attacks in Paris in 2015 and Nice in 2016. In 2005, the French far right argued that violence perpetrated by Muslims vindicated their anti-immigrant platform; since the riots were conducted mostly by young men of Islamic heritage whose parents immigrated from the Maghreb, the Front National claimed that the rioters—who were, in fact, mostly French citizens—could not be assimilated into French society and should thus be deported.[4] Jean-Marie Le Pen and, more recently, his daughter, Marine Le Pen, both leaders of the Front National, have styled themselves as contemporary Charles Martels in this scenario, driving Islamic immigrants—recast as a new barbaric infidel horde—back across France's sovereign/sacred borders. More recently, the influx of Syrian refugees and the refugee camp in Calais known as "the jungle" has occasioned fear of Arab bodies in motion, even as these bodies are more rightly *immobilized* than *mobile*.[5] In all these contexts, the body of the Arab immigrant or traveler becomes the field of battle upon which the ideological conflicts of Orientalism's decaying discourses are played out.

In contrast to the Front National's blatantly anti-immigrant stance is the glorification of the immigrant's revolutionary power articulated in Michael Hardt and Antonio Negri's *Empire*, where they predict the decline and fall of the current world order, asserting that "a new nomad horde, a new race of barbarians, will arise to invade or evacuate Empire" (2000, 213). The authors' reinscription of one of the oldest and most lasting tropes of the decadent imagination onto their vision of the new form of a global imperial sovereignty rehearses the positive reversal with which postcolonial discourse has so often responded to indictments of colonial decadence. Their transvaluation of the "barbarian," from Europe's enslaved inhuman other into a liberatory posthuman self, reiterates the familiar gesture of global anti-colonial discourse—with a difference. *Empire*, the first book in their trilogy, argues that in the age of global capitalism, the barbarians are always already within the gateless immanence of the new virtual field of power, a fact which requires the formulation of a new concept of the proletariat and a new anti-imperialist politics. Their conception of "the plural multitude of productive, creative subjectivities of globalization" (60) contrasts with the unitary notion of "the people" that has heretofore served as the subject of democratic political thought (316). "The multitude" serves as the password for the globally mobile working class created by economic restructuring and the constantly shifting networks that both deliver and withdraw capital from site to site across the globe. In this scheme, immigrants, who represent the extreme cases of mobile workers in a world labor market that requires more fluidity and mobility from everyone, "invest the entire society with their subversive desires" (Hardt and Negri 2004, 134). The agency of the multitude lies in its power to circulate and its ability to "evacuate" the sites of power; their subversive movement along the routes defined by global networks is indeed the new shape of communism outlined by Hardt and Negri: "A specter haunts the world," the text declares in its rewriting of Marx, "and it is the specter of migration" (2000, 213).

One core argument that runs through *Decadent Orientalisms*, that the "success" of postcolonial Orientalism is proven by its disintegration into a multiplicity of micro-discourses, is germane to Hardt and Negri's claim, which they borrow from Deleuze, that "imperial rule functions by breaking down" (2000, 202). Their theory of a migrant multitude that is both internal and resistant to imperial power reads Marx through a distinctly Nietzschean lens. They situate their attempt to account for the rise and fall of Empire partly within the genealogy of French Nietzscheanism, understood as a radical effort to think decadence *otherwise*. The concept of corruption developed in *Empire* aims beyond the moral categories of good and evil, and, instead, becomes "a strict argument about form" (2000, 202): "Empire is characterized by a fluidity of form—an ebb and flow of formation and deformation, generation, and degeneration" (202). Generation is the multitude's "collective apparatus of desire" (389), while corruption has no ontological reality, but is rather only "what separates a body and a mind from what they can do" (390).[6]

These broad theorizations about the role of the multitude of "new barbarians"—as agents of postmodern imperial decadence—motivate the specific questions that the current chapter seeks to answer. To begin with, what is the use-value of immigrant desire for theorists like Hardt and Negri, and how does the practice of this desire relate to its theorization? How might we connect the multiple lines of Nietzschean thought concerning decadence and forms of empire to extra-European understandings of decadence, as well as to actual articulations of transnational subjectivity? And more specifically, how might the ethnic, racial, and religious singularities that their text both affirms and erases in its sweeping claims be foregrounded as tactical *techniques* deployed against imperial control? In order to suggest possible answers to these questions, our analysis will wind its way through the crossing circuits of Abdelwahab Meddeb's first two novels, *Talismano* (1979/1987) and *Phantasia* (1986). Meddeb's critique of postcolonial decadence performs symbolically what Maghrebian immigrants accomplish physically: both inject Arabic and Islamic techniques of circulation into networks of power inherent within the postcolonial nation-state. The "nomad thought" enacted in Meddeb's text reveals the erasure of the Arabic language and Islam as the price to be paid for their virtual recirculation within the world cultural system. Meddeb's diagnosis of the maladies of Islamist *intégrisme* and the spectacles of Orientalist media finds the symptoms of postcolonial decadence to be omnipresent, forming an inextricable knot of internal and external signs, whose meanings depend, as they did for Nietzsche, on one's position within the system.

Meddeb's return to Nietzsche in his poetic elaborations of Maghrebian immigrant subjectivity allows him to critique colonial decadence in its various forms, from that of the academic Orientalist to the repressive postcolonial nation-state. First, it should be noted that Nietzsche's understanding of decadence was a radical departure from the long tradition of accounts that anthropomorphized decadence by equating the rise and fall of civilizations with the growth and aging processes of the human body. Nietzsche dislocates power as such from the realm of mimetic representation—which had served to regulate previous forms of political sovereignty—and instead relocates it in the body's volatile and unrepresentable singularity. My analysis of the paths traced in Meddeb's texts suggests new ways of imagining the political agency of the immigrant body traveling within, against, and away from the currents of global capital. Second, Nietzsche's radical revisions of decadence undermine the very concept that allows the diagnostician to take the measure of the world—namely the *symptom*—which, in the context of Arabic decadence, has manifested itself as a knot binding race to language. The textual strategy of what I am here calling *virtual secularization*—as a translation of Islamic cultural practices from Arabic into French—allows Meddeb both to affirm Islam and to sever the fantastic knots that would make the Arab or Muslim subject a symptom of any larger entity, whether it be a monolithic conception of Arabs, the Orient, or of Islam. Finally, as Meddeb received both the traditional Islamic education of his Tunisian youth and lived in the milieu of Parisian writers and intellectuals since he moved to France in 1968 until his death in 2014, Nietzsche and his centrality to French thought of the 1960s and 1970s are simply an unavoidable aspect of his own intellectual formation. The unique way that Meddeb crosses specifically Nietzschean ideas and methods with the practices of Arabic calligraphy and Islamic iconoclasm prompt a brief diversion through one of Nietzsche's most astute French readers, Pierre Klossowski.

In *Nietzsche and the Vicious Circle* (1997), Klossowski argues that Nietzsche bases his entire philosophy on the affirmation of the symptoms and idiosyncrasies of the body in all its singularity. He claims that Nietzsche deployed his own oscillating states of lucidity and delirium to initiate a "conspiracy" against Western culture and society in general. For Klossowski, all of Nietzsche comes out of the assertion of a "fundamental impulse," an impulse that took its cue from Nietzsche's body. In this view, the body's self-affirmation becomes the force driving all philosophy, all culture. Nietzsche, according to Klossowski's account, reveals that all philosophers—including himself—have not "quested for truth," but rather have engaged in "a secret concern to express the movements of their own moods" (4). "What did Spinoza or Kant do?" asks Klossowski, standing in for Nietzsche, "Nothing but interpret their dominant impulse" (5). Klossowski determines Nietzsche's "dominant impulse" or "idiosyncrasy" as "the sovereignty of an incommunicable emotion" (12), which leads Nietzsche to assert a "culture of affects" over and against "culture" as it had previously been theorized—negatively—and imposed from without. Nietzsche's reading of decadence, therefore, does not merely invert or project his own moods onto the world of culture, but rather conspiratorially deploys his body's changes against that world. Klossowski does not read the Nietzschean text for symptoms of mental illness, as many crude "diagnoses" of Nietzsche have tried to do.[7] Instead, he listens for the ways that Nietzsche passes on the instability of his own physiological condition to the discourse of interpretation—and especially to the interpretation of maladies: "The symptoms of decadence he revealed in the contemporary world, or in its apparent history, correspond to his personal obsession with what he was feeling and observing, in himself, of his own impulsive life and his own behavior" (75).

Nietzsche's articulation of decadence as an ambivalent force intimately tied to the singularity of an actually existing human body becomes transformed by Hardt and Negri into the generative power of the multitude defined as "the universality of free and productive practices" (2000, 316). Whereas their account drains this singular body of color and cultural affiliations, the desiring body that circulates throughout Meddeb's own discourse of decadence is distinctly marked as Arab, Islamic, and Maghrebian. My analysis of *Talismano* and *Phantasia* will show that this migrant body's "productive practices" are indissociable from Arabic writing and Islamic iconoclasm understood as techniques for disrupting imperial command, which, in the context of Maghrebian immigrants in contemporary France, refers to anti-Arab, anti-Islamic, and anti-immigrant racism in civil society and the state. Meddeb's texts also take aim at the complicity between the postcolonial nation-state and the corruptions of Islamist groups, both of which seek to separate the immigrant body from its subversive power. The singular use of Islam by Meddeb, who described himself as a "Muslim atheist" whose subjectivity was formed "by the symbolic and imaginary structuration of habitual reading of the Qur'an" (*fréquentation coranique, Libération,* May 6, 2006), represents an act of both radical and critical secularization.[8]

Meddeb's creative and critical output in multiple genres and media—novels, poetry, essays, translations, as well as his weekly radio show on France Culture, "Cultures d'Islam"—reveals the strategic moves required of the critical secularist caught between European Orientalist racism and the invented simplifications of Islamist groups.[9] As a singular voice within the global project of a transnational, postcolonial critique, Meddeb deploys Nietzschean "double science" to reverse the Orientalist claims of Islamic decadence, while he also "marks the interval" between colonial and postcolonial concepts of decadence with a textual practice that performs the virtual secularization of Islam.[10] This complex rhetorical move can be illustrated by an interview that Meddeb gave five days after the attacks of September 11, 2001, in which he theorized that an American military response to the attacks in New York and Washington was a structural inevitability within the logic of a globalized "society of the spectacle." "For 'aesthetic' reasons," Meddeb predicted, "America has to act and will act, in a manner I foresee as very violent, and there needs to be counter-images of the same type" (2002, 19).[11] Having "accurately thought through the relays of the event's diffusion as image," the perpetrators of the attacks had displayed a mastery of technique—"the optimum use of current means" (4). They had, in short, exploited the increasingly global addiction to the spectacular in order to instantly disseminate their message. This dissemination of violent images required not merely a speedy diffusion of "counter-images," but an aesthetic and technological upgrade of such images, which were amply provided by global media coverage of America's "war on terror." In this sense, the ongoing war on terror has been less about accomplishing specific military or political goals, and more about manufacturing more spectacularly violent images than the enemy.

While Meddeb's assessment of the situation echoes similar media-based critiques in France (Jean Baudrillard's "L'esprit du terrorisme," in *Le Monde*, November 3, 2001, for example), he is careful to contextualize his remarks not just in terms of the technological dynamics of Western global capitalism, but also from within the perspective of Arabic and Islamic political and cultural history. Over the course of the interview, Meddeb carefully traces the "double genealogy" of the relationship between power and thought in the Arab world, while simultaneously debunking the Orientalisms that have been revived in the wake of September 11. He intervenes in this past in order to de-essentialize and to rehistoricize it. His sketch of the material and intellectual history of Islamic societies refutes, for example, the claim that in Islam there is a fundamental consubstantiality between religion and politics.[12] His non-essentializing perspective of Islamic history becomes mediated through the figure of Nietzsche, as Meddeb deploys the notion of *ressentiment* from *On the Genealogy of Morality* to describe the attitude of the Arab Islamic world vis-à-vis the technological superiority of the colonizing West (5). Rather than playing the role of the active affirming innovator, the Arab world, according to Meddeb, has been forced into the role of a reactive negating consumer.[13] The September 11 attacks both confirmed this reactive role and illustrated a desperate attempt to escape it. Meddeb's critique thus crosses two distinct narratives of social evaluation: The discourse of decadence that emerged from Europe in the latter part of the nineteenth century, with Nietzsche as a pivotal theorist, and the discourse surrounding the *nahda* in the Arabic world, related to a revival of the Arabic language in literature, attempts to modernize and reform Islamic *turath*, and a growing Arab nationalist consciousness, all occurring in the context of the encounter with Europe.

The intersection of these two discourses allows Meddeb, in both his theoretical texts and literary texts, to employ a *détournement* of both narratives of decline against a variety of targets. On the one hand, he uses the

Nietzschean critique of the nihilism of Western scientific progress to intervene in the rise of the imbricated fundamentalisms of globalization and religious reform movements. On the other hand, he exploits the premises of the *nahda* to intervene into the legacy of colonialism and what he sees as the decadent condition of the postcolonial Arab Islamic nation-state. Over the course of this double critique, he articulates the tension between cultural production and consumption—between creation and technique, which has been a concern shared by other Arab writers. Meddeb's theorization about the state of postcolonial Arab culture both follows and diverges from that of the Syrian poet Adonis in his *Introduction to Arabic Poetics*. Since the *nahda*, Adonis argues, the modern Arab poet (and by extension, Arab culture as a whole) has been under a "double siege," combining a dependency on the West with "a foetal relationship" with Arab Islamic tradition (1990, 79–81). In short, he claims that while "the prevailing Arab culture derives from the past in most of its theoretical aspects . . . its technique comes mainly from the West" (80). By viewing modernity as something primarily technological in nature, writers in Arabic fostered a dependency on Western models, even as they made gestures of reviving ancient Arabic forms. Instead of deploying the Arab modernity of Abu Nuwas or Abu Tammam, Adonis argues that writers and thinkers of the *nahda* fused a delusional relationship with the Arab past—as a static, ahistorical object—with a dependent and imitative relationship with Western technology and cultural forms.[14]

Whereas Adonis argues that only the Arabic language may function as the instrument of an authentically Arab modernity, Meddeb exploits French in order to conduct what is in some ways an even more radical inquiry into the notion of authenticity itself. *Talismano* and *Phantasia* transform the French language into the passive medium for forms of innovation and technique that are specifically Arabic and Islamic, but which also reveal the threads of precolonial, pan-Mediterranean forms of cultural *métissage*. Both the hegemony of French and the near-absence of Arabic in the text, however, only reinscribe such cultural techniques into the realm of the virtual. By superimposing ("transgraphing") the gestures of Arabic calligraphy and the practice of walking through the city onto the neural networks of memory and desire, Meddeb inscribes Arab cultural practices into French at the level of the trace. His text reinhabits Arab-Islamic cultural practices such as calligraphy, whose meanings, like any cultural activity, derive from the specificity of situation and context, but which the West has misrecognized as "arabesques" that it has often interpreted as merely ornamental signs of the nonunitary mental deportment of Arab peoples.

Meddeb crosses Arabic and European critiques of decadence as his text performs a Saidian exposé of Orientalism's "formless" mutations in the context of globalization. As Meddeb makes the French language play host to invasive cultural practices of Islam, he also contaminates the dualistic notion of a healthy Occident encountering a sick Orient, an action he performs with the Nietzschean viruses of multiplicity and genealogy. *Talismano* and *Phantasia* both theorize the disease of the postcolonial Arab state and trace the steps of a possible cure, cutting through the trauma of a malignant past and affirming a virtual Islam in the very space opened by its erasure.

Meddeb's first two novels submit the conventional structures and syntax of the French language to the idiosyncrasies of the narrator's body as it moves through a variety of landscapes, navigating between the worlds of Tunis and Paris, between two discourses of decline. Whereas *Talismano* maintains a loose connection to a plot during its extended foray through the medina of Tunis, *Phantasia*, in a somewhat less fractured prose that leans more toward the form of the poetic essay, wanders mostly through the streets and metro stations of Paris. In her essay on *Talismano*, Dina Al-Kassim explores how the entwined circuits of walking and writing in the novel represent an attempt to reconfigure the narrative pathways that have led to the current impasse of the North African postcolony. The itinerary followed in *Phantasia*, which begins by superimposing the neural network of memory and the drives onto the chronotopic "networks of travel" (walking-writing in time and space—or "calligraphesis") developed in *Talismano*, allows us to take Al-Kassim's stimulating analysis even further. She defines Meddeb's reconfiguration of the postcolonial imagination as a hybrid structure that fuses the spiral path of the medina with the grid of the Western city. However, a reading of both novels together shows that, rather than joining, fusing, or simply grafting together elements of divergent cultures, the texts superimpose such elements onto each other so that each cancels out the other, yet both remain as traces in the cancellations performed by the text. In the space cleared by this mutual cancellation, Meddeb's writing describes the path of a truth that only applies at the moment of its operation, what Alain Badiou has called "situational truth" (2002, 16, 129), and which disarms the totalizing fantasies of both the colony and the postcolony.

Talismano commences with the narrator suddenly in the middle of the signifying labyrinth of the medina "Here I am back again expressed daedal city, moved to be distracted by childhood: to rediscover old tastes through the diversions of Tunis" (Me voici de retour exprimé ville à dédale, ému à me distraire d'enfance: a retrouver des saveurs anciennes à travers les déduits de Tunis) (15).[15] The reader is instantly thrust, *in media res*, into the "expressed daedal city" which superimposes layer upon layer—the text upon the city upon the narrating subject—all traveling through the labyrinth of memory. *Phantasia*, on the other hand, begins with a creation *ex nihilo* of the narrating voice in the middle of the signifying labyrinth of the body's neural network:

> When the body is immobilized in the lava boiling up within it. Nerves vibrating molten steel heating a thousand fires that mill the head. Pile of grain, dust skull. Exposed, the brain abandoned to reconstruct rags and faces. Visions are superimposed then eclipsed before they reappear piercing, tumultuous, unforeseen.

> Quand le corps est immobilisé dans la lave qui en lui bouillonne. Nerfs vibrant coulée d'acier chauffant mille feux qui égrugent la tête. Tas de grains, crâne poussière. A vif, le cerveau abandonné à reconstruire des lambeaux et figures. Se superposent les visions, puis s'éclipsent avant de reparaître lancinantes, bruyantes, imprévisibles. (11)

The text immediately overlays the circuits of this "labyrinth shot through with nerves" onto the circuits *within* the images that are circulating through the network of memory. The narrating subject recalls the pathways of a garden filled with jasmine and pomegranate trees, evoking the Tunisia of Meddeb's childhood, as these pathways become cancelled by the straight and narrow lines of a French garden that shares the geometry of a modern French city. The opening passage of *Phantasia* describes the process by which the idyll of the narrator's Maghrebian childhood becomes internalized and entered into the realm of the symbolic, and from which it reemerges only as a muted and restricted ghost of itself:

Garden of orange and pomegranate trees, jasmine and roses. Avenues cut across it, disturb its harmony, change its cadence. The thick lines, it seems, smother the melody. Hidden, the rhythm is discovered as the object becomes internal. The time of an impregnation, and the connection is revealed. In my garden, the pathways, avenues without the space for their deployment, compel the rhythm and obscure it. They superimpose a pseudo-imperial order upon it, strangled like an imperative uttered by a hoarse voice inside a crater. Paths traced following the gesture of the commander. (11–12)

The networks of compulsive memory become a phantasmagoria of culturally marked external spaces that are haunted by specters driven to return in compulsive and obsessive ways. The paths and walkways of this garden of nerves also maintain control over a mysterious and indeterminate music; the well-worn paths, however, "superimpose a pseudo-imperial order" on this memory music, and instead follow "the gesture of the commander" (12).

Meddeb's garden of foreclosed music clearly evokes psychoanalytic models of the unconscious, with its repressions, returns, and superego. This gesture of locating the psychic past among the ruins of Empire also occurs in Freud's *Civilization and Its Discontents*. To illustrate the past's imperishability within the mind, Freud takes his reader on a tour of Rome, whose ruins "are found dovetailed into the jumble of the great metropolis," just as the remnants of a subject's past would still be embedded in the very structures of his or her present mental life (18). Freud immediately retracts the visual representation of his tour through Rome, however, claiming the impossibility of "representing [mental faculties] in pictorial terms" (19). Both Freud and Meddeb present their itineraries as chronotopes that condense time and space into a composite allegorical image that each of them proceeds to cancel out in different ways. Meddeb sketches out the beginnings of a panoptic map of his imperial mind-garden, but he overlays this sketch on top of so many other images in such rapid succession that the images blur and only the gesture of overlaying itself remains. Freud plays a game of *fort/da* with his deliberately faulty map of Rome, first sketching a vivid picture of the city, then snatching it away, leaving only a negative image as proof of our passage through the ruins. Whereas Freud's cancellation imprints a ghostly image of imperial decay in the mind of his reader in historical time, Meddeb traces the virtual paths of symbolic annihilation in corporeal time.

The most crucial difference between Meddeb's and Freud's psychic tours, however, lies in the significance that Meddeb attributes to Islam's iconoclasm as a primary motivator for his writing practice. *Talismano* and *Phantasia* both conceive of the gesture of calligraphy as a traversal of the medina in terms of a necessary loss of primal, compulsive images: "I look behind things as the calligrapher who studies, inside the letter, the image that gave birth to it. In the memory of the hieroglyph, the ideogram, what excites the calligrapher's eye facing his alphabet if not the loss of the image, mourning of the letter" (*Je regarde derrière les choses comme le calligraphe qui scrute dans la lettre l'image qui lui a donné naissance. Au souvenir du hiéroglyphe, de l'idéogramme, qu'agite l'oeil du calligraphe face à son alphabet sinon la perte de l'image, deuil de la lettre*) (1986, 20). Meddeb does not simply oppose the itinerary of calligraphy to the map of the image, à la Michel de Certeau, but rather he positions the map, the image, the representation—all of which imply a panoptic surveillance of the symbolic networks of city-garden-writing-nerves—both in front of and within the gesture of writing. In Lacanian terms, the image in Meddeb's reading of Islamic aesthetics functions as the primary signifier, the unsaid word of the traumatic real that motivates the entire chain of signifiers surrounding it. Meddeb does not require explicit recourse to psychoanalysis, however, as he foregrounds this practice of suppressing representational images as being interior to the practice of everyday life in societies that derive from the symbolic structuration of Islam. The traversal of the space of the medina as a kind of three-dimensional physiological calligraphy emerges, in Meddeb's texts, as the process by which the prohibition of figural representation structures the symbolic and imaginary fields of the Islamic subject.

Against these networks of everyday Islamic life, Meddeb describes the panopticon of the postcolonial state, which seeks to create a totalizing map of the city and its movements. Near the beginning of *Talismano*'s tortuous excursion through the medina of Tunis, the text presents the reader with a series of perspectives that reach successively higher, each attaining a wider purview than the last. Beginning with the narrator's view as a *promeneur solitaire*, whose "senses splatter the itinerary's coherence," the text takes a brief detour through "cellars and labyrinths of torture" inside the "civilian prison." Meddeb attributes such labyrinths to the "one-eyed and other bruisers" (des borgnes et autres cogneurs) who fight to preserve their "tribe of privilege" through the "nationalization of repression" (17). The text points toward how the postcolonial nation-state has reproduced colonial discipline and carceral punishment (and within the very prisons built by France during the colonial era). The next level up reveals the walls and watchtowers of the medina, whose limited perspectives are destroyed and blinded by the panopticon of the prison: "Razing the walls and the watchtowers: the civilian prison bloodies the gaze" (17–18). Above the prison, however, is a repository of disease that eats away at the very faculty of sight: "the prison is surmounted by the institute that treats trachoma. To the gangrene that separates the body from its energy is added the plague that gnaws the eye right through to the blood" (18). The walking narrator's street-eye view, however, internalizes a birds-eye view that oversees and pierces even this diseased and violent kingdom of the blind:

> But eagles aren't affected by incarceration and the narrowness of the cells. But screeching eagles don't let themselves get plucked. The eye multiplying glances, omnipresent, unruly, traversing the walls, laying

waste to the narrow windows, frightening the guards, immobile yet global, present in every detail, in this sovereign lucidity that never sees things divided into segments to travel through then abandon to lend attention to some other moment or place, watching with such acuity of presence all the floating cells, moving, projections and memory . . . free in ample wingbeats at the moment of ascent enlightened nocturnal, endless journey to the heights, to the eventual quest for prey; the journey alone asserts itself eloquent motif. (18)

This passage makes visible the violent repression of the postcolonial state that strives to makes its violence invisible. The text replaces the sovereign eye of police surveillance with the fluid totality of the text's own "sovereign lucidity." Meddeb accesses the eagle's eye in order to pierce the walls of the prison, unscrewing the locks from their doors, as it were, thereby revealing the guards inside the prison's panopticon, making them the object of its gaze. In the same way that the calligrapher's pen is motivated by the loss of the image, Meddeb's text is motivated by the eagle's view of the world, a view that is impossible to represent but whose gestures are traced in the gestures of the allographic journey.

Just as the itineraries of *Talismano* traverse the map generated by the corruptive power of the postcolonial Maghrebi nation-state (exemplified by the prison), so too does the text combat the resuscitated representations used in Islamic reformist and Arab nationalist discourses. The text explicitly opposes its own bodily writing practice, whose power emerges through its own "decadent" singularity, to the practice of embodiment, understood as an ontological representation of the body viewed externally. Meddeb concretizes this metaphor of embodiment in scenes that depict the narrator's battle against a monstrous idol created by an apocalyptic-minded street preacher (reminiscent of both Wattar's Bu al-Arwah and Djaout's time-traveling Ibn Tumart, discussed in Chapter 4). He uses the idol to illustrate the grotesque impossibility of the very concept of the revival of cultural authenticity, which, he clearly suggests, has marked not only the discourse of the *nahda*, but also contemporary nationalist discourse in Islamic societies and the Islamists' crude attempts to revive the past. Meddeb's radical view of a polyphonic Islam, on the other hand, develops a situational truth that privileges the perennially disruptive force of the monotheistic message. During a digression on Islamic grammatology, Meddeb explicitly aligns his textual practice with the poetics of calligraphy: "We don't write with the intention of embodying an idea, of merging with a theoretical generation, of formulating a truth, of preparing minds to welcome a message, but of setting into truth [*mettre en vrai*] the possibility of laying out in a single gesture the One that ensures our long-term stability" (111). Contrasted to Meddeb's transgressive view of Islam is that of the fanatical preacher who created the idol, and who incites a crowd to stitch together bits and pieces from exhumed corpses, while urging them to rally around their monstrous creation, which they do in a kind of orgiastic anarchy. To fight this chaos, the narrator enlists the help of an Arab goldsmith, Maître Mahmud, and a Jewish goldsmith, Ya'qub, in an attempt to mummify the "fetish body" of this "anthropomorphic reconstitution of myth" (83). In this way, the text thus endorses a multicultural coalition of living forces against a vision of community stitched together from the exhumed remains of the past.

Talismano opposes its own gestural practice to the grotesque and failed representation of the Islamic past embodied by the idol, and Meddeb clearly locates this opposition within the domain of Islamic thought that theorizes the divine as unrepresentable and prohibits attempts to embody, imitate, or represent it. Al-Kassim rightly points out that Meddeb's aesthetic concerns are not, as some critics have argued, primarily metaphysical and postmodern in some disembodied, ahistorical sense, but have everything to do with a creative and historicizing engagement against the postcolonial state (2001, 128, 136). Her own argument, however, obscures the importance of the cultural specificity of Islam for Meddeb, whose project is not just a more liberating and disruptive reading of Islamic tradition, but also an Islamization of French, an embedding of specifically Islamic practices in the heart of the European imagination: "Those who Islamize calligraph more than they paint [ceux qui s'islamisèrent calligraphient plus qu'ils ne peignent]; or rather dissolve the sense of the written by the full and joyful gesture of the calligrapher" (110). To "Islamize" is thus to perform an ecstatic abrogation of the law in the very gesture of inscribing it, a double gesture of inscription and erasure, wherein a virtual image is all that remains.

This combat between the urban calligraphers, pitting the narrator, Mahmud, and Ya'qub against the taxidermists of tradition worshipping the idol, reaches its climax when Mahmud clashes with Muhammad 'Abduh (1849–1905), one of the leading proponents of Islamic modernism and reform. As the crowd marches through the streets, and everything begins precipitating toward orgiastic and violent excess, Meddeb revives this historical icon of Islamic reformism in order to stage an exhortation against the decadence of the Arab world since the *nahda*. Faced with the spectacle of the savage crowd, 'Abduh asks:

What will civilized people say? We have called you to the renaissance by means of a return to our pure sources, to the fundamentals of our religion, to the age of justice; we have, using [the method of jurisprudential] agreement, shown how our Book contains all the technological miracles that are transforming the century. (229)

Shocked at the revelry of the crowd, 'Abduh rehearses the clichés of Islamic reform in the era of the *nahda* in a way that vividly illustrates Adonis's notion of the "double siege" of Arab culture—between a rigid Islamic past supplying theory and a progressive Western present supplying technology. 'Abduh's claim that *fiqh* can reveal how the *Qur'an* anticipates all the inventions of modern science reiterates the efforts of early Islamic modernizers, including those of the historical Muhammad 'Abduh, to prove that Islam was not incompatible with Western science.[16] Meddeb's presentation of this scene transforms 'Abduh himself into the very idol rousing the crowd to ever-increasing levels of debauchery and disorder, which in turn fuels his outrage. Despite Mahmud's respect for the great man, the goldsmith cannot keep from bursting into laughter and affirming the Islam of blasphemy and drunken revolt while saying that "men of god and of reforms should be thrashed" (230).

Meddeb's text revels in such transgressions, but in a way that is necessarily linked to a foundational word as the impetus, or organizing principle, of this transgression. Adonis claims that true Arab modernity has always been not just an impotent criticism of the past, which is what the *nahda* ultimately amounts to for him, but a forceful refutation of the past (78), which is seen not just in Abu Nuwas but in the *Qur'an* itself. Meddeb theorizes Arab modernity in a similar way, saying that "all that's great in Islamic culture, all that's beautiful, came about not by the application of the Islamic letter of the law, but rather through the transgression or at least the skirting of that letter, in a will to forget and ignore it" (2002, 8). Instead of measuring decadence by temporal distance from the originary text, which is what Adonis claims the notion of the *nahda* ultimately accomplished, both Adonis and Meddeb conceive of decadence as the freezing of the disruptive power of writing and mobility as a situated practice. This revised mode of cultural evaluation conceives of decline in terms of a separation of the body or the text from its potential energy. Mahmud's praise of the transgressive strain within Islam echoes Meddeb's emphasis on the history of dissent behind the very rise of Islam, seen, for example, in the political struggles for Medina. Responding to 'Abduh's typically condemnatory exhortation, Mahmud joyously affirms the crowd's transgressive qualities: "We are drunks and blasphemers; we will not give ourselves over to speculators; we have participated in the rapture of the black stone; what do I see around me if not Zanj and Qarmatians" (1987, 229). Meddeb traces two moments in the genealogy of transgressions organized around the Islamic letter when he has Mahmud evoke the series of revolts of black slaves (*al-zanj*) during the seventh to ninth centuries against their Iraqi masters, and the establishment in 899 of the Qarmatian state, which was based on egalitarian sexual relations and a conception of history as cyclical, self-renewing, and ascendant. The text thus aligns its own transgressive practices with those of an Islamic past whose renewal has traditionally occurred through acts of revolt and transgressions of the letter, not in impotent returns to or reformations of it.

The Arabic-Islamic modernity that Meddeb's text traces neither draws a transcendent map of the networks of everyday life, nor manufactures a mimetic embodiment of a fixed truth. In its conception of temporality, the past does not become an immovable point providing an absolute measure by which the present may be evaluated; instead, the past functions as the heterogeneous element that circulates within the homogeneous time of technology and the abstract space of the modern European city. Adonis reveals that his interest in certain forms of ancient poetry comes from the potential of such forms to intervene in the mechanical notion of a temporality that is only determined by the state of technology. In this way, Meddeb demonstrates how alternate experiences of modernity function to chip away at the Euro-centric model of modernity, revealing it disintegrating and coming apart at the seams. Réda Bensmaïa, in his essay on the site of the medina in Maghrebi writing, asserts that "to write/live the médina is to travel through time, to reinscribe the time of history and that of the '*durée*' of the steps of walking, in the abstract non-time of the concept-city" as it was theorized by Michel de Certeau (2003, 118). The practical time of Meddeb's writing comes close to what Dipesh Chakrabarty in *Provincializing Europe* has called a "timeknot": an entanglement of temporalities (2000, 111–13, 243) where the past coexists within the present as its supplement. Meddeb's narrator, whom Bensmaïa categorizes as a "*médinant*,"[17] weaves such a knot as he walks and writes through the city of the text, visiting the gestures of Arabic calligraphic art onto the French text, cognitively mapping Islam onto the networks of both "old" Tunis and "new" Paris. We are left with the speculative, critical specter of colonial modernity.

Bensmaïa claims that even though "the medina has nothing to do with Baudelaire's melancholic Paris," the *médinant* nonetheless represents "a new type of flâneur" (2003, 166). The overmapping that occurs in *Phantasia*, however, reveals an uncomfortable overlap between these two spaces and the different practices associated with them. Instead of simply privileging the *médinant* over the flâneur, or viewing them as two opposed figures lacking a common element, Meddeb's text invites us to read the *médinant* with the *flâneur*. For Benjamin, the experience of the nineteenth-century European city is distinguished by a stalling of time—and the dialectic of history—brought about by the phantasmagoria of urban images and the shock effects of urban mechanization. By traversing the symbolic space of the "abstract city," Meddeb's text reinscribes the lived practices of Islam into the circuits of a Paris ruled by what Benjamin theorizes as empty, universal, homogeneous time. Likewise, he reinscribes these same practices into the homogeneous time articulated by Arabism and Islamism. By writing Islam without Arabic, which even a radical innovator like Adonis concedes as the chief guarantor of an authentic Arab modernity, Meddeb challenges the primacy of the Arabic language as the unifying element in Arab identity, and subverts the history of privileging Arabs as being closer to the "pure" Islam of the Prophet Muhammad. Meddeb also disrupts the cultural continuity and political agency that Arabic was supposed to sustain, while reinscribing this disruption as a trace that motivates his own French text. The pathways of the city function as utopian dream-spaces for the *flâneur*, spaces that alienate him and strand him in ambiguity, despite the apparently intimate relation these spaces bear to him and his past: "The street conducts the flâneur into a vanished time . . . into a past all the more spellbinding because it is not his own, not private. Nevertheless, it always remains the time of childhood" (1999, 416). The writing of the medina is also a writing of childhood and the past, but in a way that seeks a cure for the trauma of individual and collective history in the gesture of traversing symbolic space in all its traumatic intimacy.

The most uncomfortable area of overlap between the *flâneur* and the *médinant* lies in their related ways of reading and evaluating the signs and images of public (symbolic) space. Benjamin relates his fascination with the figure of the *flâneur*, and with Baudelaire as a peculiar type of *flâneur*, to the practice of walking through the European city and the emerging importance of symptomology in the nineteenth century. The *flâneur* reads the surfaces of people (but also things, buildings and places), and by superimposing the succession of images, he hallucinates phantasms that he then categorizes into *types*. Differences become erased in this inductive hallucination, as what is most distinct gets reduced to the exemplar of a type. The universal claims of this process of typology are anchored in the singularity of the individual, however, as the truth that is derived by the flâneur "becomes something living; it lives solely in the rhythm by which statement and counterstatement displace each other in order to think each other" (Benjamin 1999, 418). The *flâneur* overlaps the *médinant* precisely in the operation of a situational truth that emerges with the movements of the idiosyncratic body. Yet for Meddeb's *médinant* the itinerary through the text (and the city) does not arrive at a terminal image whose value is that of a commodity to be exhibited, which is precisely the endpoint of Benjamin's theoretical path. Rather, the *médinant* cuts through the images of colonial and postcolonial fantasy, inscribing the gestures of calligraphy within the French text and the French city that have produced these fantasies.

Meddeb's texts formulate their task in terms of the severing of such fantastic knots that both evokes and subverts the language of the psychoanalytic cure. *Talismano* theorizes its own textual practice as a "talking cure" that seeks to "correct the social body" of postcolonial Maghreb and "to rectify the orientalist consensus by eliminating the spy-crazed virus [*le virus de l'espionite*] from its organism" (1987, 57). *Phantasia* locates its task at the malignant intersection of racism, power, and *ressentiment*:

> Between the power that sees in you a sub-being and the humiliation that defies revenge; between the warlike means that crush you and the harassment of the weak ripened by blind hatred, a monstrous nodule is concealed, which it is up to me to sever. In order to conceal the ground beneath the scowling eye of the fitful ones who occupy the political territories of Islam, it would be appropriate to work to make this territory interior to Europe. (1986, 118)

The text performs this cure in a way that partially resonates with Lacan's version of the psychoanalytic cure, "traversing the fantasy," which aims to disrupt the subject's fantasy by crossing through language to show how it supports the traumatic real. Whereas the psychoanalytic talking cure seeks to insert the subject into the position of the unconscious ("*Wo es war, soll Ich werden*" in Freud's famous phrase), Meddeb's *walking* cure seeks to insert the Islamic subject into the symbolic networks of Europe. His textual project thus aligns with the socioeconomic reality of Maghrebian immigrants who "invest" French society—as site of imperial power—with what Hardt and Negri called their "subversive desires." Like Meddeb, Lacan describes fantasy as a kind of tumor that gradually accrues around the symbolic: "a tissue . . . envelops . . . the network in which, on occasion, something is caught." The only way to understand this process of tumorous obstruction, Lacan claims, is "to map the network," to go back and forth over one's ground, to cross one's own path, and to check and recheck it always in the same way (1998, 45). Meddeb's text describes the path of this journey that begins with the opening up of desire and proceeds towards what Žižek describes as the "closure" of the drives, a movement whose satisfactions derive from "endlessly repeating the same failed gesture" (1997, 30). The cure for imperial decadence proposed by Meddeb ultimately reinscribes the new fantasy of a virtually secularized Islam in the place of the old fantasies crossed out by his text.

The migrant desire described in *Talismano* and *Phantasia* traverses the fantasies of French Republican universalism, Arab-Islamic nationalism, and Islamic fundamentalism, which, if we read them in Žižek's terms, appear as articulations of public law requiring the transgressive and more coercive supplements of unspoken law to sustain them (1997, 28–29). "Fantasy," Žižek writes, "designates precisely this unwritten framework which tells us how we are to understand the letter of the Law" (29). Just as the "universal" *droits de l'homme* declared by the French Revolution tacitly privileged white, male property owners, so, too, does the Republican ideal in contemporary France (as *"une et indivisible"*) still favor those who are *français de souche* ("of French stock"), a fantasmatic euphemism for "white." The fantasies that prop up the Maghrebian Arab states and Islamist groups, which both promise liberation from foreign domination, can also divide society against itself across lines of race, ethnicity, and gender. Meddeb's text allows us to suggest that the migration of "new barbarians" across these fantasies has led to the violent attempts to reinforce them, ultimately resulting in the catastrophic violence that accompanies this traversal.

Phantasia performs the cognitive mapping of its "cure" by traveling through the symbolic networks of the metropole, creating a fantastic montage of images, gestures, and languages, all superimposing childhood memories of the medina onto contemporary Paris. After a hellish sojourn beneath Paris, the narrator climbs a broken escalator out of the Place de la Nation metro station:

> A TV screen in my head broadcasts a fantasia on the arid steppe, fleet horse race, galloping on the moving ground. The dust clouds constrict my larynx. Only with effort does man lift himself up onto animals. The dust spreads out. Shivers bristle the skin. The smell of the fray sickens me. The stallions rear up. The race stops at the level of the tent. The stage disappears behind the curtain of smoke and dust that is assimilated into the gray veil of Paris. (136)

The text first enters the labyrinth through the network of mass media, replacing the television images (discussed earlier in the chapter) of Arab-Islamic *ressentiment*—car bombs, "maniacal Ayatollahs"—with the heroic image of the equestrian *fantasia*: an orchestrated display of Arab horsemanship and military skill, an image famously orientalized by Delacroix. Meddeb's use of the word "fantasia" also evokes the *lingua franca* of the Maghreb, a language emblematic of the multicultural *métissages* of precolonial North Africa, which were obscured by the bicultural *métissage* brought about by French colonialism.[18] To the phantasms of Orientalist mass media, Meddeb adds the phantasm of a common language haunted by the specters of Spanish, Italian, Arabic, and Turkish. Here, and in many other passages that evoke various forms of transcultural practices, Meddeb reverses the direction of the truth that Benjamin's flâneur establishes. Instead of superimposing many faces to create a single type, the path traced by the *médinant* opens a space for difference without falling into the destructive fantasy of types or races. While for Benjamin the masses are the "agitated veil" through which Baudelaire sees Paris (1969, 168), the homogeneous gray veil of Paris "assimilates" the visions of *métissage* dreamed up by the metropolitan *médinant*. The veil that both reveals and conceals the Orientalist fantasies of the metropole feminizes the city and distinguishes it from the *fantasia*'s masculine theater of war.

This veil's assimilation of powerful images from the Arab imaginary awakens the narrator's anguish, which compels him to retrace his steps in a different space. As he ascends the stairs out of the Paris Metro at Place de la Nation, which is dominated by Aimé-Jules Dalou's 1899 monument *Le Triomphe de la République*, the narrator superimposes his memories of Tunis onto the images of the French capital:

> Inside the urban décor an obsession torments my being and transports me to the long street that divides the medina of Tunis between north and south. A series of stops line the way to the school. The talkative barber, the lascivious grocer, the girls in pink smocks, the generous aunt's balcony, the hammam's noria,[19] the blind mule, the underground bakery, the courtyard of initiations, square of Eros, the green mosque, the ruined mausoleum, the dark corridor, the public latrines, the squalid garbage, the stairway rising over the walls, the boulevard crossed by white Filibus bicycles, the mountainous street, the dead-end that terminates at the school across from the gardens whose enclosures crumble beneath bougainvillea and hibiscus. Endless visions, leaving the bomb shelter, I advance between the shop-windows, beneath the

awnings of the bistros, exhausted by a carnivorous desire, enclosed in the circle of beatings, where blood trickles down, in the rites of mutilation, at the level of instinct, the window of love orients a sudden beam of light that disarms the minotaur in the labyrinth. (1986, 137)

As the narrator emerges onto the scene of metropolitan erasure and hallucination, the neural networks "transport" him along the established paths of obsessive memory of his Tunisian childhood. As in the description of the garden discussed above, the text spirals down into the circuits of travel that function *within* the images shuttling through its own circuits of memory: The stairs rising over the medina walls resonate with the narrator's steps up the escalator, while the Filibus bicycles crisscross in front of the Parisian street traffic. Despite the precise affection evoked in this memory, however, the path still leads to a dead end. By mapping this montage onto the "assimilating veil" of Paris, however, the text disarms the threat within the networks it traces (the threat of an imperialistic superego?), even if it does not finally escape from the labyrinth. On the contrary, *Phantasia* ends with the promise of an even deeper foray into the winding passages of the Tunisian text-city. Possibly also referring to the revision of *Talismano*, completed the same year that *Phantasia* was published, the narrator says that "tomorrow morning I will redo the itinerary of *Talismano*" (*Le lendemain matin, je refais l'itinéraire de* Talismano) (208). Meddeb's textual practice does not seek to escape from the trauma of an interrupted genealogy, nor to get lost within the melancholic maze of exile; rather, it would, in the words of Abdelkebir Khatibi, "keep a space open to war" (1993, 6), where the panoptic eye cannot follow, and where the tracing of the network reconfigures the meaning of the trace itself: "To give ourselves over through the written without giving you up, to exhaust your eye through the arabesque of words, to propose networks of travel to you, to enjoin fracture upon everything that offers itself to the eyes" (A nous livrer par l'écrit sans vous donner prise, à vous fatiguer l'oeil par l'arabesque des mots, à vous proposer les réseaux du voyage, à vous enjoindre fêlure à tout ce qui s'offre aux yeux) (1987, 243).

The value of immigrant desire is revealed in Meddeb's affirmation of the body's subversive singularity. This singular body is also shot through with myriad networks of specific shared practices that make possible the virtual confluence of the multitude. The question of culture, which Hardt and Negri almost entirely evacuate from their critique of Empire, reappears in Meddeb as both a technique for circulating in ways contrary to imperial demands, and also as coordinates for cognitively mapping one's position within the global system. The symbolic structures of Islam, the joyful gestures of calligraphy, and one's footsteps through the medina all may serve to virtually link the idiosyncratic productive power of Maghrebian immigrants in France and beyond. Meddeb's texts offer a combative writing that would exhaust the panoptic Orientalist view, whether it aims to exhibit the contents of the "Arab mind" or to expose the interior of domestic spaces using bombs and television cameras. In the age of war, terror, and spectacle, Pierre Klossowski's rear-view affirmation of Nietzsche helps clarify Meddeb's intersecting discourses of cultural health and morbidity. According to Klossowski, Nietzsche "predicted that this future [the nihilistic twentieth and twenty-first centuries] would be convulsive, to the point where our own convulsions are caricatures of his thought" (1999, 15). In a similar way, one can say that the machinery of the spectacle has since provided ample confirmation of Meddeb's prediction concerning the aesthetic necessity of a violent response to September 11 and subsequent attacks. Auguring from the perspective of the social diagnostician, both Meddeb and Nietzsche deploy discourses of decadence to articulate a future that is already inscribed in the past. For Nietzsche, the world will fall victim to the familiar convulsions of fin-de-siècle European decadence, while for Meddeb, the indifferent eye of globalized technology will seek equilibrium through violent spectacle. Meddeb's "networks of travel," however, engineer different ways of seeing and understanding the world in order to imagine a future emerging within the predictable circuits of power and spectacle.

CONCLUSION

Toward a Contrapuntal Double Critique of Colonial Modernity

Viewed from an exclusively internal (noncomparative) perspective, any individual narrative of decadence is necessarily marked by what Edward Said has called "the rhetoric of blame" (1993, 18). While he attributes this rhetoric primarily to the attitudes of intellectuals and writers from the formerly colonized world, this phrase quite accurately describes the entire range of discourses that I have discussed in this study, from the colonial and anticolonial accusations of decadence emerging from the language of authenticity and the symptom to the postcolonial reiterations and traversals of this discourse. It is as an alternative to this rhetorical impasse that Said proposes his often-imitated critical method of "contrapuntal reading," which is a way of accounting for the "intertwined and overlapping histories" (18) that constitute the subject not just of comparative literature but of the global political economy. The diverse styles of social evaluation that determine the epistemological structure of colonial decadence can *only* be read contrapuntally, I would argue. In other words, they can be read neither from a purely internal perspective nor from the external perch of a supposedly objective observer. Instead, any attempt to achieve a broader view of a planetary discourse of decadence requires one to account for the ways that the rhetoric of blame seeks to appropriate the discourse of the other and to transpose the synchronous enmities and contradictions generated by global capitalism into a temporal *narrative* of power.

The primary reason for trying to account for something like a discourse of planetary decadence in the first place is precisely so that we may more clearly be able to differentiate this narrative, which is characterized by its fantasmatic unhistorical misrecognitions, from something that can more properly be called *history*. Slavoj Žižek can help us understand how the *nahda*'s narration of the "awakening" of an Arab subject of history emerges from the acute awareness of the Arab world's very state of abject decay. "The paradox to be fully accepted," writes Žižek, "is that when a certain historical moment is (mis)perceived as the moment of loss of some quality, upon closer inspection it becomes clear that the lost quality emerged only at this very moment of its alleged loss" (1997, 12–13). What the Arabic intellectual of the nineteenth century perceives as his lost authenticity appears only at the instant of claims regarding its disappearance, which, as I have tried to demonstrate, has both everything and nothing to do with the "influence" of European liberal thought. Furthermore, the specific accounts of "awakening" or "renaissance" peculiar to Arabic discourse— from 'Abduh and al-Kawakibi to al-Shidyaq and Antun—attempt to resolve the deeper antagonisms generated by the clash of nineteenth-century imperialisms into narratives of progress *or* decadence. It is only by reading these antagonisms contrapuntally (simultaneously) that what Žižek calls their "absolute synchronicity" may be reinscribed in the history of colonial modernity as a traumatic genealogical interruption. The discourses of French *décadence* and Arabic *nahda* both fail to account for the complex structure of the historical disruptions produced by colonial modernity. The difference between *narrative* and *history* reveals itself here in the discrepancy between discourses of lost authenticity and the radical paradigm shifts that have indeed transformed the globe in the wake of European colonialism. "A true historical break," Žižek tells us, "does not simply designate the 'regressive' loss (or 'progressive' gain) of something, but *the shift in the very grid which enables us to measure losses and gains*" (13). The ultimate expression of Orientalism, the Holocaust,[1] was precisely such a break, whose immeasurable human losses have radically transformed the narrative and evaluative tools we use to understand the event itself. By demonstrating how a select group of texts has configured collective losses and gains in different periods and contexts, this study has endeavored to trace the very *decay* of decadence, reimagined as a "shifting grid" that may be used to measure the profound antagonisms that structure contemporary political and economic global relations.

Conclusion: Toward a Critique of Colonial Modernity

In making the case for the importance of "decadence" for an understanding of the political and cultural traffic between France and the Arab world since the nineteenth century, this book has necessarily run up against the perils of comparative analysis and critique. If "ideology," in Louis Althusser's formulation, "represents the imaginary relationship of individuals to their real conditions of existence" (109), the work of global comparativism must navigate the ways that the imaginary relationships established through Orientalism and decadence circulate, and how they distort, disintegrate, defamiliarize, and cancel out events, ideas, and entire societies and continents. In this sense, contrapuntal reading can never be a mere juxtaposition of two iterations or expressions of historically specific being, understood as positivist objects of cultural analysis. What is needed is a way of reading that can travel between the positive signs of fantasy and the negative spaces that would constitute a postcapitalist, postcolonial relationship between society and the material conditions of life. This would be a contrapuntal reading with the ability to deconstruct the oppositions constitutive of the field of imperialist discourse, but which does not disable oppositional, anti-imperialist critique—a kind of decolonized deconstructive mode of contrapuntal reading.

The work of Moroccan writer Abdelkebir Khatibi opens up precisely such a critical path, and one which will return us to Saidian contrapuntal reading. In his 1974 theoretical analysis of Moroccan popular culture, *La blessure du nom propre* (The Wound of the Proper Noun/Name), Khatibi elaborates on the term that represented his critical procedure in its most condensed form, the *intersigne*:

> Intersign signifies: mark, indication, "mysterious connection between two facts" (le Robert); for us: multifaceted sanguine crystal, precision-cut, and whose glassy and fragile iridescence wounds the body and the *Nom propre* [both the "proper noun" and the "first name"], reinscribing the crystalline symmetry otherwise: identity/difference. Between the first definition and the second, the entire question of the sign is played out; from a positivist semiotics to a transversal semiotics, it is still the concept of writing that will have to be invested in the body while checking it against the Qur'anic text and the Arabic language. (Khatibi 1974, 16)

The *inter-* of *intersign* signifies an interstitial site between signs, languages, utterances, and critical strategies; but it also *acts*: It refracts, wounds, destructures, disfigures all these levels of signification. It is a procedure for a certain mode of reinscription. Yet the *intersign* is no mere sign, composed of a signifier and a signified. It is no mere *product* of a signifying event. Nor can its function be reduced to that of multiplication or the production of diversity. Khatibi's *intersignatures* radically reroute the possibilities of critique, of thought, of language(s), but also of fiction, poetry, that is, of *genres* of all kinds. The critical method developed in *Decadent Orientalisms* has likewise aimed to trace the outlines of the mutual disfigurations of decadence as an engine of colonial modernity, and to think through the interference generated in the exchanges circulating between France and the Arab world.

The book for which Khatibi is best known in North America, *Amour bilingue* (translated as *Love in Two Languages*), generates its particular kind of static or interference (*brouillage*) in the shuttling back and forth between genders *and* genres. The intimate dialogue of the text is uttered in a split tongue that superimposes the male and female protagonists onto one another in the creation of something like an androgynous subject of reading. Likewise, the text superimposes literary genres, namely prose fiction and the essay, text and metatext. We are left with the static caused by superimposed genres, through which Khatibi is able to force the conventions of these genres, codes, languages, and signs to broadcast their interference, the noise that one must suppress in order to maintain the integrity of each "semiotic system" in artificial isolation. Yet this noisemaking is neither a purely negative gesture nor some kind of experimental noise-for-noise's-sake. Rather, the static of the *intersign*, created through the simultaneity and superimposition of male and female, of text and metatext, is a Derridian *espacement*, an opening in the overdetermined structures of language and discourse; it is the invention of what Khatibi calls a "space of hospitality" within the language of the other. *Decadent Orientalisms* has also focused on the porousness of discursive structures in order to articulate the "absolute synchronicity" of the Arab world and France, fraught with misrecognitions and fantasmatic appropriations at the various levels of style, discourse, and epistemology.

The intersemiotic transects both close reading and its double, distant reading. If the *intersign* is operative *within* Khatibi's work, his oeuvre is also an *intersign* that can be read in broader contexts. In "Counterpoint and Double Critique in Edward Said and Abdelkebir Khatibi: A Transcolonial Comparison," Françoise Lionnet makes a welcome call for a renewed interest in Khatibi's work for comparative critique, and more specifically, for the study of postcolonial and transnational literatures. She reexamines Khatibi's critical work, focusing on the key chapters in *Maghreb pluriel*, alongside the work of Edward Said. Lionnet begins by comparing Khatibi's "double-critique" and Said's practice of "contrapuntal reading" but ends

Conclusion: Toward a Critique of Colonial Modernity 163

with an appraisal of the two authors' different approaches to the critical practice of *contrepoint*, arguing that while both thinkers should be lauded for having opened new avenues of reading, rendering minor or marginalized voices audible amidst the din of colonial and neocolonial babble, Khatibi ultimately offers a more convincing model for critique:

> Therein I believe lies the principal difference between Khatibi and Said: for although Said is interested in how "a particular type of research and knowledge begins to build up" allowing for the study of culture 'as contrapuntal ensembles' of hybrid identities (Said 1993, 52), ultimately he can only address their common ground of translatability, whereas Khatibi wants to allow for an as-yet-unthought exteriority beyond the "archeology of silence" that represses *other* languages, genders, and peoples in their unheard difference. For Said, what is translatable is that which is discernible within the overall arrangements of literary and musical high culture as the site of a historic face-off between the imperial west and those who resist its claims in their "disparities and discrepancies" (Said 1993, 114) which must eventually come to order and harmony, as in the musical interplay or counterpoint of the concert performance. (Lionnet 2012, 404).

Whereas Said's model of contrapuntal reading, first announced at the end of *Culture and Imperialism*, would seem to betray his excessive concern for "high culture" which would somehow determine what has value for academic research, Khatibi's understanding of *contrepoint*, Lionnet points out, takes its lead not from Western classical music but rather from the work of weaving and sewing, such as that done by Moroccan carpet makers. While such a claim does have a certain appeal—that Khatibi's weaving metaphor draws upon local practices while honoring women's work—Lionnet's contention here also dismisses what is distinctive about Said's understanding of counterpoint, namely its capacity to elaborate the very historical processes through which knowledge is "built up" in specific languages but not in others.

Indeed, there are valuable reasons to pursue the kind of argument Lionnet hints at here. For instance, one could read Khatibi's insistence on the *contrepoint* specific to Moroccan carpet making as an *invention of technique* that would not simply be borrowed from "Western" techniques or procedures of thought (from Nietzsche to Derrida, say); that is, by articulating his thought in relation to the work of Moroccan women who weave carpets, Khatibi is not simply filling "foreign" theory with local content, but rather he is elaborating a practice of portable reading. Chapter 6 of *Decadent*

Orientalisms works through this precise argument in the contemporary context of immigrants in France. Yet Lionnet does not base her argument on such an interpretation. Instead, she simply misreads Said's notion of contrapuntal critique and offers Khatibi's *contrepoint* of weaving in its place as a self-evidently superior critical model. The question thus becomes, are Khatibi's transversal intersemiotics—developed through readings of carpets, tattoos, literature, calligraphy, proverbs, and jokes from Moroccan and Islamic contexts—good only for reading Moroccan, Maghrebi, minor, or marginal cultural artifacts? In other words, *can Arab(ic), Islamic, or Maghrebi theory travel?* Can it travel to the self-appointed "centers" (the metropole or capital)—and there constitute itself as an exilic territory? This has been one of the questions guiding *Decadent Orientalisms*, where I have sought to reverse the direction of theoretical traffic originating in Europe, while demonstrating how non-Western writing and thought denature the discourses originating in France that dealt in the binaries of progress and decadence, modernity and development, of a "healthy Occident" and a "sick Orient."

One should not stop here, however. While there may be any number of contingent reasons for preferring the *contrepoint* of a carpet to that of a fugue, I am not entirely convinced that there is anything inherent to a beautiful Moroccan carpet that would necessarily make it a better theoretical model for transnational and transcolonial comparison than a Bach fugue. The inverse of such an affirmation would also of course be true: namely, that nothing guarantees that the hermeneutic resources of a Bach fugue would be superior to those contained within a Moroccan carpet. After all, in his text on the intersemiotics of such carpets, Khatibi set out "to study this imagination in the space of the carpet, as one studies a page of Aristotle, with the same seriousness, exposing aesthetic theories dedicated to the imaginary and the symbolic" (Merino 2013, 123–24).

This constellation of texts points in the direction of a *contrapuntal double critique*, which would cross close reading with distant reading, making selective use of the kind of poststructuralist tools that Khatibi himself develops and repurposes, but it would not stop there. Rather, such a critique would instead continue to listen for the "unheard differences" that are both interior *and* exterior to the texts and cultural products under consideration. It is Said, I would argue, more than Khatibi who prompts us to take this historical step back from the object of our analysis. A valuable instance of this kind of reading can be seen in Aamir Mufti's *Forget English! Orientalisms and World Literatures* (2016), which understands Said's philology as a kind of contrapuntal close reading that emphasizes precisely the processes of historical sedimentation which operate at multiple levels within the text *and* outside of it (discussed in this book at the end of Chapter 3).

Taking a contrapuntal double critique seriously would mean examining the textual self-disappropriation that Khatibi discusses, and which also animates his experiments with simultaneity, with distance and closeness, but it would also mean stepping back to think about the continuing predominance of dispossessed languages and discourses which Said, as well as Khatibi himself, both foregrounded in their work. (One thinks immediately, for example, of Khatibi's essay on Jacques Berque, "L'orientalisme désorienté" from 1976, two years before Said's *Orientalism*.) So instead of a "bad," Western *contrepoint* (Said and Bach) versus a "good," Maghrebi *contrepoint* (Khatibi and the Moroccan carpet), we have instead *two competing modes of simultaneity*. On the one hand, there is Khatibi's singular kind of *espacement*, what he calls "*le tissage par la syntaxe*" (weaving through syntax), a practice more on the side of superimposition, of interference or static, capable of opening up an exilic form of "hostage" within the text. On the other hand, we have Saidian simultaneity, which is perhaps more temporally and historically oriented, less about resolution, to be sure, than perpetual disruption; like exile, the simultaneity of Saidian counterpoint plays along the seams of what he calls an "unhealable rift" (Said 2000, 175), concerning itself with the historical dimensions of *planetary* relations. "Exile," Said writes, "is life led outside habitual order. It is nomadic, decentered, contrapuntal; but no sooner does one get accustomed to it than its unsettling force erupts anew" (Said 2000, 186).

So we might therefore say that Said's notion of counterpoint is primarily but not exclusively temporal-historical in nature, bound to musical forms of expression, which serve as a theoretical point of *departure*. It imagines new reading practices that can attempt to account for mobile structures of silencing as well as echo-chamber effects and divergent variations on multiple themes that seem to all be happening at once, although they are in fact each played in accordance with their own distinct time signatures. This critique—or shape of critique—occurs alongside *and at the same time as* Khatibi's somewhat more spatial understanding of counterpoint, perhaps more akin to weaving or sewing, and, in particular, articulated in places in relation to the art of Moroccan rug making. What, then, might a *contrapuntal double critique* look and sound like?

In its examination of how French and Arabic discourses of decadence and colonial modernity have cannibalized and distorted each other, *Decadent Orientalisms* takes a few tentative steps toward such a critique. The following reading of Khatibi's own reflections on exile, francophonie, pseudonymy, and syntax open up further paths of future reading. Let us first consider what he has to say about the linked questions of literary and linguistic forms of hostage, hospitality, and self-dispossession. In "The Language of the Other," Khatibi examines the particular case of "francophone writers":

> The literature whose name we bear, whatever our origin, citizenship, or nationality, has been constrained by its production and especially by its poetic works, to constitute a territory that belongs to no one, but that politics has claimed as if it were private property, so effectively that in certain public meetings one gets the rather curious impression that "Francophones" are a community of hostages. But of whom and of what? (Khatibi 2010, 1005)

Francophone writers write under the constraint of the utopian condition of "their" language. This is a precondition of so-called "francophone" literature, which in turn becomes a point of arrival for a philosophical meditation on languages in the plural. For Khatibi, the francophone writer is caught in an interstitial space, between the nowhere of utopia and the political instrumentalization of languages. Instead of answering the questions he asks at the end of this passage, Khatibi evokes the "weaving through syntax" that allows him to "widen the space of hospitality" in his "own" text:

> It is syntax that is my aim, my point of connection and the wake I leave in the time of each vocable. Syntax: a unification in movement of the target language. Thanks to this simultaneous translation, to this process of grafting, I record what returns to me from memory without forced reservation. In this way, I investigate the forces of silence between languages, the erasure of traces and their rest stops, their becoming ash. So if I sing the praises of syntax, it is because it widens the space of hospitality where the writer is received in his own text as a guest, in the shadow of the writer.[2]

For Khatibi, syntax is the privileged site of poetic procedures: internal, simultaneous translation, the grafting of diverse elements, and "the erasure of traces." It allows him to bypass the impasses of philological sedimentation and the symbolic politicization of language. He confesses to feeling "an affinity with a language . . . stronger than the sentiment of belonging" (117), and in general, his work aims to sabotage any deterministic relationship between language and ownership, between language and property, provoking a perpetual rupture in the pact between language and the nation. Writing in the "language of the other" is always an act of "self-disappropriation" for Khatibi, but also a way of asserting that "language is not property." One could say that Khatibi here agrees with Derrida and the notion of "monolingualism" being a "prosthesis" for an origin that is always irrecuperable and lost to memory and language. But Khatibi describes, performs, and traces the seams that mark the disappropriation of this monolanguage, moving from "monolanguage" to "bi-language" and beyond.

But we cannot stop here either, because within the synchronic virtual silences of these texts we find diachronic silences, determined by the historical process of the silencing or accumulation of languages and knowledge practices. This process is precisely what this book has explored under the title of *decadent orientalisms*: a colonial politics that institutes the study of comparative languages and literatures, including those of "the Orient", under the very sign of these languages' supposed decadence, and, ultimately, their disappearance. As we have seen, this kind of orientalism is both descriptive and prescriptive: a discourse that functions by breaking down, that integrates only to disintegrate. The ambivalent nature of this discourse prompts us to *also* pay attention to the philological context at work here, even when reading texts as fragmented and radically decentered as those of Khatibi. The *armes miraculeueses* of the Khatibian text "record" the memory of other languages, and the author "investigates the powers of silence between languages," but the fact that this investigation takes place *in French* remains a significant element of the inscription of silence in history and in the world that this text performs. Are dialectal Arabic or Tamazight at liberty to circulate in the same global spaces and think according to the same techniques or procedures as can French? The virtual apparition of other languages and signifying practices in the francophone text coincides precisely with their *mise en marge*, with their virtualization. The disappropriation Khatibi writes about is thus haunted by the politics of assimilation and the colonial notion of *francophonie* as instances of attempts at *diversity* in French. The French language remains a world in itself, a "*littérature-monde*" (to allude to the title of the 2007 book by Michel Le Bris and Jean Rouaud), just as "Global English" or "Anglophone literature"—rubrics that serve to satisfy the demands for diversity put on the canon. This means that rendering French heterogeneous and nonidentical to itself is inseparable from a homogenization of textual practices and procedures of thought into the "globalized" form of a monolingual "world literature." Should we borrow a rhetorical move from Derrida, and boldly affirm that Khatibi is in fact the most "minor-transnational" of all francophone writers?[3] After all, from the perspective of the hexagon or North American "French Studies," his texts might be said to satisfy a certain demand for otherness, opening out onto the Arabic language, Moroccan popular culture, and Islamic mystical traditions without requiring any Arabic whatsoever from the critic. Such a claim is not intended as a critique of Khatibi, but is instead aimed at certain critical approaches to francophone literature. Thus the challenge of reading Khatibi today, and, by extension, a field such as francophone studies, is to acknowledge the extraordinary diversity of rhetorical techniques employed in these texts without celebrating this as diversity *tout court*. As with Khatibi and francophone studies, so, too, with comparative literature.

Another way of framing this argument is that Arabic calligraphy, *darija*, Tamazight, and other local practices (tattooing, proverbs, jokes, and the like)—those things that serve as the poles that Khatibi uses to make French or francophone practices render their static and generate the opacity or interference of the *intersign*—may well have a higher redemption value in the "world republic of letters" when uttered *in French*. That is, the self-disappropriation that Khatibi transforms into something like a virtue of literary asceticism borders on complicity with the forms of disappropriation that are also still very much operative in the world literary system, albeit in a more brutal and far less theoretical way. The asymmetrical structures of the institutions of world literature, relating to, among other things, values attached to certain "global" languages, the system of "consecration" by which an author from the margins must be recognized and praised by writers, critics, and publishing houses at the center (Paris, London, New York, and so on) continue to regulate who reads and writes what and in what languages. I do not point out the obvious facts of the situation in order to pass judgment on francophone writers from the Maghreb such as Khatibi. Quite the opposite: I would say that it is precisely *because* Khatibi has taken this problematic of language conflict further than any other writer of his generation that we must not stop at a celebratory appraisal of his singular rhetorical inventions—which is a common strategy when reading writers "from the margins"—nor is it advisable to transform this singularity into a theoretical model to follow.

We might undertake a contrapuntal reading with Khatibi by continuing to expand upon the notions of linguistic "hostage" and self-disappropriation that he articulates. Let us begin with Khatibi's superb essay on Jean Genet's *Un captif amoureux /A Prisoner of Love* ("Ultime dissidence de Genet"), a novel whose title posits its author, Genet, as a *different* kind of prisoner

Conclusion: Toward a Critique of Colonial Modernity 169

who articulates his desire that France, the French language, and French critics (including Sartre and Derrida) *disown him*—a desire articulated in what has come to be seen as nothing less than a landmark text of contemporary French literature! Khatibi's rather astounding and highly ambivalent account of Genet's text itself demonstrates one possible approach to the kind of reading I am suggesting. Khatibi delineates the intricacies that constitute this textual "card game without cards," disassociating the textual play of Genet's language from the highly charged political context to which it would seem to give voice. "The history of Palestinian Palestine," Khatibi writes "has nothing to do with this work, which is the fragmented autobiography of a great writer" (Khatibi 2008, 193). Rather, Khatibi tells us, "the essential is to decode *Un Captif amoureux* as a *palindrome*" (163): palindrome of the saintliness granted Genet by Sartre in his *Saint Genet*, and at the same time his own funeral oration sung in the form of a palindrome. One example of Khatibi's palindromic reading demonstrates how Genet himself inhabits the spaces between French and Arabic when Genet plays with the letters that form the acronym of the Palestinian political party, *Fatah*—which spells *hatf*—or "natural death" when written in Roman characters from left to right (181). Khatibi's text generates static out of the political element in Genet, created in the space opened between the critique of the other (Genet) and the writing of the self (Khatibi). An expanded version of my argument would look beyond the critical "metatext" in order to think about its variance with Khatibi's literary oeuvre. Such a reading would need to think about the kind of textual disorientations and self-disappropriations operative in a work such as Khatibi's *A Summer in Stockholm / Un été à Stockholm*, a novel from 1990 that operates by the law of the *intersign*, performs a *double critique*, and aims toward the horizon of a *pensée-autre*, other-thinking.

This novel centers around the character of Gérard Namir, an "professional foreigner" who travels to Stockholm to work as a simultaneous translator at an international conference on Swedish political neutrality. The protagonist's Franco-Maghrebi name is just one of the *intersigns* in the dense intersemiotic network of the text. Beginning with the "living museum" of the airplane that takes Gérard Namir to Stockholm, the text deconstructs the geographical and ethnic identifications of both the Arabic travel narrative—or *rihla*—and those found in European travel fiction. In two essays from the 1990s, Khatibi detailed the Oulipian formulas used to generate the novel (allegorical characters set in motion through a magic square), the superimposition of mobile images in the spirit of Bergman and Baudelairean flânerie, and the organization of all the elements of the novel into a distributed network of affective relations through syntax; one can easily imagine why he titled a chapter in the novel *extase froide*, "Cold Ecstasy." The narrator's admission, toward the end of *Un été à Stockholm*, that "this narrative is not a *roman à clef*" (156) doubtless holds the key to the play of clarity and opacity, of light and shadows, that Khatibi's essays and novel project onto each other: The key used to generate the novel cannot be used to decode it.

The traveling theory that generated this novel, which was developed in relation to procedures of thought and the "transversal intersemiotics" opened by practices such as the *contrepoint* of Moroccan carpet making, provided a platform, where, Khatibi tells us, "the least Mediterranean part of my memory was revealing itself to itself" (2010, 1009). But where, then, *is* the Maghreb in this text, and how might we locate it? Instead of making the Maghreb the referent or object of these texts, Khatibi instead wields the Maghreb—understood as a site of crossing, of multiplicity, of violent and/or productive tensions of all kinds—as the generative *subject* of the text, but a subject whose traces will have been blurred by the intersemiotic writing ("blurred" in the sense of *une piste brouillée*). The Maghreb does not serve as *content* to fill a foreign *form* (the novel, say), but rather, as was the case with Kateb Yacine's *Nedjma*, we see an invention of Maghrebi *technique, une science maghrébine de l'écriture*. *Un été à Stockholm* takes this to its limit, where the purported "content" is not just European, but indeed *nordic*, specifically Swedish, and Swedish in a way that reveals the supposed neutrality of Sweden, of Swedish, and of Stockholm as themselves *local particularities*.

Such are the double-sided versions of hostage and disappropriation at work in Khatibi: a kind of self-disappropriation that generates the text as a *dwelling place* of language in exile. The "place of hostage" created by the static of the *intersign* opens a horizon within the text, even as this horizon remains haunted by the specters of disappropriation. That is, Khatibi's critical elaborations show us the seams and fissures in modernity, where Orientalism continues both to decay as a discourse about the world and to cause disintegration in the world. The task of transcolonial comparativism, then, would involve attending to both the negative and positive forces emanating from these sutured worlds. Bringing together Saidian contrapuntal reading and Khatibian double critique can indicate modes of silencing and erasure across the ensemble of discursive and cultural production, demonstrating how phonemes and syntax are never entirely autonomous from world-historical processes. Simultaneously, close attention to the awakenings, inventions, and transgraphings of Orientalized writers and thinkers provides ample evidence of a will to escape, disturb, and act through language within the overdetermining structures of Orientalist diagnoses of decadence. Contrapuntal double critique aims beyond the rhetoric of blame that plagues discussions of postcolonial language politics and the mirrored accusations constitutive of decadence itself, where mimetic forms of nationalism continue to reproduce iterations of colonial sovereignty in the postcolonial world. It affirms the right of theory, thought, and language to travel outside established networks or circuits, even as one must continue to pay close attention to those theories, thoughts, and languages whose mobility has been slowed or blocked entirely. Ultimately, this mode of critical work illustrates how the experience of subjugation co-constitutive with colonial modernity spurs on the invention of what Aching calls the "creative possibilities for autonomous action and for sovereignty" (44) dialectically emerging from the decay of colonial modernity.

ACKNOWLEDGMENTS

When I began this book well over a decade ago, I would have been both humbled and amazed to know how many people and institutions would come to play such diverse roles in its writing. Initially born out of my desire to puzzle out the lack of discussion linking the French decadent writers of the 1880s and the obsession with decline and decay internal to Arab and Muslim societies at the same time, this project was guided throughout by Aamir Mufti. His critical renewals of Edward Said's investigation of philology, secularism, literature, and empire helped me formulate the questions this book explores.

Emily Apter's graduate seminar at UCLA on "the dark side" of decadence was decisive and pathbreaking for my own thinking. Eleanor Kaufman rescued this book at several crucial junctures, and her insistence that I cleave to the nonbinary comparative mode made all the difference. I owe a large debt of gratitude to Michael Cooperson, whose attention to detail and astounding capacity to straddle ninth-century Baghdad and nineteenth-century Lebanon proved indispensable. I would also like to thank Dominic Thomas, who gave me his copy of Fanon's *Les damnes de la terre* within minutes of our first meeting and later introduced me to Abdelwahab Meddeb; Andrea Loselle for her guidance regarding Celine and racism; Kenneth Reinhard for clarifying my thinking regarding Nietzsche, decadence, and fantasy; Samuel Weber for his exquisite readings of Walter Benjamin; and Gil Hochberg for pointing in the direction of the ramifications of the Semitic hypothesis in the Maghreb. Stathis Gourgouris, Ali Behdad, and Nouri Gana provided support, conversation, and thoughtful suggestions. Thanks are due to the late Michael Heim, who offered suggestion on some of the longer translations that appear in this volume.

Colleagues at UCLA were a sustaining force during the research and writing of this book from its earliest stages. I would especially like to acknowledge Chris Shaw for his unique way of accentuating Lacan, the category, and primitivist modernisms. Deep thanks for their thinking friendships go out to Magdalena Edwards, Leah Feldman, David Gabriel,

Claire Gallou, Karen Grumberg, Jenny Gully, William Hendel, Edwin Hill, Rebecca Hopkins, Ryan Kernan, Anna Kornbluh, LaShonda Long, Nahrain Al-Mousawi, Charlton Payne, Leila Pazargadi, Therí Pickens, Jeff Schroeder, Hoda El Shakry, Guilan Siassi Pinaud, Amy Tahani-Bidmeshki, Loli Tsan, and Erin Hyman, whose memory remains vibrant among those who knew her.

Sections of this book were first presented at Cornell University, Harvard, Princeton, Penn State, NYU, UCLA, the University of Illinois Urbana-Champaign, USC, and at numerous meetings and panels under the aegis of professional organizations such as the ACLA, MESA, and the MLA. I have benefitted greatly from discussions and comments at these arenas from Michael Allan, Tarek El-Ariss, Anna Ball, Anna Bernard, R.A. Judy, Waïl Hassan, Kamran Rastegar, Bruce Robbins, Jeff Sacks, Richard Sieburth, Susan Slymovics, and Gayatri Spivak. Karim Mattar has offered many insightful comments and much moral support over the years. During my tenure as an Andrew W. Mellon Fellow in French and History across the Disciplines at Cornell University, I was lucky to enter into the orbit of Laurent Dubreuil's uncompromisingly iconoclastic scholarship and friendship. Snowy and isolated Ithaca was fashioned into a warmly welcoming place to think and write thanks to Esther Fernandez, Laurent Ferri, Mat Fournier, Heather Furnas, Alex Lenoble, Ruth Mas, Tracy McNulty, Natalie Melas, Bob Proehl, Camille Robcis, Shawkat Toorawa, and Jonathan Culler, who first suggested Fordham for this book. Hélène Cixous opened several doors and suggested ways of looking through them during her residency at Cornell. Chris Garcès became a deeply valued interlocutor and collaborator, and I would like to recognize and thank him for his general brilliance and for specific comments on various sections of this book.

During my sojourn at Sarah Lawrence College, Angela Moger's divine intervention helped keep this book alive, and Sebastian Kelso and Corie Marshall met my teaching with such keen and expansive learning that our work together remains a model of intellectual reciprocity and liberality. I have learned much from colleagues at the Université Mohamed Premier in Oujda, Morocco: Soumia Boutkhil, Larbi Touaf, and especially Chourouq Nasri. To the poet Sameh Derouich: thank you for your Arabic haiku. The Stevens Foundation and the SUNY COIL Center funded workshops and travel to Cairo and Oujda that benefitted this book.

By keeping me so busy, SUNY College at Oneonta has taught me the unfungible value of writing time. I have also greatly profited from several travel grants administered through the College that have allowed me to do research in France and Morocco. Colleagues at SUNY Oneonta have provided much-needed intellectual agitation and companionship. To Alejandra Escudero, Mette Harder, April Harper, Brett Heindl, Achim Koedermann, Ho Hon Leung, Jonathan Sadow, Bianca Treddenick, and Loli Tsan (encore): thank you! Olivia C. Harrison, who unmasked herself as one of the anonymous readers of the manuscript for Fordham, offered incisive suggestions that helped shape the final form the book has taken. Tom Lay has been a supportive and patient editor at Fordham.

Thanks to Houssein Miloudi and L'Atelier 21 for permission to use the cover image. Sections of this book, sometimes in quite different form, have appeared in *boundary2*, *The b20 Review*, *Dalhousie French Studies*, and *Expressions maghrébines*. I am grateful to these venues for permission to republish this material here, and for numerous editors and readers at these journals for their incisive comments and suggestions, especially Paul Bové, Arne DeBoever, Marta Segarra, Christa Jones, and Anissa Talahite-Moodley. I have been graced with the love and support of my sisters Sandy Fieni, Lisa Price, Carol Lutz, Robin Ideström, and Lynne Yost. John and Barbara Gossett have been a constant source of material and moral support. I do not know how I could ever adequately thank my late mother and father, Janice and Tony Fieni—for everything.

My most profound recognition I reserve for Nancy Rose Gossett, who has sustained this book and its writer with sacrifices unspeakably great and unseeably small, with her love, attention, and uncompromising intellect. *Et merci infiniment à ma licorne rêveuse bleu ciel, Ella, et à mon petit dragon rouge et féroce, Margot.*

NOTES

INTRODUCTION: ORIENTALIST DECADENCE

Note on Arabic transliteration: Throughout this book I have used a simplified version of the *International Journal of Middle East Studies* transliteration system. The chief diacritics used are a closed apostrophe (') for 'ayn and an open apostrophe (') for hamza, except when it occurs at the beginning of a word.

1. The full text of this speech can be found at the official White House website: https://georgewbush-whitehouse.archives.gov/news/releases/2005/11/20051111-1.html. Accessed June 22, 2018.

2. I take the phrase from Ali Behdad's book *Belated Travelers: Orientalism in the Age of Colonial Dissolution* (Durham, NC: Duke University Press, 1994). Behdad describes the phenomenological "belatedness" of European travelers in the east (such as Nerval and Flaubert) in order to account for the "all-inclusiveness of [Orientalism's] epistemological field and its ability to adapt to and incorporate heterogeneous elements" (13). My analysis of Orientalism differs from his in that whereas he analyzes Orientalism as a closed system, I aim to show how the discourse of power in the Arab world is intimately implicated with Orientalism even as it emerges within the specific historical and material contexts governing Arabic societies.

3. I refer here primarily to the second section of *Orientalism*, "Orientalist Structures and Restructures."

4. For more on the relation between Orientalist scholarship and the Nazi state, see Pollock (1993).

5. Albert Hourani (1962) explores the problem of translation between European and Islamic conceptual paradigms in various sections of *Arabic Thought in the Liberal Age*. For example, he explains how 'Abduh and other Islamic intellectuals of the period (mis)translated certain concepts of European provenance: "*maslaha* gradually turns into utility, *shura* into parliamentary democracy, *'ijma* into public opinion" (144). In *Dominance without Hegemony*, Ranajit Guha analyzes how the "differentiation between two idioms" functioned in the context of colonial India, where the slippage between British and Indian intellectual paradigms served as crucial structural

supports in the configuration of colonial power; see esp. 23–62. We are reminded that this problem is still very much with us every time the compatibility between "democracy" and "Islam" is debated in the media or the lecture hall.

6. Muhsin al-Musawi's extraordinary book *The Medieval Islamic Republic of Letters* (2015) arrives at a similar conclusion after a systematic analysis of the literary system that obtained during the period of Ottoman rule (1258–1919), one that has long been relegated to the dustbin of Arabic literary, and thus cultural, "decadence." Al-Musawi critiques the way that "the architects of modernity" have collapsed "political loss" and "cultural decadence" to such a degree that they have given false evidence to regressive forces in is Islamic societies. "The cultural and historical gap that results" from such a conflation of the political and the cultural, al-Musawi writes, "can easily induce architects of regression to involve regions and peoples in schisms and disorder" (11).

7. See Gourgouris (2003).

8. Said describes his much discussed concept of "contrapuntal reading," which he first articulated in *Culture and Imperialism*, as a method of reading "with a simultaneous awareness both of the metropolitan history that is narrated and of those other histories against which (and together with which) the dominating discourse acts" (51). This book is an exercise in this method, although I cannot claim to achieve the "concert and order" that Said claims may ultimately emerge from this technique. I return to contrapuntal reading in the Conclusion.

9. The term "Arabic" will be used throughout instead of the adjective "Arab" in order to distinguish a conception of authenticity that is linked more closely to the Arabic language as the divine and authentic instrument of revelation in the Qur'an than to European ideas about race (to be discussed later in conjunction with Ernest Renan). By including al-Afghani, who was in fact Persian, under this heading, I mean to suggest the importance of the category of Arabness and the Arabic language to his conception of Islamic reformism, as well as his immense influence on subsequent Arabic thought. The connection between the constructedness of the notion "Arab" and the hundreds of millions of people who use this term to describe themselves represents another step in the manifold historical processes that constitute identity formation after the colonial age. When the word "Arab" is used in these pages, it is done to indicate those who self-identify as "Arab."

10. Both Emily Apter's "Acting Out Orientalism," in *Continental Drift: From National Characters to Virtual Subjects* (Chicago: University of Chicago Press, 1999), and Ali Behdad's "Allahou-Akbar! He Is a Woman: Colonialism, Transvestism, and the Oriental Parasite," in *Belated Travelers*, view Orientalism as a kind of cultural transvestism.

11. For a sampling of treatments of French literary decadence, consult the following: Asti Hustvedt, "The Art of Death: French Fiction at the Fin de Siècle," *The Decadent Reader: Fiction, Fantasy, and Perversion from Fin-de-siècle France*, ed. Asti Hustvedt (New York: Zone Books, 1998); Jean Pierrot, *L'imaginaire décadent*, trans. Derek Coltman as *The Decadent Imagination, 1880– 1900* (Chicago: University of Chicago Press, 1981); David Weir, *Decadence and the Making of Modernism* (Amherst: University of Massachusetts Press, 1995); Barbara Spackman, *Decadent Genealogies: The Rhetoric of Sickness from Baudelaire to Annunzio* (Ithaca, NY: Cornell University Press, 1989).

12. For two treatments of Arabic-Islamic decadence, see Ghali Shukri, *al-Nahda wa al-suqut fi al-fikr al-masri al-hadith* [The Rebirth and Decline in Modern Egypt of Modern Thought] (Beirut: Dar al-Talia, 1978), and Muhi'idin Subhi, *Al-Umma al-mashlula: tashrih al-inhitat al-'arabi* [The Crippled Nation: Anatomy of Arab Decline] (Beirut: Riad El-Rayyes Books, 1997). Hourani's *Arabic Thought in the Liberal Age* remains the standard English language overview of the period, and much of what it covers relates to questions of decadence and rebirth. For a recent treatment of the literary Arabic *nahda*, see Rastegar (2013) (ed.) and El-Ariss (2013 and 2018, ed.). For works that examine the issue of loss in modern Arabic literature, see Sacks (2015) and Gana (2011).

13. See Donald Quataert's *The Ottoman Empire, 1700–1922* (Cambridge: Cambridge University Press, 2000) for a discussion of the clothing laws in Ottoman lands, esp. 141–42.

14. George Antonius's classic treatment of the rise of Arab nationalism, *The Arab Awakening* (1939), is largely responsible for promoting this translation of *nahda* in an English-language context.

15. For two examples of this view in French and English language treatments of the *nahda*, see Muhammad Badawi's *A Short History of Modern Arabic Literature* (Oxford: Oxford University Press, 1993), in which Badawi suggests that Napoleon "awakens" the Arab world from the sleep of its decadence, whose literature is that of an "exhausted, inward looking culture," and is characterized by an "absence of originality and a loss of vigor," p. 2; and Henri Pérès's "Les premières manifestations de la littérature arabe en Orient au XIXe siècle" from 1935, which opens with the following sally:

> Parmi les causes qui ont provoqué le réveil de la littérature dans le Proche-Orient au XIXe siècle, on ne saurait passer sous silence l'expédition de Bonaparte en Egypte; si les résultats politiques furent contestables, par contre, les conséquences intellectuelles eurent une portée dont on ne mesure les effets avec quelque exactitude qu'a plus d'un siècle de distance. La majorité des lettres égyptiennes, ceux que n'aveugle pas un nationalisme exagéré, reconnaissent que le vieux monde oriental, figé dans une existence

> qui datait du Moyen Age, a reçu la « chiquenaude » qui l'a remise en marche du jeune ambitieux dont les desseins politiques, si hardis fussent-ils, s'appuyaient sur la science la plus réfléchie.
>
> Among the causes that provoked the awakening of literature in the Near East during the nineteenth century, one cannot remain silent about Bonaparte's expedition in Egypt; if the political result was debatable, the intellectual consequences, on the contrary, had an impact that one can only measure precisely after a century of distance. The majority of Egyptian letters, those not blinded by an exaggerated nationalism, frozen in an existence dating to the Middle Ages, was suddenly switched back on by a flick of the wrist of the ambitious young man whose political designs, however bold, were based on the most well thought-out science. (233)

Hourani's classic *Arabic Thought in the Liberal Age* also gives Napoleon the privileged position of agent of awakening.

16. Many scholars of Islam have made this argument about Islamic reform movements from the nineteenth century to the present day. Hourani's *Liberal Thought* provides repeated examples of how reformists like al-Afgani and 'Abduh transform Islamic doctrine by equating it with "natural law." Both of Keddie's books on Afghani amply demonstrate the novelty of his understanding of Islam, as does Kedourie's *Afghani and 'Abduh* in a somewhat more polemical manner. Al-Azmeh, in *Islams and Modernities*, asserts that "after this naturalistic and utilitarian interpretation, little remains, in substantive terms, of Islam how as it existed; what remains is a symbolic order" that can be manipulated at will (38). Laroui's *La crise des intellectuels arabes* argues that more recent manifestations of what has been called "fundamentalist" Islam have tended to gain support as external aggression against Muslims have increased.

17. Tomiche, "Naissance et avatars du roman arabe avant *Zaynab*," *Annales Islamologiques* (Cairo: Institut d'archéologie du Caire, 1980), 16:321–51.

18. Hourani argues that the influence of Guizot on Afghani can be seen in the latter's change of focus on Islam as a religion to Islam as a civilization (114); 'Abduh lectured on Guizot's *History of Civilization in Europe* (132).

19. See Tarek El-Ariss's superb reading of al-Tawhtawi and Benjamin in *Trials of Modernity* for another recent example of this critical gesture (esp. 21–28).

20. See especially "Dream World of Mass Culture" in Buck-Morss (1989).

21. While the apparent lack of logical connection between the elements of Benjamin's theory may be attributed to the unfinished state of the *Arcades Project*, it is also possible to understand this tentative theory of history as a

new way of affirming the literary quality of historical narrative itself, and even as a radical new kind of "popular history," that would combine the rigor of Marxist analysis with the accessibility of both cinema and the fairy tale. Buck-Morss suggests that "awakening" for Benjamin was a way of breaking the spell of history placed on the dreaming collective, just as the hero of the fairy tale uses cunning to break the spell put on him or her. She cites his 1934 essay on Kafka: "Fairy tales are the way of handing down the tradition of victory over the [forces of myth]" (1989, 273).

22. See Benjamin's *The Origin of German Tragic Drama*, trans. John Osbourne (London: Verso, 1998); "Central Park," *New German Critique* Winter 4 (1985): 32–58; "Convolute J: Baudelaire," *The Arcades Project*; and "On Some Motifs in Baudelaire," *Illuminations* (New York: Schocken Books, 1968), 160–61.

23. See Jameson (1981).

24. Quoted in Gore (1970), 292; originally published in "Après M. Renan," *Heures d'histoire* (Paris: 1893), 287.

25. I return to both debates in Chapter 1. See also Stephen Sheehi, who provides an excellent comparative reading of these two debates in *The Foundations of Modern Arab Identity* (2004), chap. 5.

26. The translation in *Nation and Narration*, ed. Homi K. Bhabha (London: Routledge, 1990), has become a standard reference for English language treatments of the essay.

27. *Le Monde*, May 4, 2017, "La 'poulpe' Ernest Renan." http://www.lemonde.fr/livres/article/2017/05/04/le-poulpe-ernest-renan_5122036_3260.html accessed June 27, 2017.

28. Etienne lists a few of these errors, including Renan's misguided view of Islamic mysticism. See also the reference to the *Encyclopedia of Islam* article on Ibn Rushd later in this chapter.

29. Johannes Fabian, *Time and the Other: How Anthropology Makes Its Object* (New York: Columbia University Press, 1983).

30. For a discussion of this aspect of Renan's intellectual personality, see Shapiro (1982), to which I refer in Chapter 1.

31. The great irony in such a conception of social responsibility is that by transferring the requirements of morality to the collective, Renan is, in a sense, absolving the individual of responsibility, and placing the moral burden onto institutions.

32. Shapiro (1982), 197. "The model of continuous and organic development in Renan's *History [of the Origins of Christianity]* seems to be a parody of Hegel."

33. In *Peau noire, masques blancs* (1952), Fanon famously summed up why Hegel's master-slave dialectic breaks down in the context of the colony:

The master doesn't demand the slave's recognition, Fanon tells us, just his labor (179).

34. Gore analyzes the role of the 1848 Revolution in *L'avenir de la science*, which was subtitled "Pensées de 1848." Gore points out that Renan was excited by the revolution, but only intellectually and somewhat reluctantly, as if he had been forced by French history to equate revolution with progress, without believing in anything remotely resembling the ideal of *égalité*. See Gore (1970), 106–7. Gore later argues that "after about a dozen years, a political regime becomes respectable in his view, from the very fact of having maintained order, the condition of true progress" (au but d'une dizaine d'années, un régime politique devient respectable à ses yeux, du fait même d'avoir maintenu l'ordre, condition du vrai progrès) (295).

35. Renan's use of Islam as a fantasmatic cardinal point from which to critique European institutions in general and French Catholicism in particular draws on a long history of which Montesquieu's *Lettres persanes* (1721) is perhaps the best-known example.

36. The line "there is no document of civilization which is not at the same time a document of barbarism" comes from Benjamin's thesis VII of his "Theses on the Philosophy of History," anthologized in *Illuminations* (1969).

1. FRENCH DECADENCE, ARAB AWAKENINGS: FIGURES OF DECAY IN THE *NAHDA*

1. See Mufti (2010). I am here following through on Mufti's reading of Said's philological impulse: "Said's project at least from *Orientalism* onward implies not a rejection but rather a radicalization of philology—that is, it calls for a radically historical understanding of language and the forms of its institution in literature, culture, and society" (493).

2. Renan (1995 [1890]), 71. All translations from this work are mine.

3. Shapiro (1982).

4. Ernest Renan (1949 [1852]), 85. All translations from this work are mine.

5. Said (1978), 120.

6. The gesture of orienting the world map according to the coordinates of a community's sacred sites is also repeated in Arabic geography, most notably for the purposes of the current discussion, in the third section of al-Tahtawi's introduction to his account of his expedition to Paris. Renan's "secular" mapping is striking precisely for the way it reproduces the schema of medieval Christian geography.

7. See Fabian (1983).

8. Keddie (1968), 10. Keddie speculates that Afghani's "main reason for claiming Afghan birth was probably to avoid identification with the minority,

Shi'i, branch of Islam." Kedourie's Afghani and 'Abduh implies that Afghani's Sunni name might be an element of his overall lack of orthodox belief. See Kedourie (1966).

9. Al-Afghani (2003), 43–44.

10. The microfilm of the *Journal* at the BNF François Mitterand in Paris reveals that the original lecture was published on March 30, and not on March 29, as most, including Keddie, have asserted.

11. In his rejoinder to Afghani, Renan writes, "It is largely the conversation I had with him that convinced me to choose the connections between the scientific spirit and Islam as the subject of my Sorbonne lecture" (C'est en grande partie la conversation que j'eus avec lui qui me décida à choisir pour sujet de ma conférence à la Sorbonne les rapports de l'esprit scientifique et de l'islamisme) (2003, 50).

12. From the introduction to Afghani's response in the May 18 edition of the *Journal des Débats*, 3.

13. Kedourie (1966), 42–25; Keddie (1965), 85.

14. Keddie (1972), 24–26.

15. Ernest Renan, "Qu'est-ce qu'une nation?" in *Becoming National: A Reader*, ed. Geoff Elay and Ronald Grigor Suny (New York: Oxford University Press, 1996), 41–55. I refer to the following passage: "A nation is therefore a large-scale solidarity, constituted by the feeling of the sacrifices that one has made in the past and of those that one is prepared to make in the future. It presupposes a past; it is summarized, however, in the present by a tangible fact, namely, consent, the clearly expressed desire to continue a common life. A nation's existence is, if you will pardon the metaphor, a daily plebiscite, just as an individual's existence is a perpetual affirmation of life" (43).

16. Gilles Deleuze, "Pensée nomade," in *Nietzsche aujourd'hui* (Paris: Union Général d'Éditions, 1973). Translated as "Nomad Thought" in *The New Nietzsche*, ed. David B. Allison (Cambridge, MA: MIT Press, 1985). The trope of nomadism is developed at great length in *A Thousand Plateaus*, particularly in the "Treatise on Nomadology."

17. In his analysis of the chapter "What Is Religious?" from *Beyond Good and Evil*, Shapiro points out that "Nietzsche's parallels between religious and ethnic identities here are just the reverse of Renan's" (1982, 212). He adds: "For Nietzsche the genuine northerners play the skeptical role which Renan attributes to the Greeks, while the Celts are fundamentally anomalous, much as Renan had seen the Jews as an anomaly in both the ancient and the modern worlds" (212).

18. Shapiro also argues that Nietzsche calls Renan his "antipodes" because religion exists in his thought as a kind of "return of the repressed" (1982, 214).

19. Charles Bernheimer's *Decadent Subjects* argues that the discourse of decadence in fin de siècle Europe ended up contaminating even the efforts of those, like Lombroso and Nordau, who worked hardest to develop a hygiene of normalcy. Renan belongs to this group of social hygienists. On the subject of decadence, Bernheimer isolates no fewer than nine distinct meanings for the word *"décadence"* in Nietzsche (see esp. 26–27).

20. I will return to the figure of Nietzsche as nomadic philosopher in Chapter 6 and its discussion of Maghrebian immigration, where I connect his ideas about the degenerate human body to the bodies of immigrants that circulate within the networks of global power.

21. Al-Kawakibi (1899), 155–57.
22. Rahme (1999), 159–77, esp. 166.
23. Kedourie (1974), 107. See also Haim (1974), 27–29.
24. Laroui (1974), 107–8.
25. Reid (1975), 105–6.
26. Antun and 'Abduh (1982 [1902]).
27. Reid (1975), 80–93, and Hourani (1962), 253–59, both provide analyses of Antun's understanding of Ibn Rushd, as well as the debate with 'Abduh. See also Sheehi (2004), chap. 5.
28. Arnaldez (1998). This text reads Ibn Rushd in his properly Islamic historical context, as does Benmakhlouf (2000).

2. AL-SHIDYAQ'S DECADENT CARNIVAL

1. This famous phrase is taken from Nietzsche's "On Truth and Lies in an Extramoral Sense" (1873); I derive my position on the relationship between the body and language in Nietzsche from Pierre Klossowski's *Nietzsche et le cercle vicieux* (trans. as *Nietzsche and the Vicious Circle*; Chicago: University of Chicago Press, 1997). See Chapter 6 for a brief discussion of Klossowski's account of the body, language, and "decadence" in Nietzsche.

2. Although Humphrey Davies has recently published his monumental four-volume edition of the novel, the translations used here are my own. See Shidyaq, *Leg over Leg or The Turtle in the Tree Concerning the Fariyaq: What Manner of Creature Might He Be*, ed. and trans. Humphrey T. Davies (New York: New York University Press, 2015).

3. Mattityahu Peled's article "Al-Saq 'ala al-Saq—A Generic Definition" claims to solve the troubling problem of genre by demonstrating that al-Shidyaq's text conforms to the eleven criteria that Northrop Frye uses to distinguish "Menippean satire" (43–46).

4. I thank Aamir Mufti for insisting on the importance of "indigenous forms" over and above the kind of erasure of such forms articulated by Franco Moretti in "Conjunctures on World Literature," where the novel

functions as a kind of European-made suitcase into which third-world writers would simply pack their local baggage. For Moretti's article, see *New Left Review* (January–February, 2000): 54–68. The singularity of the novel's form has also been affirmed by Nadia al-Baghdadi, who asserts that, like Sterne's *Tristram Shandy*, it should be considered "a genre of its own." See her article "The Cultural Function of Fiction: From the Bible to Libertine Literature—Historical Criticism and Social Critique in Ahmad Faris al-Shidyaq," in *Arabica* XLVI (1999): 394.

5. For an account of the novel's reception in Arabic criticism, particularly al-Shidyaq's use of rhymed prose, see Sulaiman Jubran, "The Function of Rhyming Prose in *al-Saq 'ala al-Saq*," *Journal of Arabic Literature* 20, no. 2 (September 1989): 151–53.

6. The Ahmad Faris al-Shidyaq Research Project, organized through the Central European University, organized two workshops in 2008 in order to rectify the general lack of accurate scholarship on al-Shidyaq. See the project website, http://www.ceu.hu/afsrp. More recently, Sacks (2015) has provided an excellent and theoretically attuned account of the importance of al-Shidyaq in discussions of literature, loss, and philology.

7. Sacks (2007), 41.

8. Khatibi (2010), 1006.

9. In some ways the text resembles the medieval prose genre of *adab*, an open format first developed in the Umayyad court, which consisted of anecdotes, quotations, and poetry.

10. This assertion appears in a 1919 letter Joyce wrote to Harriet Weaver quoted in Richard Ellman's *James Joyce* (New York: Oxford University Press, 1982), 46.

11. Such a view of language is also symptomatic of a much larger problem: the politicization of the Arabic language as the primary instrument of Arab modernity and Arab nationalism.

12. Peled (1991), 132–34, provides a discussion of this text and its meaning for *al-Saq*.

13. It should be noted that there are two different kinds of word lists in the text. The first features synonyms that may or may not be phonetically related: Each word is isolated on the right-hand side of the page, followed by a half-inch of blank space and a short definition. These lists reflect the more functional, conservationist nature of the novel, even as they are inserted in the middle of the narrative. The second kind of lists appear in paragraph form, and are sometimes separated by periods, and sometimes are strung together without punctuation. The text I analyze here belongs to this second kind of list.

14. For an overview of public health in Egypt during the nineteenth century, as well as more about the 1831 epidemic, see LaVerne Kuhnke's

Public Health in Nineteenth-Century Egypt (Berkeley: University of California Press, 1990). For an account of the profound effects of the bubonic plague of 1347 in the Middle East, which suffered frequent recurrences and a more severe population reduction than did Europe, see Michael Dols's *The Black Death in the Middle East* (Princeton: Princeton University Press, 1977).

15. It is important to emphasize that Bakhtin seems to be most concerned with the type of "violence" that erupts in the context of the "carnival symbolic," that is, in the specific context of the novel, and his description of its constitutive elements, ranging from "grotesque realism," and "universal laughter" to "the language of the marketplace," aims to elucidate what happens when the energies of carnival begin to inform the genre of the novel. Mbembe's (2001) critique of Bakhtin can be considered a brilliant update of the latter's argument only to the degree that both texts theorize about real bodies and not mere texts. What Mbembe calls "Bakhtin's error" is that in the context of the African postcolony carnivalesque transgression constantly reproduces the "convivial" simulacrum that regulates power relations, instead of opening up liberating pathways beyond monological authority. He argues that public life in postcolonial Africa reveals an inversion of the Bakhtinian understanding of the carnival burlesque, where the masses "clothe themselves in cheap imitations of power" while "power . . . makes vulgarity and wrongdoing its main mode of existence" (133). Such a critique itself reproduces most of Kristeva's reading of Bakhtin in *Le texte du roman*, where she claims that carnivalesque speech is but a "pseudo-transgression" that continuously enriches the power of the law through its very dependence upon it. It is when the energies of such speech enter the prism of the novel that the apparent binarism of carnival ambivalence, which operates on the level of a simple inversion of power, as a mockery and exposé of official authority, becomes doubled again into "polyphony" (1970, 176). Slavoj Žižek reads the relationship between laughter and the prevailing ideology in a similar way, asserting that "in contemporary societies, democratic or totalitarian . . . cynical distance, laughter, irony, are, so to speak, part of the game. The ruling ideology is not meant to be taken seriously or literally" (1989, 28). My argument is that while Célinian laughter (discussed in Chapter 3) powerfully affirms this thesis about the incestuous relationship between the masses and the ruling elite in fascist or totalitarian contexts, the laughter of al-Shidyaq's text is notably different. The carnival of *al-Saq 'ala al-saq*, in contrast to what we see in Céline, articulates the productive singularities of the Arabic language as the desire for public dialogue, not as a regression *inward*.

16. Geoffrey Roper argues that al-Shidyaq's detailed study of the Arabic and Syriac texts when he worked as a professional copyist and his awareness of the "corruptions" common in hand-copied texts convinced him that

"the revival of Arabic literature and culture depended on bypassing the old scribal tradition" and making the leap to the printed word (1995, 212). It is interesting to note that the importance of scribal culture distinguishes al-Shidyaq's situation from both the carnivalesque traditions of renaissance Europe, and the carnivalesque discourse of *créolité*, both of which exploit the *oral* text to regenerate the *printed* text. By contrast, al-Shidyaq carnivalizes the handwritten text in his printed work. A similar gesture is made in Abdelwahab Meddeb's texts, which are the focus of Chapter 6. Meddeb's work, however, makes the gesture of Arabic calligraphy transform the printed *French* text.

17. I refer to Aamir Mufti's article, "Global Comparativism," *Critical Inquiry* 31, no. 2 (Winter 2005), 472–89, which describes the critical practice of the title phrase as the kind of "opening up and crossing over" of given cultural practices and literary "traditions" (exemplified in the work of Edward Said), which function as "utterly historical operations that at the same time transgress the categories of traditional historicism" (477). I situate my analysis of Céline and al-Shidyaq on the critical terrain of this methodology in order to show that "all ideas of cultural autonomy and autochthony are fantasmatic in nature" (477–78).

18. My argument attempts to confirm Homi Bhabha's speculation that the ideologies of difference that emerged in colonial discourse prefigure the concerns of "postmodern" critical theory. "My growing conviction," Bhabha writes, "has been that the encounters and negotiations of differential meanings and values within 'colonial' textuality . . . have anticipated, *avant la lettre*, many of the problematics of signification and judgment that have become current in contemporary theory." See "The Postcolonial and the Postmodern," in *The Location of Culture* (London: Routledge, 1994), 173.

3. FROM DREYFUS IN THE COLONY TO CÉLINE'S ANTI-SEMITIC STYLE

1. Hochberg (2016), 202, 219.
2. See Anidjar (2008), 18–19, and Massad (2015), chap. 5.
3. Anidjar's claim is that Nazism produces the de-Semitization of Jews and the Semitization of Arabs, even as the term "anti-Semitism" comes to refer exclusively to anti-Jewish racism after World War II (2008, 19).
4. Jeffrey Herf's *Nazi Propaganda for the Arab World* (New Haven: Yale University Press, 2009) details this important instance of spreading anti-Semitism in the Arab World during World War II. As such, Herf's book can be said to function as a kind of twentieth-century corollary of what this chapter demonstrates, albeit operating within vastly different conditions and on different terrain.

5. The political maneuvering behind the Exposition reveals the hidden economic propellers of racial politics in this period in France. In *The Origins of Totalitarianism*, Hannah Arendt attributed to the 1900 Exposition the role of a kind of deus ex machina in the Dreyfus affair, since fears that the Expo would be boycotted due to the injustice of the French government led rather quickly to Dreyfus's exoneration in July 1899, whereas daily editorials by Clemenceau, Zola's "J'accuse," speeches by Jaurès, and much popular sentiment against anti-Dreyfusard clergy had failed (1973, 119).

6. In Zeev Sternhell's account, most French newspapers during the 1880s were anti-Semitic (1978, 217).

7. Quoted in Hammerschlag (2010), 38.

8. For more on Zola's role in the affair, especially within a nuanced and forceful critique of the long tradition of the "French intellectual," see Shlomo Sand, *The End of the French Intellectual: From Zola to Houllebecq* (London: Verso, 2018).

9. Nothing is known about either of these two authors other than what one might surmise based on the texts under consideration. It seems possible that "Hugolin" is a pen name, perhaps chosen because Saint Hugolin was a Franciscan monk who was martyred near Ceuta, in Morocco, in the year 1227.

10. While the text refers to Isaïe Levaillant, a prominent Jewish French politician and writer, as its inspiration for this sentiment, the burlesque could easily be aimed at the author of *Le Juif Algérien*, who espouses the same kind of assimilationist faith that Levaillant preached in France.

11. It is possible that the author of the *Pétition* was inspired by *The Talmud Unmasked*, published in 1892 by Justinas Bonaventure, which was itself cribbed from an 1871 work by August Rohlings. The longevity and persistence of this form of anti-Jewish polemic is attested to in the fact that the Anti-Defamation League saw fit to systematically refute the claims made in such screeds as recently as 2003.

12. See, e.g., "Petits métiers algériens," in *Algérie artistique et pittoresque* (1893), 5–6.

13. Aamir Mufti's *Enlightenment in the Colony* is the best exploration of the relation between the Jewish Question and the fractured legacy of the Enlightenment in colonial nationalist thought. Mufti's title, as well as the overall trajectory of his work, have both served as guiding inspirations for my own title and work.

14. See Hammerschlag (2010), 29, 42.

15. From an undated letter to Lucien Combelle, presumably post-1947, cited in Gibault (1985), 157.

16. My chief sources for biographical information on Céline are McCarthy's chapters, "Céline the Pamphleteer," "Occupation and Exile 1940–51" and the middle volume of Gibault's authoritative *Céline* (1985).

17. Léon Daudet, in *Action française*, February 10, 1938; also cited in Séebold (1985), 66. The connection between Céline and the renaissance is not simply an ideological position voiced by certain of his readers, but also has a substantive basis; in *Les verbes de Céline: Étude d'ensemble*, the first in a multivolume study of Céline's lexical inventions, Alphonse Juilland asserts that in Céline there is "*un foisonnement de néologismes sans précédent depuis Rabelais*" (1985, 2).

18. See, for example, Isabelle Blondiaux, "Céline: A Clinical or a Critical Case," in Scullion, Solomon, and Spear (1995), 13–28.

19. In *Céline: Portrait de l'artiste en psychiatre* (Paris: Société d'études Céliniennes, 2004), Isabelle Blondiaux argues that Céline's use of madness as a thematic and stylistic choice pathologizes the creative act itself. She contrasts this to the way that critics since Milton Hindus have tended to cross a certain objective line of analysis and forgive Céline by declaring him psychotic and paranoid.

20. It is interesting to note that Derrida's own admitted fascination for the word "resistance" comes partly from connotations of heroism and bravery developed during the Resistance of World War II. Céline's own activity during the occupation can be very literally considered a resistance of nonresistance.

21. Both Fredric Jameson's assessment of Céline as a detective-like collector and analyst of personal, moral details (as discussed in McCarren 1998, 218), and Walter Benjamin's pronouncement of Céline as an "anthropological" or "clinical nihilist" (*Arcades Project*, K7, a2 and N8a,1) frame Céline as a kind of social analyst.

22. The function of the Célinian neologism is brought into sharp relief when compared to a passage from a renaissance defender of French, Geoffrey Tory, the humanist printer and translator. There are four kinds of men, Tory claims, who try to "*corrompre et difformer*" the French language: "*Ce sont écumeurs de latin* ["Latin pirates"], *plaisanteurs et jargonneurs* [an allegation leveled against Villon]," and worst of all are the "*innovateurs et forgeurs de mots nouveaux. Si tels forgeurs ne sont rufians, je ne les estime guère meilleurs. Pensez qu'ils ont une grande grâce quand ils disent après boire qu'ils ont le cerveau tout encornimatibulé et emburlicoqué d'un tas de mirilifiques et triquedondaines, d'un tas de gringuenaudes et guilleroches, qui les fatrouillent incessament!*" (in *Premiers Combats*, p. 53). The charm of Tory's passage resides in the epithets ("*écumeurs de latin*") and the imitation of the object of his critique, an imitation good enough to incite Rabelais to plagiarize from his section on the "Latin pirates." Céline is guilty of all these corruptions and deformations; his ideal might be to commit all four at once if possible. The gratuitous fifth crime would be plagiarism of such a text, whose accusations he would have aimed at himself as he does in *Bagatelles pour un massacre*.

23. Cited in Séebold (1985), 63. Hammerschlag's book explores this idea at great length, ultimately asserting the critical power of a certain kind of "figural Jew."

24. Especially interesting evidence of this is a letter from Céline to Dr. Walter Strauss, dating from 1937 or 1938, where Céline writes: "*Ce qui vous arrive est absolument affreux* [Nazi persecution]." Gibault claims that Céline offered the Doctor help, while at the same time warning him that he is "*abominablement antisémite*" (quoted in Gibault 1985, 166–67). This same situation forms the framework for many of the tirades in *Bagatelles pour un massacre*.

25. See the essays collected in Scullion, Solomon, and Spear (1995) for engagements with these problematic readings of Céline's political style.

26. Jean-Guy Rens, "Voyage no. II—Rogodon par L.-F. Céline," 1971; quoted in Dauphin (1976), 173.

4. RESURRECTING COLONIAL DECADENCE IN INDEPENDENT ALGERIA

1. We see this mutation, or splitting of Orientalism-as-anti-Semitism, in the difference between Muslim and Christian reactions to the Dreyfus affair (see Chapter 3). In general, Muslims sympathized with Dreyfus, whereas many Arab Christians transferred the racism of French anti-Semitism, which originally applied to both Arabs and Jews, and took an "anti-Semitic" view of Dreyfus. See Lewis (1986), esp. 26–28 and 133–34. D. Kimon's *La pathologie de l'islam et les moyens de la détruire* (1897) adopts the broadly defined racist tropes developed in the Orientalist laboratory and applies them exclusively to specific groups: Turks, Arabs, and Muslims, and Jews.

2. Throughout *L'an V de la révolution algérienne* (English translation, *A Dying Colonialism*), for example, Fanon repeatedly refers to the effects of the anticolonial war in terms of physiological "mutations" of the nervous systems of the colonized: "La puissance de le Révolution algérienne d'ores et déjà dans la mutation radicale qui s'est produite chez l'Algérien" (2001 [1959], 14).

3. The complex relationship between what goes by the name of *nahda* in the Arab East in comparison with the Maghreb is beyond the scope of this chapter, but there appears to have been less of an attempt to distinguish Islamic reformism from the more cultural and secular focus on reviving Arabic language and literature that occurs in Egypt and the Levant (the presence of a strong Christian minority in the latter countries being one clear possible reason for this difference). See Murtad (1983 [1979]), which conflates the revival of the Arabic language and Islamic reformism under the banner of *al-nahda*. Merad's study of Algerian Islamic reformism also uses 1925 as its point of departure but does not make use of the term *nahda*. Jacques Berque points out the push to revive Arabic had long been established in Tunisia since the beginning of the twentieth century (as witnessed by the

Khalduniyya Tunisian Cultural Association, founded 1896), but was only still being established in Algeria in the early 1930s (Berque, 1967). When examining the causes and champions of the revival of Classical Arabic in the Maghreb, one should take with a grain of salt the praise allotted to the role of French Orientalists, such as Régis Blachère, who, according to Berque, "fought manfully in support of the Classical traditions of the East" while teaching in Rabat (360).

4. Many writers have pointed out the secularist roots of Algerian Arabization, often, it seems, to reveal the ironies in the genealogy claimed by groups like the FIS (Front Islamique de Salut, "Islamic Salvation Front") in the name of political Islam. For an example, see Gafaïti (2002), 40.

5. The genealogy of the meaning of the word "Arab" is enormously complex, but many have indicated the role of the British, in particular, in crafting what this word has come to mean. For one account of this complexity, see Leila Ahmed, *A Border Passage: From Cairo to America—a Woman's Journey* (New York: Penguin, 2000), 266.

6. MSA is the modernized, "streamlined" form of the Arabic language that was engineered during the nineteenth-century Egyptian-Levantine *nahda*. It is distinct from both Algerian dialectical Arabic and Classical, Qur'anic Arabic.

7. This situation of Berber (or Amazigh) languages has been slowly improving since the mid-1990s. In 2002, Berber was declared a "National language" by the Algerian government, and it was elevated to an "official language" in 2016. See http://www.centredeerechercheberbere.fr/statut.html (accessed July 1, 2018).

8. Stora (2000), 151–60; Gafaïti (2002), 35.

9. This interview was also aired in the UK as part of a BBC program, "Shooting the Writer." This comment is discussed in Cox (1997), 94, 108; Dobie (2003), 34; Gafaïti (2002), 40–41; Geesey (1996), 271, 278; and Carlier (2002), 90. Wattar's comment also provides an uncanny echo of Camus's famous Nobel Prize acceptance speech from 1957: "I have always denounced terrorism. I must also denounce a terrorism which is exercised blindly, in the streets of Algiers for example, and which one day could strike my mother or my family. I believe in justice, but I shall defend my mother before justice." Herbert R. Lottman, *Albert Camus: A Biography* (New York: Doubleday, 1979), 618. In this context, Wattar would be preemptively placing Camus's words in the mouth of Djaout's daughter (who will be featured later in my discussion of Djaout's novel) as a representative of francophone Algerian society that is to be excluded from the national project, as were the Harkis and the pieds-noirs. His comment pits the Algerian family against Algeria as a national family in a way that resonates with similar statements throughout the history of French Algeria.

10. This legerdemain also allows him to get away with publicly critiquing aspects of Boumédienne's government, a point Debbie Cox takes up in her essay on Wattar. She argues that the regime tolerated Wattar's criticism because the temporary alliance between the Parti d'Avant-Garde Socialiste (PAGS) and the FLN during the agrarian revolution provided a new degree of freedom for those on the left. The global critical success of Wattar's novels proved the success of Algerian *ta'rib* (1997, 106).

11. See Michael Cooperson's 1998 essay on Arabic time travel narratives for an extended discussion of this topic.

12. Roger Allen has pointed out that the "Period of Time" to which the text refers (and which was the working title as it was being published periodically) corresponds to Cromer's tenure as Consul-General during occupation. See Allen's introduction to his translation (1992, 72).

13. The translations of passages from Wattar's novel are mostly my own, but I also rely on and use William Granara's translation and give page numbers from his edition first, followed by the page numbers in the Arabic edition. When only one reference is given, the English text is being indicated.

14. Anouar Majid, in his critique of the uses and abuses of secularist ideas in relation to Islam, suggests that Laroui's reliance on the term "Arab" demonstrates how he has become "trapped in the very epistemologies [he] seek[s] to overcome." Majid argues that "the Arab intellectual crisis simply indicates that Arabs have not been able to theorize their own identity within the bifurcations and polarities engendered by the colonial experience" (2000, 60).

15. This reading of the novel's lead character adds another layer to Réda Bensmaïa's conception of the *médinant* as a kind of Maghrebi *flâneur*, who, unlike Walter Benjamin's European *flâneur*, reinscribes the heterogeneous time of the body into the spaces of the medina. As opposed to Meddeb's narrator, taken as an example of the *médinant*, Bu al-Arwah suffers the shock of a postcolonial city that has been radically reordered in ways that resonate with Benjamin's writings on Baudelaire. For more on this topic, see my discussion of the *médinant* in Chapter 6.

16. Compare this to a stanza from Baudelaire's famous "Correspondences":

> Comme de longs échos qui de loin se confondent
> Dans une ténébreuse et profonde unité,
> Vaste comme une nuit et comme la clarté,
> Les parfums, les couleurs et les sons se répondent.

17. In her essay on the gendering of MSA and dialect in Algeria, Anne-Emmanuelle Berger argues that dialectical Arabic—as the chief "mother

tongue" in Algeria—is given a feminine and maternal role in contemporary language politics of Algeria. She compares the language enforced by Arabization, MSA, to the *hijab*—as a kind of phallic symbol of power imported from the Arab East: "It is because modern Muslim women are thus made into the guardians of the symbolic border of the Islamic world that the newly veiled women acquire a sense of power" (2002, 73). She goes on to point out that "the adoption of standard Arabic is also an attempt to shield and sever the speaking subjects of Algeria from the infantilizing effect of a dialect construed as weak, impure, and improper" (74).

18. Like Bu al-Arwah, Wattar left Algeria near the beginning of the war to study at the Zaytuna Mosque in Tunis. For a brief biographical note on Wattar, see F. Ladkany's entry in Jamel-Eddine Bencheikh, *Dictionnaire de littératures de langue arabe et maghrébine francophone* (Paris: Presses Universitaires de France, 2000), 422–23.

19. This masculinization of national language can also be seen in his assertion that only Djaout's wife and children would mourn his passing, which suggests that, in Algeria, French only signifies for women and children.

20. I am borrowing this distinction between the pedagogical and performative functions of narration from Bensmaïa, who borrows it from Homi Bhabha's essay "DissemiNation: Time, Narrative, and the Margins of the Modern Nation," in *Nation and Narration*, ed. Homi K. Bhabha (New York: Routledge, 1990), 139–70.

21. The obvious contemporary parallel to Ibn Tumart is the rise of Algerian Islamist groups, which, like the colonial nightmare, haunt the margins of Djaout's text. Other recurrent themes in the text more explicitly parallel the story of the lost empire of the puritanical Almoravids, from the vanished paradise of the author's Algerian childhood to lyrical passages celebrating the flight of birds, as well as the career of the child-poet Rimbaud, whose journey to Aden Djaout also attempts to retrace.

5. ALGERIAN WOMEN AND THE INVENTION OF LITERARY MOURNING

1. Abraham and Torok's "renewal" of Freud's famous 1917 essay "Mourning and Melancholia" has itself proved to be fecund ground for subsequent analyses, including that of Derrida's foreword to their reinterpretation of Freud's reading of the Wolfman, "Fors: Les mots anglés de Nicolas Abraham et Maria Torok," in Abraham, Torok, and Derrida (1976), 7–73. Freud's essay both contrasts and complicates the distinction between *mourning* as a "successful" way of dealing with loss (in which the lost object becomes psychically "assimilated" by the subject in the process of "working through") and *melancholia*, as a kind of "failed mourning" or a pathological

state that occurs when the subject is unable to successfully mourn the lost object. On the one hand, Derrida deconstructs this distinction, while on the other hand, he affirms "failed" mourning as an ethical gesture that does not idealize the lost object but retains its singularity in material form. In *Spectres of Marx*, Derrida writes that "mourning is not one kind of work among others. It is work itself, work in general, the trait by means of which one ought perhaps to reconsider the very concept of production—in what links it to trauma, to mourning, to the idealizing iterability of expropriation, thus to the spectral spiritualization that is at work in any *tekhne*" (1994, 97). This provocative suggestion concerning the link between the work of mourning and *tekhne* speaks to the concerns of the present essay, which in addition aims to consider the gendering of the work of mourning in relation to the work of art.

2. For an extended discussion of the cave as a symbolic resource and as a thematic element in Maghrebi literature and folk traditions, see Jones (2012).

3. All translations of Méchakra's novel are mine.

4. See Pears's (2004) discussion of the way the text deploys the two versions of this name ("ARRIS" as the toponym, and "Arris" as the personal name) as the word shifts its reference and allows Méchakra to blur the line between generations and different kinds of objects of loss (77).

5. From the date of publication (1993), if not from the date of completion of the manuscript, given in the text as 1988.

6. Harrison (2016) gives a virtuoso reading of *The Algerian Trilogy*, of which *Dhakirat al-Jasad* is the first book. Harrison contextualizes Mosteghanemi's work within the rubric of what she calls the "transcolonial exotic," a kind of repackaging of Maghrebi history and social life for a Mashreqi audience. See esp. 61–78.

7. Translations of Mosteghanemi are from the edition by Baria Ahmar Sreih. In some cases I have made slight modifications, which are explained in the essay. When two distinct page numbers are given, the first references the English translation, and the second references the Arabic.

8. The Arabic does not specify that the martyrs are not "mass-produced," but rather uses the indefinite plural, *shuhada'*, "martyrs," as distinct from the singular form, *shahidan*. Sreih's published English translation has been retained here, since it clarifies the main idea being expressed that would otherwise be difficult to translate.

9. Gilroy (2005) examines this broad problematic from the perspective of the European center, in this case, contemporary multicultural Britain attempting to come to terms with the loss of its empire. For those who need "race" to "keep their bearings" in the new world, Gilroy writes, "there can be no working through this problem because the melancholic pattern has become the mechanism that sustains the unstable edifice of increasingly brittle and empty national identity" (106).

10. See Khanna (2006).

11. Much criticism has focused on precisely the complex relationship between these two terms as apparent opposites, whereas Derrida, for example deconstructs this opposition. For two other examples of critical approaches to this question that view mourning and melancholia as existing on a continuum rather than in opposition, see Eric Santner, *Stranded Objects: Mourning, Memory, and Film in Postwar Germany* (Ithaca, NY: Cornell University Press, 1990), and Gana (2011).

12. Page numbers following English text refer to Peggy Kamuf's superb translation of Cixous's text, which has been used throughout.

13. The establishment of the Décret Crémieux on October 24, 1870, represented the culmination of the first phase of a struggle for citizenship for the Jews of French Algeria. However, the decree aggravated conflicts between the Jewish minority and the Muslim majority while also speeding up the assimilation of Jews. In October 1940 the Vichy government abolished the decree, and Algerian Jews were stripped of French citizenship. It was abrogated a second time in March 1943 and then reinstated, after much controversy, in October 1943. For more on the complex citizenship history of Jews in Algeria, see Stora (2006) and Arendt (2007 [1943]).

14. I take my lead here from Khanna, who speculates that this may in fact be the case: "Given the shared theoretical roots of nation formation, colonial policy, and psychoanalysis, we may want to conjecture that psychic assimilation itself is a colonial formation that is a catachresis in the former European colonies" (2008, 169).

15. See "Khatibi's 'Place of Hostage,'" in Khatibi (2010), 1006.

16. All translations from Djebar are mine. The text has also been translated as *Algerian White*, trans. David Kelley and Marjolin de Jager (New York: Seven Stories Press, 2000).

17. The translation reads: "There, on American soil, our French from before the dawn flows just as simply, after all, as the mother tongue we share" (20–21).

18. Such a technique harkens back to Djebar's reworking of the frame-tale structure of *A Thousand and One Nights* in her own *Ombre sultane*. The framing of this oral account of the impromptu occupation-turned-militant celebration of the dead thus represents a specifically *literary* technique deployed in this mixed-genre text.

19. For one account of traditional mourning practice in Algeria and the role played by gender, see chap. 5 of Jansen's *Women without Men*.

20. This was the answer that Cixous gave to the author, who asked the original question. The exchange took place at a conference dedicated to her work at Cornell University on September 20–21, 2010, entitled "Writing at a Distance: With Hélène Cixous."

6. VIRTUAL SECULARIZATION: ABDELWAHAB MEDDEB'S
"WALKING CURE" AND THE IMMIGRANT BODY IN FRANCE

1. See Karen Miller's August 30, 2006, article from the Associated Press Worldstream, "Arab Man in New York Airport Denied Plane Entry for Wearing Arabic Script T-Shirt."

2. For a review of such statements that appeared in the French media immediately following the first *affaire des foulards Islamiques*, see David Beriss, "Scarves, Schools, and Segregation: The *Foulard* Affair," in *French Politics & Society* 8, no. 1 (Winter 1990): 1–13. Notably, Beriss references an interview with Gilles Deleuze in *Libération*, October 26, 1989, where Deleuze asks whether the wearing of headscarves might be "a concerted effort, of which the headscarf is but the first step."

3. One must nonetheless examine the accusations of a "new anti-Semitism" in France, primarily among Franco-Maghrebi youth, and coming from figures like Alain Finkelkraut, with a degree of critical circumspection. In his analysis of the problem, Paul Silverstein (2008) examines ways that the genuine problem of anti-Jewish anti-Semitism coming from Franco-Maghrebi youths becomes inflated through misdefinitions and misleading statistical reporting. Silverstein concludes that "in the majority of cases [of anti-Semitism in contemporary France], it is clear that it is far-right xenophobia directed at both Jews and Muslims that still remains the greatest danger to French civil life" (23).

4. For example, see Kim Willsher's article from November 13, 2005, in *The Sunday Telegraph* (London), "Le Pen Benefits from Unrest with 'Wave of Far-Right Recruits,'" 29.

5. For a discussion of the mobility and immobility of refugees and migrants, see David Fieni, "Tagging the Spectral Mobility of the Stateless Body: Deleuze, Stasis, and Graffiti," *The Journal for Cultural Research* 20, no. 4 (October 2016).

6. Their argument about Empire's "formal" decadence evokes Georges Bataille's celebrated entry for *informe* in his *dictionnaire critique*. Bataille's political economy of the "formless" anticipates both the decentralized shape of imperial sovereignty, and also the attributes of an abject and stateless multitude which lacks all recourse to citizens' rights:

> Formless.—A dictionary would begin as of the moment when it no longer provided the meanings of the words but their tasks. In this way formless is not only an adjective having such and such a meaning, but a term serving to declassify, requiring in general that every thing should have a form. What it designates does not, in any sense whatever, possess rights, and everywhere gets crushed like a spider or an earthworm. For academics to be satisfied, it would be necessary, in effect, for the universe to take on a

form. The whole of philosophy has no other aim; it is a question of fitting what exists into a frock coat, a mathematical frock-coat. To affirm on the contrary that the universe resembles nothing at all and is only formless, amounts to saying that the universe is something akin to a spider or a gob of spittle.

(Georges Bataille, "Informe," in *Oeuvres complètes* (Paris: Gallimard, 1988), 1:217. For an attempt to apply Bataille's concept to modern art, Yves-Alain Bois and Rosalind Krauss, *Formless: A User's Guide* (New York: Zone Books, 1997).

7. The classic diagnosis of Nietzsche as being himself degenerate occurs in Max Nordau's widely read "medical study" of the nervous disorders of the European elite, *Degeneration*, which exemplifies the clinical confidence that facilitated the transference of medical terminology onto larger cultural phenomena during the fin de siècle. This confidence becomes immediately apparent in the five main categories used by Nordau, who was himself a practicing physician, to structure his book: "The Symptoms," "Diagnosis," "Etiology," "Prognosis," and "Therapeutics." As his example of cultural decadence or nervous degeneration among philosophers, Nordau cites Nietzsche, who had succumbed to a severe mental breakdown three years prior to the book's publication in 1892. Nordau reads Nietzsche's text precisely as the fin-de-siècle clinicians had trained themselves to read the human body: the text exhibits symptoms that authorize Nordau to diagnose Nietzsche as a sadistic, hysterical ego-manic, with "a mania for contradiction" (1993, 447–50). He uses this diagnosis of Nietzsche to demonstrate that the social organ of philosophy has itself become infected.

8. I adopt the term "critical secularism" from the title of a special issue of *boundary2* edited by Aamir Mufti, which revisits the Saidian ground of "secular criticism" in order to think the secular beyond they ways it has been abused as a tool of colonial or imperial control.

9. The radio show, which was first broadcast on October 12, 2001, was launched as a vehicle that would demystify Islam for French listeners struggling to understand the links between what occurred on September 11 and Islam in general. The original program description for "Cultures d'Islam" (which was deleted from the France Culture website in the wake of Meddeb's death in 2014 and the arrival of new host, Ghaleb Bencheikh) indicates something of Meddeb's virtual secularization of Islam:

> Ce n'est pas par hasard ou par accident que l'islam est devenu la deuxième religion de France. Toute une histoire a convergé vers cette présence désormais interne à l'Hexagone. Or, hormis une série de clichés, peu de choses sont connues de cette civilisation : pourtant en langue française, le corpus qui la concerne est tout aussi dense que séculaire.

Nous souhaitons avec cette émission participer à la levée d'une méconnaissance pour que les références islamiques circulent dans le sens commun.

Nous approchons l'islam en tant que phénomène de culture et civilisation. Cette disposition n'occulte pas les questions religieuses et dogmatiques telles qu'elles sont apparues à travers les tensions et les dérives qui se sont manifestées dans le cours de l'Histoire et qui visitent avec constance la scène de l'actualité. Notre approche est ouverte, moderne, polyphonique.

See the *France Culture* website for "Cultures d'Islam," where one can access archives of Meddeb's past shows: https://www.franceculture.fr/emissions/cultures-dislam

10. My reading of Nietzschean "double science" is here indebted to Alan Schrift's reading of Derrida. In "Nietzsche's French Legacy," Schrift traces the ways that Foucault, Derrida, Deleuze, and Lyotard used Nietzsche, and draws a connection between the method of deconstruction, in particular, and Nietzsche's own critical method. Like deconstructionists, Schrift argues, Nietzsche deploys what Derrida terms a "double science," a movement of thought and writing that consists of two related moments. The first moment is a reversal or inversion of the received values within a given binary pair: just as Nietzsche, in *The Genealogy of Morality*, inverts the received values of "good" and "evil," so too does Derrida, in *De la grammatologie*, invert the values within the binary pairs of writing/speech, and presence/absence. To assume that Nietzsche's (or Derrida's) analysis satisfies itself with this inversion of values, Schrift says, would be to misread Nietzsche in the same way that Heidegger did when he "accused Nietzsche of 'completing' the history of metaphysics with an 'inversion' of Platonism" (1996, 337). In Derrida's words, the second moment has the force of an imperative: "we must now mark the interval between inversion . . . and the irruptive emergence of a new 'concept,' a concept that can no longer be, and never could be, included in the previous regime" (336). Schrift locates this "marked interval" in Nietzsche at the intersection of his perspectivist attitude and his refusal of "an unmediated, non-interpretive apprehension of 'reality'" (337). "The question," Schrift concludes, "is no longer whether a perspective is 'true' or 'false'; the sole question that interests the Nietzschean genealogist is whether or not a perspective enhances life" (337).

11. Much of the content of this interview was later collected with additional material and published as *La maladie de l'Islam* by Éditions du Seuil in 2002. Like the interview, the text is critical of militant Islamist groups, while also praising the creative force and aesthetic beauty of Islamic *culture*. It won the 2002 Prix François Mauriac and was the first book by Meddeb to be translated into English: *The Malady of Islam*, trans. Pierre Joris and Ann Reid (New York: Basic Books, 2003).

12. The importance and complexity of this point warrants citing a large selection from the interview, in which Meddeb discusses the political uses of Islam and Christianity as a supplement to temporal power:

> The facts of the material history of Islam help disprove something usually perceived as dogma, namely the concept repeated everywhere again and again according to which Islam is in its essence articulated on the structure of authority based on the consubstantiality of the religious and the political. Many European Islamologists share this belief with the fundamentalists; it is an idea that haunts the press and the media. But it is false! Historical fact does not verify it. Political power has very often been exercised by the military man who becomes emir. And who then had to negotiate the kind of relationship he will have with the man who represents religion, the one called the *'alim*, the scholar in theology, who represented the juridical-theological instances.
>
> When one has an essentialist vision of things, one invokes the Prophet of Islam who was a warrior-prophet, founder of a political society; one says that in the very genesis of Islam, at its very foundations, one detects the consubstantiality which, indeed, existed and which continued with the creation of the figure of the caliph, the successor, the delegate of the Prophet. This caliphate is characteristically Islamic: one succeeds the Prophet in the fullness of His functions, as leader of the community. That is the ideal figure of the caliph, as it existed for a brief period of time. Very early on, starting with the first Arab empire centered in Damascus, with the Umayyads (640–750), the caliphate could have been tempted to resolve this problem of the legitimacy of power by a separation between the temporal function (assumed by the Meccans of Koraish) and the spiritual function (assumed by the imam, the descendant of the Prophet). I locate these premises in a poem by the official poet Farazdak (d. 728), which separates these two figures, attributing temporal prestige to the one and spiritual charisma to the other. Add to this that the very concept of the caliphate had been emptied of its substance by the end of the tenth century, the era of that institution's decline, which saw the extension of the caliphal function to three figures: besides the caliph of Baghdad, two others declared themselves caliphs, namely the Umayyad prince of Cordoba and the Fatimid Mahdi of Cairo. This function, after having become an empty shell invested with various utopias, will be restored by the Ottomans, but in a totally symbolic manner, precisely to signify that the religious function comes to add itself as a supplement to the figure of the sultan, whose first function is imperial.
>
> We can find a useful indication in the monograph Ernst Kantorowicz devoted to Frederic II, Germano-Roman emperor (1212–1250), who had major conflicts with the papacy and especially with Innocent III. Toward 1220 one of the great quest ions was to know who, the emperor or the pope,

was the *vero imperator*. This conflict led to a civil war that lasted the whole of the thirteenth century, with various ups and downs. Dante himself both witnessed and was part of it: Florence was divided between the whites and the blacks, partisans of the pope and partisans of the emperor, Guelfs and Ghibellines, and Dante, backing the emperor, was expelled from Florence and had to live in exile. These elements pervade his work and he composed a major theoretical essay, *De monarchia*, which tries to think through that will to create two courts, separated but linked by a network of causalities — the court of the emperor and the court of the pope. The problem of the separation of the spiritual and the temporal is thus a problem common to Christianity and Islam. The same Frederic II, as leader of the sixth crusade (1229), negotiated with the Ayubides, the descendants of Saladin, in Jerusalem, Palestine, and he was given royal authority over Jerusalem, Bethlehem, and Nazareth. He then negotiated with Fakhreddine, the local governor of the Ayubid sultan Al-Kâmil who was in Cairo, and came to a peaceful understanding. At that time the caliph in Baghdad was a totally symbolic personage and was considered by Frederic II as the equivalent of the pope because he no longer had any political or military power. This caliph protested loudly and vituperatively against the treatise but he had no means of coercion. And Frederic II is reported to have exclaimed: "It's extraordinary, their pope protests in vain!" For indeed his protest had no effect whatsoever; the emperor treats military and political questions with the military and political powers, and "their pope" is completely powerless. Frederic II was dreaming of nearly the same thing for the Occident. You can see that if we take historic facts into account, it is at least necessary to complexify the so-called dogma of the consubstantiality of the political and religious.

But fundamentalism and Wahhabism restore the idea of the consubstantiality of the political and religious by recalling the mythic model of Medina, a model that factual history contradicts and dismantles. And of course when every political action is determined by religion, the effect is devastating. For politics, which is a human endeavor, by becoming a divine endeavor turns more dogmatic and intolerant. God is never wrong. (10–13)

13. Meddeb's focus on the ideas of active and reactive forces in Nietzsche suggests that he is reading Nietzsche through Deleuze. See Deleuze (1983) for Deleuze's explanation of these ideas.

14. Tarek El-Ariss's superb book, *Trials of Arab Modernity* (2013) provides an extended meditation on the fraught relationship between theoretical and technological innovations erupting in events marking Arab cultural production since the *nahda*.

15. I have used my own translations of Meddeb's novels throughout. Jane Kuntz's translation of *Talismano* was published by the Dalkey Archive in

2011. The text's opening words echo those of the most famous "walking text" of the French canon, Rousseau's *Les rêveries du promeneur solitaire* (1782), which begins, "Me voici donc seul sur la terre, n'ayant plus de frère, de prochain, d'ami, de société que moi-même" (35). Meddeb's urban trek through the medina teeming with signs of social and historical filiations contrasts sharply with the utopic mental spaces described by Rousseau.

16. Albert Hourani discusses various Arabic authors of 'Abduh's circle who tried to show that Islam "had hidden in it all the modern world thought it had discovered" (1962, 162). Another point of contention between 'Abduh and Meddeb, whose writing reveals an intimate relationship to the works of Ibn 'Arabi, is revealed in the fact that 'Abduh kept Ibn 'Arabi's *al-Futuhat al-makkiya* (The Keys to Mecca) from being published because 'Abduh saw mysticism as antithetical to the building of a strong *umma*. See Hourani (1962), 150.

17. Bensmaïa adapts the term from Khatibi's analysis of Meddeb in his essay on the latter's work, "Incipits," in *Du bilinguisme*.

18. Dakhlia (2000). Dahklia cites the titles of Meddeb's novels, as well as texts by Maghrebian francophone writers Assia Djebar, Mohamad Khaïreddine, and Abdelkebir Khatibi as evidence of an unconscious resurfacing of this lingua franca in the postcolonial period. It is also interesting to note that Meddeb provides two spellings of the same term, *fantasia/phantasia*, to illustrate the further multiplicity of Maghrebian language practice. Djebar's *L'amour, la fantasia* (1985) was published a few months before Meddeb's *Phantasia* (1986).

19. A *noria* is a large waterwheel.

CONCLUSION: TOWARD A CONTRAPUNTAL DOUBLE
CRITIQUE OF COLONIAL MODERNITY

Sections of this conclusion were first published in French as "Désappropriation de soi et poétique de l'intersigne chez Khatibi," in *Expressions maghrébines* 12, no. 1 (Summer 2013): 1–17, as part of a dossier on Khatibi. This material was then repurposed and modified for publication in *The b20 Review*, on December 11, 2018, as part of a dossier directed by Olivia C. Harrison, "The Maghreb after Orientalism."

1. I borrow this assertion about the Holocaust from Pollock (1993), 86.

2. Khatibi (2010), 1005. I have slightly modified Catherine Porter's excellent translation in this second passage.

3. This performatively ironic assertion about Khatibi's "identity" comes from Derrida's lecture on "la francophonie outside of France," published in *Le monolinguisme de l'autre*, where he declares himself "the most franco-Maghrebian" of the pair (Derrida and Khatibi), and possibly even "the *only* franco-Maghrebian" (Derrida 1996, 29).

SELECT BIBLIOGRAPHY

'Abbud, Marun. *Saqr Lubnan*. Beirut: Manshurat Dar al-Makshuf, 1950.
'Abduh, Muhammad. *Risalat al-tawhid* [Treatise on Unity]. Cairo: Dar al-Ma'arif, 1966 [1897].
Abraham, Nicolas, Maria Torok, and Jacques Derrida. *Cryptonymie: Le verbier de l'homme aux loups*. Paris: Aubier Flammarion, 1976.
Abraham, Nicolas, Maria Torok, and Nicholas T. Rand. *The Shell and the Kernel: Renewals of Psychoanalysis*. Chicago: University of Chicago Press, 1994.
Aching, Gerard. "On Colonial Modernity: Civilization Versus Sovereignty in Cuba, c. 1840." In *International Relations and Non-Western Thought: Imperialism, Colonialism, and Investigations of Global Modernity*, edited by Robbie Shilliam, 29–46. Abingdon, UK: Routledge, 2011.
Adams, Jad. *Hideous Absinthe: A History of the Devil in a Bottle*. Madison, Wisconsin: University of Wisconsin Press, 2004.
Addi, Lahouari. "Les intellectuels qu'on assassine." *Esprit* (January 1995), 133–38.
Adonis. *Introduction to Arabic Poetics*. Translated by Catherine Cobham. Austin: University of Texas Press, 1990.
al-Afghani, Jamal al-din. "Réponse du cheik Gemmal Eddine." In Renan (2003).
———. "Lecture on Teaching and Learning." In *An Islamic Response to Imperialism: Political and Religious Writings of Sayyid Jamal ad-din al-Afghani*. Edited and translated by Nikki R. Keddie. Berkeley: University of California Press, 1968.
Al-Azmeh, Aziz. *Islam and Modernities*. London: Verso, 1993.
al-Kassim, Dina. "The Faded Bond: Calligraphesis and Kinship in Abdelwahab Meddeb's *Talismano*." *Public Culture* 13, no. 1 (2001): 113–38.
al-Kawakibi, 'Abd al-Rahman. *Umm al-qura: Ay dabt mufawadat wa muqarrarat mu'tamar al-nahda al-islamiya* [The Mother of Cities: Minutes from the Meetings and Decisions of the Congress of the Islamic Awakening]. Port Said, 1899.
Allen, Roger. "A Study of Muhammad al-Muwaylihi's *Hadith 'Isa ibn Hisham*." In *A Period of Time*. Reading: The Middle East Center, 1992.

al-Musawi, Muhsin Jasim. *The Medieval Islamic Republic of Letters: Arabic Knowledge Construction*. Notre Dame: University of Notre Dame Press, 2015.
al-Muwaylihi, Muhammad. *A Period of Time*. Translated by Roger Allen. Reading: The Middle East Center, 1992.
al-Shidyaq, Ahmad Faris. *Al-Saq 'ala al-saq fi ma huwwa al-Faryaq*. Beirut: Dar Maktabat al-Hayyah, 1966.
Althusser, Louis. *Lenin and Philosophy and Other Essays*. Translated by Ben Brewster. New York: Monthly Review Press, 2001.
Anidjar, Gil. *Semites: Race, Religion, Literature*. Stanford: Stanford University Press, 2008.
Anti-Defamation League. *The Talmud in Anti-Semitic Polemics*. New York: Anti-Defamation League, 2003.
Antonius, George. *The Arab Awakening: The Story of the Arab National Movement*. Philadelphia: J. B. Lippincott, 1939.
Antun, Farah. *Ibn Rushd wa falsafatuhu* [Ibn Rushd and His Philosophy]. Beirut: Dar al-Tali'a, 1981 [1902].
Arendt, Hannah. *The Origins of Totalitarianism*. New York: Harcourt Brace Jovanovich, 1973.
———. "Why the Cremieux Decree Was Abrogated." *The Jewish Writings*. New York: Schocken Books, 2007.
Arnaldez, Roger. *Averroès: Un rationaliste en Islam*. Paris: Balland, 1998.
———. "Ibn Rushd." *The Encyclopedia of Islam*. 2nd edition. Leiden: Brill, 2002.
Badiou, Alain. *Ethics: An Essay on the Understanding of Evil*. Translated by Peter Hallward. London: Verso, 2002.
Bakhtin, Mikhaïl. *The Dialogic Imagination*. Edited by Michael Holquist; translated by Caryl Emerson and Michael Holquist. Austin: University of Texas Press, 1981.
———. *Rabelais and His World*. Translated by Hélène Iswolsky. Bloomington: Indiana University Press, 1968 [1965].
Barlow, Tani E. *Formations of Colonial Modernity in East Asia*. Durham, NC: Duke University Press, 1997.
Benjamin, Walter. *The Arcades Project*. Translated by Howard Eiland and Kevin McLaughlin. Cambridge, MA: The Belknap Press of Harvard University Press, 1999.
———. "On Some Motifs in Baudelaire." *Illuminations*. Translated by Harry Zohn. New York: Schocken Books, 1969.
———. "Theses on the Philosophy of History." Ibid.
Benmakhlouf, Ali. *Averroès*. Paris: Les Belles Lettres, 2000.
Bensmaïa, Réda. *Experimental Nations, Or the Invention of the Maghrib*. Princeton: Princeton University Press, 2003.
———. "Villes d'écrivains." *Peuples méditerranéens/Mediterranean Peoples* 78 (1997): 157–67.

Berger, Anne-Emmanuelle, ed. *Algeria in Others' Languages*. Ithaca, NY: Cornell University Press, 2002.
Bernheimer, Charles. *Decadent Subjects*. Baltimore: Johns Hopkins University Press, 2002.
Berque, Jacques. *French North Africa: The Maghrib between Two Wars*. Translated by Jean Stewart. New York: Praeger, 1967.
Brett, Michael. "Legislating for Inequality in Algeria: The Senatus-Consulte of 14 July 1865." *Bulletin of the School of Oriental and African Studies* 51, no. 3 (October 1988): 440–61.
Buck-Morss, Susan. *The Dialectics of Seeing: Walter Benjamin and the Arcades Project*. Cambridge, MA: MIT Press, 1989.
Butler, Judith. *Antigone's Claim: Kinship Between Life and Death*. New York: Columbia University Press, 2000.
Carlier, Omar. "Civil War, Private Violence, and Cultural Socialization: Political Violence in Algeria (1954–1988)." Translated by Whitney Sanford. In Berger (2002), 81–106.
Casanova, Pascale. *La république mondiale des lettres*. Paris: Éditions du Seuil, 1999.
Céline, Louis-Ferdinand. *Bagatelles pour un massacre*. Paris: Denoël, 1937.
———. *L'école des cadavres*. Paris: Denoël, 1938.
Chakrabarty, Dipesh. *Provincializing Europe: Postcolonial Thought and Historical Difference*. Princeton: Princeton University Press, 2000.
Chatterjee, Partha. *Nationalist Thought and the Colonial World*. Minneapolis: University of Minnesota Press, 1986.
Chesneau, Albert. *Essai de psychocritique de Louis-Ferdinand Céline*. Paris: Lettres Modernes, 1971.
Cixous, Hélène. *So Close*. Translated by Peggy Kamuf. Cambridge: Polity, 2009.
Cooperson, Michael. "Remembering the Future: Arabic Time-Travel Literature." *Edibiyât* 8 (1998): 171–89.
Cox, Debbie. "The Novels of Tahar Wattar: Command or Critique?" *Research in African Literatures* 28, no. 3 (Fall 1997): 94–109.
Dakhlia, Jocelyne. "Mémoires des langues." *La pensée de Midi* 3 (Winter 2000): 40–44.
Dauphin, Jean-Pierre, ed. *Les critiques de notre temps et Céline*. Paris: Garnier Frères, 1976.
Deleuze, Gilles. *Nietzsche and Philosophy*. Translated by Hugh Tomlinson. New York: Columbia University Press, 1983.
———. "Nomad Thought." In *The New Nietzsche*, edited by David B. Allison, 142–49. Cambridge, MA: MIT Press, 1997.
Dermenjian, Geneviève. *La crise anti-juive oranaise, 1895–1905: L'antisémitisme dans l'Algérie coloniale*. Paris: L'Harmattan, 1986.

Derrida, Jacques. *Le monololinguisme de l'autre, ou la prothèse d'origine*. Paris: Galilee, 1996.

———. *Resistances of Psychoanalysis*. Translated by Peggy Kamuf, Pascale-Anne Brault, and Michael Naas. Stanford: Stanford University Press, 1998.

———. *Specters of Marx: The State of the Debt, the Work of Mourning, and the New International*. New York: Routledge, 1994.

Djaout, Tahar. *L'invention du désert*. Paris: Seuil, 1987.

Djebar, Assia. *Algerian White*. Translated by David Kelley and Marjolin de Jager. New York: Seven Stories Press, 2000.

———. "Il n'y a pas d'exil." *Femmes d'Alger dans leur appartement: Nouvelles*. Paris: Des femmes, 1983.

———. *The Nouba of the Women of Mount Chenoua*. Film. Distributed by Women Make Movies, 2001.

———. *Ombre sultane*. Paris: Albin Michel, 1997.

Dobie, Madeleine. "Francophone Studies and the Linguistic Diversity of the Maghreb." *Comparative Studies of South Asia, Africa and the Middle East* 23, nos. 1 and 2 (2003): 32–40.

Drumont, Édouard. *La France juive: Essai d'histoire contemporaine*. 48th edition. Paris: C. Marpon & E. Flammarion, 1886.

Du Bellay, Joachim. *La deffence et illustration de la langue françoyse*. Paris: Librairie Marcel Didier, 1970.

———. *The Defense & Illustration of the French Language*. Translated by Gladys M. Turquet. London: J. M. Dent & Sons, 1939.

Dubreuil, Laurent. *Empire of Language: Toward a Critique of (Post)colonial Expression*. Translated by David Fieni. Ithaca, NY: Cornell University Press, 2013.

Durrant, Sam. *Postcolonial Narrative and the Work of Mourning: J. M. Coetzee, Wilson Harris, and Toni Morrison*. Albany: State University of New York Press, 2004.

El-Ariss, Tarek, ed. *The Arab Renaissance: A Bilingual Anthology of the Nahda*. New York: Modern Language Association of America, 2018.

———. *Trials of Arab Modernity: Literary Affects and the New Political*. New York: Fordham University Press, 2013.

Etienne, Bruno. "Renan et Islam." In *Mémorial Renan*, edited by Jean Balcou, 427–31. Paris: Honoré Champion, 1993.

Fabian, Johannes. *Time and the Other: How Anthropology Makes Its Object*. New York: Columbia University Press, 1983.

Fahmy, Khaled. "The Anatomy of Justice: Forensic Medicine and Criminal Law in Nineteenth-Century Egypt." *Islamic Law and Society* 6, no. 2 (1999): 224–71.

Fanon, Frantz. *L'an V de la révolution algérienne*. Paris: La Découverte, 2001 [1959].

———. *Peau noire, masques blancs*. Paris: Editions du Seuil, 1952.
———. *The Wretched of the Earth*. Translated by Constance Farrington. New York: Grove Press, 1963 [1961].
Fany, C. *Le juif algérien*. Algiers, 1898.
Freud, Sigmund. *Civilization and Its Discontents*. Translated by James Strachey. New York: Norton, 1961.
Gafaïti, Hafid. "The Monotheism of the Other: Language and De/Construction of National Identity in Postcolonial Algeria." In Berger (2002), 19–43.
Gana, Nouri. *Signifying Loss: Toward a Poetics of Narrative Mourning*. Lewisburg, PA: Bucknell University Press, 2011.
Gardais, H. "Les mystères d'Alger" [Les mystères d'al-Djazaïr]. *La lutte antijuive: Organe absolument indépendent*, February 4–18, 1898.
Geesey, Patricia. "Exhumation and History: Tahar Djaout's *Les Chercheurs d'os*." *French Review* 70, no. 2 (December 1996): 271–79.
Gibault, François. *Céline: 1932–1944: Délires et persecutions*. Paris: Mercure de France, 1985.
Gide, André. *The Journals of André Gide: 1889–1913*. New York: Knopf, 1955.
Gilroy, Paul. *Postcolonial Melancholia*. New York: Columbia University Press, 2005.
Gore, Keith. *L'idée de progrès dans la pensée de Renan*. Paris: Editions Nizet, 1970.
Gourgouris, Stathis. *Does Literature Think? Literature as Theory for an Antimythical Era*. Stanford: Stanford University Press, 2003.
Guha, Ranajit. *Dominance without Hegemony: History and Power in Colonial India*. Cambridge, MA: Harvard University Press, 1997.
Hafez, Sabry. *The Genesis of Arabic Narrative Discourse: A Study in the Sociology of Modern Arabic Literature*. London: Saqi Books, 1993.
Haim, Sylvia. *Arab Nationalism: An Anthology*. Berkeley: University of California Press, 1974.
Hamacher, Werner. "95 Theses on Philology." Translated by Catharine Diehl. *Diacritics* 39, no. 1 (2009): 25–44.
Hammerschlag, Sarah. *The Figural Jew: Politics and Identity in Postwar French Thought*. Chicago: University of Chicago Press, 2010.
Hardt, Michael, and Antonio Negri. *Empire*. Cambridge, MA: Harvard University Press, 2000.
———. *Multitude: War and Democracy in the Age of Empire*. New York: Penguin Books, 2004.
Harrison, Olivia C. *Transcolonial Maghreb: Imagining Palestine in the Era of Decolonization*. Stanford: Stanford University Press, 2016.
Hewitt, Nicholas. *The Golden Age of Louis-Ferdinand Céline*. Leamington Spa, UK: Berg Publishers, 1987.

Hochberg, Gil. "Remembering Semitism" or "On the Prospect of Re-Membering the Semites." *ReOrient* 1, no. 2 (Spring 2016): 192–223.

Holquist, Michael. *Dialogism*. London: Routledge, 1990.

Hourani, Albert. *Arabic Thought in the Liberal Age: 1798–1939*. Cambridge: Cambridge University Press, 1962.

Hugolin. *Pétition burlesque adressée aux deux Chambres et aux ministres par les juifs d'Algérie, qui prétendent qu'on leur fait une guerre de religion en les empêchant d'assassiner et de voler*. Algiers, 1899.

Ibrahim-Ouali, Lila. "La ville en ruines dans le roman maghrébin francophone et arabophone: *Agadir* de M. Khaïr-eddine et *Ez-Zilzel* de T. Ouettar." *La mémoire en ruines: Le modèle archéologique dans l'imaginaire moderne et contemporaine*. Clermont-Ferrand: Presses Universitaires Blaise-Pascal, Centre de Recherches sur les Littératures Modernes et Contemporaines, 2000.

Jameson, Fredric. *The Political Unconscious*. Ithaca, NY: Cornell University Press, 1981.

Jansen, Willy. *Women without Men: Gender and Marginality in an Algerian Town*. Leiden: E. J. Brill, 1987.

Jones, Christa. *Cave Culture in Maghrebi Literature: Imagining Self and Nation*. Lanham, MD: Lexington Books, 2012.

Judy, Ronald T. "On the Politics of Global Language, or Unfungible Local Value." *boundary 2* 24, no. 2 (Summer 1997): 101–43.

Juilland, Alphonse. *Les verbes de Céline: Étude d'ensemble*. Paris: Anima Libri, 1985.

Kaplan, Alice Yaeger. *Reproductions of Banality: Fascism, Literature, and French Intellectual Life*. Minneapolis: University of Minneapolis Press, 1986.

———. "Sources and Quotations in Céline's *Bagatelles pour un massacre*." In Scullion, Solomon, and Spear (1995), 29–46.

Keddie, Nikki, and Jamal al-Din Afghani. *An Islamic Response to Imperialism: Political and Religious Writings of Sayyid Jamal Ad-Din al-afghani*. Berkeley: University of California Press, 1968.

———. *Sayyid Jamal ad-Din "al-Afghani": A Political Biography*. Berkeley: University of California Press, 1972.

Kedourie, Elie. *Afghani and 'Abduh: An Essay on Religious Disbelief and Activism in Modern Islam*. London: Frank Cass, 1966.

———. "The Politics of Political Literature: Kawakibi, Azoury, and Jung." *Arabic Political Memoirs and Other Studies*. London: Frank Cass, 1974.

Khanna, Ranjanna. *Algeria Cuts: Women & Representation, 1830 to the Present*. Stanford: Stanford University Press, 2008.

———. "Post-Palliative: Coloniality's Affective Dissonance." *Postcolonial Text* 2, no. 1 (2006). http://postcolonial.org/index.php/pct/article/view/385/815.

Khatibi, Abdelkebir. "A Colonial Labyrinth." Translated by Catherine Dana. *Yale French Studies* 83, no. 2 (1993): 5–11.

———. *Du signe à l'image: Le tapis marocain*. Casablanca: Lak International, 1995.

———. "Incipits." In *Du bilinguisme*, edited by Jillal Benanni, 171–203. Paris: Denoel, 1985.

———. *La blessure du nom propre*. Paris: Denoël, 1974.

———. "The Language of the Other: Testimonial Exercises." Introduction by David Fieni. Translated by Catherine Porter. *PMLA* 125, no. 4 (October 2010): 1006.

———. 2008. "Ultime dissidence de Genet." *Oeuvres de Abdelkebir Khatibi, III: Essais*. Paris: La Différence, 2008.

Klossowski, Pierre. *Nietzsche and the Vicious Circle*. Translated by Daniel W. Smith. Chicago: University of Chicago Press, 1997.

Kristeva, Julia. *Desire in Language*. New York: Columbia University Press, 1981.

———. *Le texte du roman*. The Hague: Mouton, 1970.

———. *Powers of Horror*. Translated by Leon S. Roudiez. New York: Columbia University Press, 1982.

Lacan, Jacques. *The Seminar of Jacques Lacan, Book XI: The Four Fundamental Concepts of Psychoanalysis*. Translated by Alan Sheridan. New York: Norton, 1998.

Laroui, Abdallah. *The Crisis of the Arab Intellectual*. Translated by Diarmid Cammell. Berkeley: University of California Press, 1976 [1974].

Lazare, Bernard, and Philippe Oriol. *Une erreur judiciaire: L'affaire Dreyfus*. Paris: Editions Allia, 1993.

Le Bris, Michel, Jean Rouaud, and Eva Almassy. *Pour une littérature-monde*. Paris: Gallimard, 2007.

Lewis, Bernard. *Semites and Anti-Semites: An Inquiry into Conflict and Prejudice*. New York: Norton, 1986.

Lionnet, Francoise. "Counterpoint and Double Critique in Edward Said and Abdelkebir Khatibi: A Transcolonial Comparison," in *A Companion to Comparative Literature*, edited by Ali Behdad and Dominic R. D. Thomas, 387–407. Chichester: Wiley-Blackwell, 2011.

———. "Introduction: The Creolization of Theory." In *The Creolization of Theory*, edited by Shu-mei Shih and Francoise Lionnet, 1–33. Durham, NC: Duke University Press, 2011.

Lloyd, David. *Irish Culture and Colonial Modernity, 1800–2000: The Transformation of Oral Space*. Cambridge: Cambridge University Press, 2011.

Longeon, Claude, ed. *Premiers combats pour la langue française*. Paris: Librairie Générale de France, 1989.

Loselle, Andrea. "Franks and Gauls in the German Trilogy." In Scullion, Solomon, and Spear (1995), 185–202.
Majid, Anouar. *Unveiling Traditions*. Durham, NC: Duke University Press, 2000.
Massad, Joseph. *Islam in Liberalism*. Chicago: University of Chicago Press, 2015.
Mbembe, Achille. *On the Postcolony*. Berkeley: University of California Press, 2001.
McCarren, Felicia. *Dance Pathologies*. Stanford: Stanford University Press, 1998.
McCarthy, Patrick. *Céline*. New York: Viking Press, 1975.
Méchakra, Yamina. *La grotte éclatée*. Algiers: ENAL, 1986 [1979].
Meddeb, Abdelwahab. "En réponse à 'l'affaire Redeker.'" *Libération*, October 6, 2006.
———. "Islam and Its Discontents: An Interview with Frank Berberich." Translated by Pierre Joris. *October* (Spring 2002): 3–20.
———. *Phantasia*. Paris: Éditions Sindbad, 1986.
———. *Talismano*. Paris: Éditions Sindbad, 1987.
Merad, Ali. *Le réformisme musulman en Algérie de 1925 à 1940*. Paris: Mouton, 1967.
Merino, Leonor. "Pour Abdelkebir Khatibi: Le visage de la terre est déjà recouvert des yeux de tant de bien-aimés disparus." *Expressions maghrébines* 12, no. 1 (Summer 2013): 121–24.
Morson, Gary Saul, and Caryl Emerson. *Mikhail Bakhtin: Creation of a Prosaics*. Stanford: Stanford University Press, 1990.
Mosteghanemi, Ahlem, and Raphael Cohen. *The Bridges of Constantine*. London: Bloomsbury, 2013.
Mosteghanemi, Ahlem, and Baria A. Sreih. *Memory in the Flesh*. Cairo: American University in Cairo Press, 2003.
Mufti, Aamir. "Critical Secularism: A Reintroduction for Perilous Times." *boundary 2* 31, no. 2 (2004): 1–9.
———. *Enlightenment in the Colony: The Jewish Question and the Crisis of Postcolonial Culture*. Princeton: Princeton University Press, 2007.
———. *Forget English! Orientalisms and World Literatures*. Cambridge, MA: Harvard University Press, 2016.
———. "Orientalism and the Institution of World Literatures." *Critical Inquiry* 36, no. 3 (Spring 2010): 458–93.
Murtad, Abdalmalek. *Nahdat al-adab al-'arabi al-mu'asir fi al-jaza'ir 1925–1954* [The Modern Arabic Literary Nahda in Algeria]. Algiers: National Publishing & Distribution Company, 1983 [1979].
"Nahda." *al-Lisan al-'arabi*. Rabat: al-Maktab al-Da'im li-Tansiq al-Ta'rib fi al-watan al-'Arabi, 1964.

———. *Arabic-English Lexicon*. Book I. Edited by Edward William Lane. New York: F. Ungar, 1955–56.
———. *Supplément aux dictionnaires arabes*. 3rd edition. Edited by Reinhart Pieter Anne Dozy. Leiden: E. J. Brill, 1967.
Nietzsche, Friedrich. *The Gay Science*. Translated by Walter Kaufman. New York: Vintage Books, 1974.
———. *On the Genealogy of Morality: A Polemic*. Translated by Maudemarie Clark and Alan J. Swensen. Indianapolis: Hackett, 1998.
———. *Twilight of the Idols*. Translated by Duncan Large. Oxford: Oxford University Press, 1998.
———. *The Will to Power*. Translated by Walter Kaufman and R. J. Hollingdale. New York: Vintage Books, 1967.
Nordau, Max. *Degeneration*. Lincoln: University of Nebraska Press, 1993.
Orlando, Valérie. *Of Suffocated Hearts and Tortured Souls: Seeking Subjecthood Through Madness in Francophone Women's Writing of Africa and the Caribbean*. Lanham, MD: Lexington Books, 2003.
Pears, Pamela A. *Remnants of Empire in Algeria and Vietnam*. Lanham, MD: Lexington Books, 2004.
Peled, M. "The Enumerative Style in al-Saq 'ala al-Saq." *Journal of Arabic Literature* 22, no. 2 (September 1991): 127–45.
Pérès, Henri. "Les premières manifestations de la renaissance littéraire arabe en Orient au XIX siècle: Nasif al-Yazigi et Faris ash-Shidyaq." *Annales de l'Institut d'Études Orientales de la Faculté des Lettres d'Alger* 1 (1934–35): 233–56.
"Petits métiers algériens." *Algérie artistique et pittoresque*, edited by Eugène Larade. Algiers: J. Gervais-Courtellemon & Co., 1893.
Pollock, Sheldon. "Deep Orientalism? Notes on Sanskrit and Power Beyond the Raj." In *Orientalism and the Postcolonial Predicament*, edited by Carol A. Breckinridge and Peter van der Veer, 76–133. Philadelphia: University of Pennsylvania Press, 1993.
Rahme, Joseph G. "'Abd al-Rahman al-Kawakabi's Reformist Ideology, Arab Pan-Islamism, and the Internal Other." *Journal of Islamic Studies* 10, no. 2 (1999): 159–77.
Rastegar, Kamran. "Authoring the Nahda." *Middle Eastern Literatures* 16, no. 3 (2013): 227–31.
———. "Literary Modernity before Novel and Nation: Transaction and Circulation between Nineteenth-Century Arabic, Persian and English Literatures." PhD dissertation, Columbia University, 2005.
Reid, Donald. *The Odyssey of Farah Antun: A Syrian Christian's Quest for Secularism*. Minneapolis: Bibliotheca Islamica, 1975.
Renan, Ernest. *L'avenir de la science: Pensées de 1848*. Paris: Flammarion, 1995 [1890].

———. *Averroès et l'averroïsme. Oeuvres complètes*, volume 3. Paris: Calmann-Lévy, 1949 [1852].

———. *L'Islam et la science*. Montpellier: L'archange-minotaure, 2003.

———. "Qu'est-ce qu'une nation?" In *Becoming National: A Reader*, edited by Geoff Elay and Ronald Grigor Suny, 41–55. New York: Oxford University Press, 1996.

Roper, Geoffrey. "Faris al-Shidyaq and the Transition from Scribal to Print Culture in the Middle East." In *The Book in the Islamic World*, edited by George N. Atiyeh, 209–31. Albany: State University of New York Press, 1995.

Rousseau, Jean-Jacques. *Les rêveries du promeneur solitaire*. Paris: Éditions Gallimard, 1972.

Russo, Mary. *The Female Grotesque: Risk, Modernity, Excess*. New York: Routledge, 1995.

Sacks, Jeffrey. "Futures of Literature: Inhitat, Adab, Naqd." *Diacritics* 37, no. 4 (Winter 2007): 32–55.

———. *Iterations of Loss: Mutilation and Aesthetic Form, Al-Shidyaq to Darwish*. New York: Fordham University Press, 2015.

Said, Edward. *Culture and Imperialism*. New York: Knopf, 1993.

———. *Orientalism*. New York: Vintage Books, 1978.

———. *Reflections on Exile*. Cambridge, MA: Harvard University Press, 2000.

Sartre, Jean-Paul. *Anti-Semite and Jew*. Translated by George J. Becker. New York: Schocken Books, 1948.

Say, Léon. "Debouchées et politique coloniale." *Journal des débats* (May 2, 1883), 2.

Schrift, Alan D. "Nietzsche's French Legacy." In *The Cambridge Companion to Nietzsche*, 323–55. Cambridge: Cambridge University Press, 1996.

Scullion, Rosemarie, Philip H. Solomon, and Thomas C. Spear, eds. *Céline and the Politics of Difference*. Hanover, NH: University Press of New England, 1995.

Séebold, Éric. *Essai de situation des pamphlets de Louis-Ferdinand Céline*. Tusson: Du Lérot, 1985.

Shapiro, Gary. "Nietzsche Contra Renan." *History and Theory* 21, no. 2 (1982): 193–222.

Sheehi, Stephen. *Foundations of Modern Arab Identity*. Gainesville: University Press of Florida, 2004.

Silverstein, Paul A. "The context of Antisemitism and Islamophobia in France." *Patterns of Prejudice* 42, no. 1 (2008), 1–26.

Spivak, Gayatri Chakravorty. "Terror: A Speech After 9–11." *boundary 2* 31, no. 2 (2004): 81–111.

Starkey, Paul. "Fact and Fiction in *al-Saq 'ala al-Saq*." In *Writing the Self: Autobiographical Writing in Modern Arabic Literature*, edited by Robin Ostle, Ed de Moor, and Stefan Wild, 30–38. London: Saqi Books, 2001.
Sternhell, Zeev. *La droite révolutionnaire, 1885–1914*. Paris: Seuil, 1978.
Stora, Benjamin. *Algeria 1830–2000: A Short History*. Ithaca, NY: Cornell University Press, 2000.
———. *Les trois exils juifs d'Algérie*. Paris: Stock, 2006.
Tomiche, Nada. "Naissance et avatars du roman arabe avant *Zaynab*." *Annales Islamologiques* 16 (1980): 321–51.
———. "Nahda." In *The Encyclopaedia of Islam*. 2nd edition. Edited by P. Bearman, Th. Bianquis, C.E. Bosworth, E. van Donzel and W.P. Heinrichs. Leiden: Brill, 2002.
Wattar, al-Tahir. *Al-Zilzal*. Algiers: Center for Publishing and Distribution, 2004 [1974].
———. *The Earthquake*. Translated by William Granara. London: Saqi Books, 2000.
Watts, Philip. "Postmodern Céline." In Scullion, Solomon, and Spear (1995), 203–15.
Weil, Patrick. "Le statut des musulmans en Algérie colonial: Une nationalité française dénaturée." In *La justice en Algérie 1830–1962*, 95–109. Paris: La Documentation française, Collection Histoire de la Justice, 2005.
Wilson, Stephen. *Ideology and Experience: Antisemitism in France at the Time of the Dreyfus Affair*. Rutherford, NJ: Fairleigh Dickinson University Press, 1982.
Žižek, Slavoj. *The Plague of Fantasies*. London: Verso, 1997.
———. *The Sublime Object of Ideology*. London: Verso, 1989.
Zola, Emile. "J'accuse." *L'Aurore*, January 13, 1898.

INDEX

'Abduh, Muhammad, 3, 9, 21, 201n16; al-Afghani and, 21, 39; Antun and, 49; al-Kawakibi and, 48; Meddeb's fictionalization of, 149–50; jurisprudence of, 13, 180n16; translation and, 177n5
absinthe, 78
Académie Française, 22, 37, 87
Aching, Gerard, 5, 135, 171
Adonis, 143, 150–52
al-Afghani, Jamal al-Din: Arabness and, 178n9; claim of Afghan birth, 182–83n8; French influence on, 180n18; homogeneous time and, 17; Islamic awakening and, 15; Renan's debate with, 16, 36–45
Alexandria (Egypt), 59–60
Algeria: French colonial, 68–69, 73–86, 89, 93, 196n13; *nahda* in, 190–91n3; postcolonial, 98–117, 119–35, 191n9
Algerian Civil War (1990s), 4, 103–5, 130, 133–35
Algerian War (1954–1962), 100, 102, 120–27
Algerian White (Djebar), 119, 130, 132–35
Algiers, 73, 77–79, 82, 115, 128–29, 190n9
allegory: Benjamin on, 18–19, 21; Cixous and, 129; Jews as, 92
Almohad dynasty, 106, 113–15
Almoravid dynasty, 113–15, 193n21
Althusser, Louis, 161
Anidjar, Gil, 4, 69, 71, 187n3
anti-Semitism, 4, 20–27, 43, 53, 69–94, 137; Algeria and, 77–85; Arab world and, 98, 187n4; Céline and, 85–92; Dreyfus Affair and, 75–77; Nietzsche and, 46. *See also* Dreyfus Affair
Antun, Farah, 13, 21, 32, 47–50
Apter, Emily, 178n10

arabesque, 12, 143, 156
Arabian Nights. See *A Thousand and One Nights*
Arabic language, 65, 83–4, 100, 135–36, 152; Arabization and, 100–6, 112, 131; carnivalesque and, 53–63; gender and, 59–60, 110–11, 192n17; *nahda* and, 12–13, 50, 190n3; Nazi propaganda and, 72; philology and, 6, 37
Arabic literature, 54–7, 106, 112, 119, 143, 178n6
Arab nationalism, 48, 99, 108, 152; Arabic language and, 100, 185n11; racialization of Arabs and, 85
Arab renaissance. See *nahda*
Arabs, 1, 39, 47, 140, 152, 192n14; colonial engineering between Jews and, 4, 8, 69–72, 98, 190n1; decadence and, 18, 56; Frantz Fanon on, 99; history of, 37; Orientalism and, 25, 34, 37, 43; the "second *nahda*" and, 108; semitization of, 187n3; tension with Turks, 59, 60
The Arcades Project (Benjamin), 13, 16–20
authenticity, 143, 148, 159; Arab, 66, 160, 178n9; colonialism and, 98; French and, 67; Indo-European, 40; Islamic reformism and, 15–17, 45, 107; national, 53
L'avenir de la science (Renan), 23, 33, 35, 39, 182n34
Averroes. See Ibn Rushd
Averroès et l'averroïsme (Renan), 21, 25–26, 39, 49
awakening, 10–23, 44–45, 48–51, 53, 181n21; Benjamin and, 17–20; *nahda* as, 38, 60, 114
al-Azmeh, Aziz, 15, 32, 180n16

Bagatelles pour un massacre (Céline), 85–92

215

Bakhtin, Mikhaïl, 53, 59, 63–67, 87, 186n15
Barlow, Tani, 6
Barrès, Maurice, 43, 80
Bataille, Georges, 196–97n6
Baudelaire, Charles, 12, 109, 152, 155, 192n15
Baudrillard, Jean, 142
Behdad, Ali, 177, 178n10
Ben Badis, 'Abd al-Hamid, 100–1
Benjamin, Walter, 152–53, 155, 180–81n21; historical materialism of, 16–20
Ben Salah, Athman, 75–77
Bensmaïa, Réda, 113, 117, 151, 192n15
Berbers, 104, 108, 114; languages of, 101, 110, 131, 167, 191n7
Berque, Jacques, 165, 190–91n3
Bhabha, Homi, 187n18
Le blanc de l'Algérie (Djebar), 119, 130, 132–35
Blanche, Jacques-Émile, 76
Bonaparte, Napoleon: *nahda* and, 13, 14, 20, 100, 179–80n15
Boumédienne, Houari, 101, 192n10
boycotts, 78, 80
The Bridges of Constantine. See *Dhakirat al-Jasad*
Buck-Morss, Susan, 17–19, 181–82n21
burlesque, 81
Burlesque Petition (Hugolin), 82–85
Bush, George W., 2–3
al-Bustani, Butrus, 14, 54
Butler, Judith, 121

Cairo, 62
calligraphy, 140, 143, 146–49, 153, 157, 164
Carlier, Omar, 101–3, 110–11
Camus, Albert, 191n9
capitalism, 6, 13, 40, 51; Arabic literature and, 111; Bakhtin and, 64
carnivalesque, 64–67; Arabic literature and, 53, 56, 60–61, 63–67
Céline, Louis-Ferdinand, 84, 85–94, 189nn17,19; anti-Semitism and, 4, 43, 80, 82; carnivalesque and, 65–67, 98; philology and, 69
Césaire, Aimé, 98
Chakrabarty, Dipesh, 151
Charlie Hebdo attacks (2015), 137
Chatterjee, Partha, 5

children and childhood: Arab Muslim, 42, 44–45; Benjamin and, 18; cholera epidemic of 1831 and, 61–62; Djaout and, 113–14, 116; loss and, 103, 121; memory and, 145, 152, 154; as metaphor for ignorance, 22–23; the postcolonial future and, 116, 130–31
Christianity, 88; assimilation and, 137; Catholic right during Dreyfus Affair, 20; Islam and, 36, 41, 182n35, 199–200n12; Judaism and, 70, 72; Renan and 21, 35, 46; secularism and, 8, 26, 35, 38
citizenship, 6, 85, 128; colonial Algeria and, 73, 74, 80; postcolonial Algeria and, 135
Cixous, Hélène, 119, 127–30, 131, 134–35, 195n20
colonial modernity, 5–6, 72; Césaire and, 98; Djaout and, 114–16; decadence and, 40, 51, 52, 132, 165, 171; Nietzsche and, 10; political theology of, 36; Žižek and, 160
comparativism, 5, 7, 53, 66, 161–72; French and Arabic decadence and, 13; Renan and, 36
Constantine (Algeria), 100, 105, 107–8, 110, 112, 123–25
constructivism, 26, 41–44, 98
contagion, 3, 67, 87
contrapuntal reading, 10–11, 159–65, 170–71
Crémieux Decree. See Decret Crémieux

Dabiq (publication of ISIS), 2–3
Daudet, Alphonse, 78,
Daudet, Léon, 87–88, 90
de Certeau, Michel, 146, 151
decolonization, 5, 24, 32, 94, 161; Algeria and, 110
Decret Crémieux, 73, 74, 80, 84
defamiliarization, 11–21, 32, 161; Arabic literary tradition and, 50, 60; history and, 38
Degas, Edgar. 76–77
Deleuze, Gilles, 45, 51, 63, 66, 138, 196n2
Derrida, Jacques, 89, 99, 105, 119, 167, 193n1
despotism, 2, 24, 26
Dhakirat al-Jasad (Mosteghanemi), 119, 122–27, 135

Index

dialectics, 11, 13, 19, 24, 34
Djaout, Tahar, 103–6, 111–17, 148, 191n9, 193n21
Djebar, Assia, 119, 130, 132–35, 195n18
Dreyfus Affair, 4, 68, 73–86, 98, 188n5, 190n1; Renan and, 20
Drumont, Edouard, 77, 78, 80, 85, 118
du Bellay, Joachim, 90
Dubreuil, Laurent, 84

The Earthquake (Wattar), 105–13, 116–17
Egypt, 10, 20, 100, 185n14; British occupation of, 106–7; al-Kawakibi and, 48; literary *nahda* and, 190n3; Ottoman Empire and, 50, 59–60; al-Shidyaq in, 60–63
Empire (Hardt and Negri), 137–39
Enlightenment, 9–11, 21, 45, 188n13
eschatology, 110
Un été à Stockholm (Khatibi), 169–70
Europe: Arab world and, 13, 26, 43, 49, 100–1; assimilation and, 73; cultural influence of, 9–12, 14, 32, 56, 160; decadence and, 2, 27, 142, 157; historical agency of, 3; imperialism of, 16, 72; material culture of, 17; medieval philosophers of, 49–50; modernity and, 5, 152; Orientalism and, 7, 11; racial difference and, 35, 47–48, 108; secular history and, 41–45
exile, 45, 112, 116, 117; al-Afghani and, 37; Antun and, 50; Céline and, 86; Cixous and, 127–29; al-Kawakibi and, 48; Khatibi and, 164–66, 170; Meddeb and, 156; Said on, 165; al-Shidyaq and, 62
l'Exposition universelle (1900), 76, 188n5

Fabian, Johannes, 22, 35
Fahmy, Khaled, 10
Fanon, Frantz, 24, 182–83n33, 190n2; Marxist analysis and, 6; national culture and, 99–100
Fany, C., 81–82
feminism, 121, 133
feminization of the negative, 118–19
flâneur, 152–53, 155, 169, 192n15
Flaubert, Gustave, 11–13
France, 3, 11, 20, 103, 169; anti-Semitic press in, 76, 78, 89; Arab world and, 162; Catholic Church in, 26; colonial policy of, 4, 39–40, 73–74; immigrants in, 157, 164; islamophobia in, 4, 137, 141; Orientalism and, 8, 13; Renan and, 22, 38; Republican ideal in, 154; writing about 9/11 in, 142
francophone literature, 112, 166–68
French language, 67, 88–92, 101–3, 111, 130–32, 193n19
French literary decadence, 11–13, 179n11
French Revolution, 23, 154
Freud, Sigmund, 2, 18, 89, 119, 126, 146, 153, 193n1
Front de Libération National (FLN), 101, 192n10
Front National (FN), 137
The Future of Science. See *L'avenir de la science*

Gafaïti, Hafid, 104–5
Gauls, 88
Genet, Jean, 168–69
genre, 36, 52–55, 57, 64–65, 162
Gide, André, 75–76, 89
Gilroy, Paul, 124, 194n9
Gourgouris, Stathis, 10
graffiti, 90, 115
the grotesque, 8; gender and ("female grotesque"), 120–22, 125, 129, 130, 133; realism and, 61–62, 64, 186n15
La grotte éclatée (Méchakra), 119–23, 130–31
Guha, Ranajit, 177–78n5

Hafez, Sabry, 56
Hamacher, Werner, 93
al-Hamadhani, Badiʿ al-Zaman, 55, 57, 106
Hardt, Michael, 63, 137–39, 141, 153, 156
Harrisson, Olivia O., 194n6
Hebrew, 25, 68, 83–84
Hegel, Georg Wilhelm Friedrich: Renan and, 11, 22–25
Hochberg, Gil, 70, 72, 84
Holocaust, 73, 160
hospitality, 54, 131, 135, 162, 166
Hourani, Albert, 177n5, 179n12
Hugolin, 81–83, 86, 89, 91, 188n9
Hussein, Saddam, 2
hysteria, 12, 88, 91, 92

Ibn Rushd: Antun on, 49–50; Renan on, 21, 25–26, 32, 34, 42

Ibn Tumart, 105, 112, 114, 115–16
immigrants, 115, 137–39, 141, 153, 156–57
India, 15–16, 37, 41
indigène (colonial legal status), 74
L'invention du désert (Djaout), 105–6, 107, 112–17
Islam, 16, 20, 32, 152; aesthetics and, 147; decadence and, 141; historiography and, 142; iconoclasm and, 140, 141, 146, 149; Islamic intellectuals, 9, 11–12, 15–16, 21, 31, 47–51; Islamic jurisprudence, 9, 13, 49; Islamic reformism, 14–18, 41–45, 47–51, 148; Islamist movements, 2–3, 102–3, 111, 139, 141, 148; "Islamo-fascism", 2–3; the Maghreb and, 74, 100–1, 103, 105–17; mobility and, 136–37, 139–40, 144, 153; *nahda* and, 14, 149–50; Orientalism and, 22–27, 34–40; puritanical, 135; *ressentiment* and, 155; Semitism and, 70; theory and, 164; transgression and, 149–51; transnational, 10; women and, 118–19. *See under* al-Afghani; Christianity; religion; secularism
islamophobia, 4, 70–71, 72, 84, 85, 137

Jameson, Fredric, 6, 19, 189n21
Jews, 46, 47; Algerian, 67–94, 127–28
Joyce, James, 55
Journal des débats, 21, 38–39, 44
"Judeo-Christian" concept, 38, 72,
Judy, R. A., 102, 111–12
Le juif algérien (Fany), 81–82

Kanoui, Simon, 84
Kaplan, Alice, 85–86, 90
al-Kassim, Dina, 144, 149
Kateb Yacine, 170
al-Kawakibi, 'Abd al-Rahman, 18, 32–33, 47–49
Khanna, Ranjana, 125–26, 128, 135, 195n14
Khatibi, Abdelkébir, 54, 129, 156, 161–70, 201n3
Klossowski, Pierre, 140–41, 157
Kristeva, Julia, 53, 58, 86, 91, 186n15

Lacan, Jacques, 147, 153–54
Laroui, Abdallah, 48, 97, 108, 116, 180n16, 192n14
Lazare, Bernard, 77, 85

Lebanon, 22, 55
La Libre Parole, 76–77, 85
Lionnet, Françoise, 162–64
Loti, Pierre, 10–13
Lloyd, David, 6, 93
La lutte antijuive, 78–79

Maghreb, 4, 100, 141, 154, 164–65, 170; anti-Semitism and, 75–76; *l'Exposition universelle* (1900) and, 75–76; history of, 113–15; Islam and, 115; lingua franca of, 155; Mashreq and, 190n3; postcolonial nation-state in, 148, 153–54
Mahfouz, Naguib, 111
Majid, Anouar, 192
maqamat, 55–59, 106
Martel, Charles, 137
Marx, Karl, 2, 6, 17, 18, 64, 138, 194n1
marxist theory, 6, 23, 102, 111, 181n21
Mashreq, 194n6; France and, 4; *nahda* in, 100
Massad, Joseph, 69
Mbembe, Achille, 186n15
McCarren, Felicia, 88, 91
Méchakra, Yamina, 119–24, 130–31, 134
Meddeb, Abelwahab, 135, 139–57, 187n16, 197–98n9, 199–200n12
Mediterranean, 143, 170
médina, 109, 144–48, 151–57, 192n15, 201n15
melancholia, 119, 121, 124–26, 129–31, 133–35; exile and, 62, 156
Memory of the Body (Mosteghanemi), 119, 122–27, 135
minority, 68, 84–86, 94; Christian, 48, 49, 65; French colonial, 73; 190–91n3; Jewish, 93, 195n13
Morocco, 100, 161, 163–65, 168, 170
mourning, 118–33
"Mourning and Melancholia" (Freud), 126, 193–94n1
Mosteghanemi, Ahlam, 119, 122–27, 131, 134, 194n6
Mufti, Aamir, 38, 93, 164–65, 182n1, 187n17, 188n13
al-Musawi, Muhsin, 178n6
Muslims, 1, 85; Algerian, 74–77, 81, 83, 84; citizenship and, 80–81; Indian, 16, 41; racialization of, 190n1; vilification of by the French far right, 137, 196n3; violence against, 180n16
al-Muwaylihi, Muhammad, 106–7

Index

nahda, 4, 13–17, 32, 37–38, 142–43, 160; Adonis and, 150; ambivalence of, 9–10, 26, 87; awakening and, 20, 114; defined, 13–14; Islamic reformism and, 40, 100, 102, 107–8; in Mashreq compared to Maghreb, 190n3; "nomad thought" and, 45–51; al-Shidyaq and, 53, 54, 56, 57, 60, 61, 66. *See also* second *nahda*
Napoleon III: colonial policy of, 73; anti-Semitic conspiracy theories and, 79
national culture, 94, 97, 99–100
nationalism, 5, 32, 45, 48, 84–85, 124–26, 171
Negri, Antonio, 137–39, 141, 153, 156
negritude, 98, 99
Nietzsche, Friedrich, 2, 10, 37, 63, 139–44; decadence and, 63, 157, 184n19, 197n7; "double science" and, 198n10; nomadism in, 32, 45–49; Renan and, 35, 37
nomad thought, 10, 32, 37, 45–51, 137–39
Nordau, Max, 197n7

Oran, 73, 77, 84
Orientalism (Said), 7, 22
Ottoman Empire, 7, 47; decline of, 11–13, 37, 39; the fin de siècle and, 31; *nahda* and, 47–51, 56, 59–60

Palestine, 72, 169
pan-Arabism. *See* Arab nationalism
Paris: arcades of (*passages*), 19, 40; exile and, 114–16; human progress and, 17; Meddeb and, 144, 151–52, 154–56; Orientalism and, 33, 37; al-Tahtawi in, 12; terrorism in, 137; World's Fair (1900), 76
pathology, 27, 97, 115, 144; Céline and, 86, 88, 91, 189n19; gender and, 128, 134; language and, 56, 60–63, 98; *mal de siècle* and, 88; melancholia as, 193–94n1; Nietzsche and, 150, 157; Orientalism and, 144, 164
performative language, 9, 32, 52, 71, 87, 98
Phantasia (Meddeb), 139, 141, 143–46, 152–56, 201n18
philology, 4, 22, 31–33, 69–70, 81, 93–94; Arabic, 71; Orientalism and, 46, 51, 66–67, 87; Semitism and, 8, 22, 82–84

philosophy of history, 4, 20–22, 25–26, 33, 36, 46
pieds-noirs, 73, 84
political theology, 36, 53
Pollock, Sheldon, 93
Proust, Marcel, 18
psychoanalysis, 89, 118–19, 126, 134, 146, 153

al-Qur'an, 49, 109–10, 112, 141, 150, 161

Rabelais, François, 53, 54, 57, 59, 66–67, 87
race, 32–39, 41–44, 72; degeneracy and, 21–26; Dreyfus's guilt and, 80; political theology of, 36, 53
Rahme, Joseph, 48
Rastegar, Kamran, 54
reformism, 100, 107, 143, 148–51; Egyptian legal, 10; Islamic 11, 14–17, 40–41, 45, 47–48, 50, 52, 98, 190n3
religion, 25–26, 42–47, 70; Algerian women and, 119; Arab nationalism and, 100–1; decadence and, 1, 2–3; hypocrisy and, 106–10; Islam as, 180n18; legitimacy of, 16; race and, 32, 34–36; rationalism and, 39; secularism and, 21, 38, 49, 142, 199–200n12; al-Shidyaq and, 54, 63, 65; violence and, 105
Renaissance (European), 53, 65, 87–88, 90, 187n16, 189n22
Renan, Ernest, 3, 11, 18, 31, 49–52, 80–81, 118; al-Afghani's debate with, 16, 36–45, 183n11; anti-Semitism of, 20–27, 70, 72, 73; Antun and, 13; decadence in, 33–36; Nietzsche and, 46–47, 189n17; progress in, 12, 17, 182n34; racism of, 15; secularism and, 20, 26, 33, 35–36, 38, 41, 45
Rimbaud, Arthur, 112, 193n21
Rome, 146
Rousseau, Jean-Jacques, 201n15
ruins, 146
Russo, Mary, 121–22

Sacks, Jeffrey, 56, 185n6
Said, Edward, 7, 20, 31–32; 53, 82, 182n1; comparativism and, 187n17; contrapuntal reading, 159–65, 170, 178n8; Orientalism and anti-Semitism, 70–71, 92; Orientalist style, 3, 11, 82;

Said, Edward *(continued)*
  Renan and, 22, 26, 34–35, 38, 71; "Semitic object" and, 4, 8, 66, 70; travelling theory of, 47
saj' (rhymed prose), 56–58
al-Saq 'ala al-Saq (al-Shidyaq), 53–67, 184n3, 186n15
Say, Léon, 39–40
second *nahda*, 97–98, 116
secularism, 15, 21, 31–32, 102, 105, 197n8; Arab nationalism and, 100; Christianity and, 8, 35, 53; Dreyfus Affair and, 20, 73; Islam and, 10, 34, 43; Islamist critique of, 3; *nahda* discourse and, 13, 21, 45–50, 65, 190–91n3; virtual secularization and, 140–41, 154, 197n9. *See also under* Renan, Ernest
semitic hypothesis, 4, 8, 69–73, 84, 87, 98, 173; Renan and the, 20–27, 34
September 11, 2001, attacks, 4, 136, 141, 142, 157, 197n9
Shapiro, Gary, 21, 46, 183n17
al-Shidyaq, Ahmad Faris, 53–67, 69; Céline and, 87, 93, 98
Si près (Cixous), 119, 127–30, 135
Spivak, Gayatri Chakravorty, 38
symptomology, 4, 36, 40, 65, 69, 152; language and, 52–53, 65–66, 84–89, 93; Meddeb and, 139–40; Nietzsche and, 10; Max Nordau and, 197n7
Syria, 20, 47–50

al-Tahtawi, 12, 17
Talismano (Meddeb), 139, 141, 143–44, 146–54, 156
tanzimat reforms, 13

terrorism, 142
A Thousand and One Nights, 75–76, 195n18
trauma, 119–22, 131, 144, 147, 152, 156; colonialism and, 97, 106, 113–15, 160; exile and, 127; fantasy and, 153; Islam and, 116; nation-state formation and, 124–25, 129, 134
Trump, Donald, 136
Tunis, 144–45, 147, 151, 155
Tunisia, 40, 134, 140, 156, 190n3
Turks, 59–60

Umm al-qura (al-Kawakibi), 47–49
United States, 1; Empire and, 9, 106; French studies in, 168; 9/11 response, 141–42

War on Terror, 1, 4, 27, 136, 142
Wattar, Al-Tahir, 103–13, 115–17, 120, 148, 191n9
Wilson, Stephen, 75–76
women, 1, 118–35; anti-Semitism against, 83; boycotting of Jewish-owned businesses and, 78; melancholia, loss, and, 118–35; national reproduction and, 110–11, 120; postcolonial theory and, 163; role in political future of Algeria, 116
world literature, 112, 167–68

Zaydan, Jurji, 13, 14
al-Zilzal (Wattar), 105–13, 116–17
Zionism, 69
Žižek, Slavoj, 154, 160, 186n15
Zola, Émile, 75, 77, 80, 90, 188n5

David Fieni is Assistant Professor of French at the State University of New York, Oneonta. He is the translator of Laurent Dubreuil's *Empire of Language: Toward a Critique of (Post)colonial Expression* (Cornell).

www.ingramcontent.com/pod-product-compliance
Lightning Source LLC
Chambersburg PA
CBHW030602020526
44112CB00048B/1092